SOCIAL SCIENCES AT HARVARD
1860–1920

FROM INCULCATION TO THE OPEN MIND

ROBERT L. CHURCH
DAVID B. POTTS
CAROL F. BAIRD
SHELDON M. STERN
ARTHUR G. POWELL

Edited, with a preface, by

PAUL BUCK

SOCIAL SCIENCES AT HARVARD

1860-1920

FROM INCULCATION TO THE OPEN MIND

HARVARD UNIVERSITY PRESS

CAMBRIDGE, MASSACHUSETTS · 1965

FOR

ELIZABETH STIX FAINSOD

CONTENTS

"THE NOTION THAT EDUCATION CONSISTS
IN THE AUTHORITATIVE INCULCATION OF WHAT
THE TEACHER DEEMS TRUE MAY BE LOGICAL AND
APPROPRIATE IN A CONVENT, OR A SEMINARY
FOR PRIESTS, BUT IT IS INTOLERABLE
IN UNIVERSITIES . . . THE WORTHY FRUIT
OF ACADEMIC CULTURE IS AN OPEN MIND,
TRAINED TO CAREFUL THINKING, INSTRUCTED IN
THE METHODS OF PHILOSOPHIC INVESTIGATION . . ."

Charles W. Eliot, *Inaugural Address*, 1869

PREFACE

THE period between the Civil War and World War I witnessed a revolution in higher education in the United States. Colleges proliferated and in some instances became universities; higher education, originally for the few, became available to many; and, most important, college teaching changed from the revelation of a fixed body of truth to the search for truth. This volume addresses itself to the third of these developments.

Too often the examination of the change in college teaching in this period records only the growth of the elective system, as if it were both the symbol and the explanation of the great transformation in higher education in America. Such accounts are too simple, for the mere recounting of the steps by which the required curriculum changed to an elective one does not advance our understanding of the history of higher education. The elective system is a product of a revolution in the conception of the role of higher education in American society and, in a sense, is the vehicle by which this changed conception declared itself. The growth of the elective system after the Civil War manifested the feeling on the part of educational leaders that the essence of higher education was the exploration—the probing—beyond the limits of accepted truth. It was this impulse, principally, that transformed Harvard from the classical college of 1850 to the great university of 1900. The configuration of the offerings of any department at Harvard in 1900 reveals the pattern: each department gave a basic general course, followed it with several courses of progressively narrower and progressively deeper scope, and capped its offerings with seminars devoted exclusively to the search for knowledge. Such patterns were not in the minds of collegiate reformers before the Civil War. A Francis Wayland at Brown or a George Ticknor at Harvard in advocating the institution of elective systems conceived of this reform as broadening the education of the student but did not envision the college as the locus of efforts to advance knowledge. It is such devotion to the exploration of truth and the advancement of knowledge that distinguishes the efforts to introduce the elective system after the Civil War from those efforts that preceded it. It is, therefore, to the development of the university's role as one of searching for knowledge that the historian must look for explanations of the elective system and of the transformation of the old-time college. The historian of higher education in the later nineteenth century must then examine carefully the intellectual influences that served to convert men to the new ideal of the university.

A further, and equally important, problem for the historian is the examination of how these new ideals were implemented in a given university. Frequently the development of the university from the college is seen as the step-by-step triumph of the fully-developed ideas of one educational reformer over the conservatism of the majority of faculty members. Again, such descriptions are too simple. That the elective system was the consequence

of a new conception of higher education points up the fact
that the transformation of the classical college was the
product of the commitment of many minds to new ideals.
In the case of Harvard it is clear that most of the faculty
and administrative officers—with the support and occasionally at the behest of the governing boards—strove to establish a university dedicated to advancing knowledge. It is
equally clear that there was no one formula for accomplish-
ing this end. President Eliot declared that "the worthy fruit
of academic culture is an open mind, trained to careful
thinking," but said very little about how to achieve this
goal. Nor were Eliot and his administration uniformly successful in their efforts to create their ideal university: not
every step was a step forward, not every department or school
measured up to the ideal. And yet, when Eliot stepped down
in 1909, Harvard had become a great university. The historian of Harvard and of late-nineteenth-century higher education must measure this success—must examine and describe
those administrative procedures which fostered, and those
which failed to foster, the exploration of truth.

The historian's is a complex task, for Harvard's administrative procedures were the creatures not of one man but of
multiple authorities: the relatively—but only relatively—
remote governing boards, and the "Immediate Government," as the faculty was formally called. The new role
of the university was furthered by the thoughts and actions
of faculty members as individuals or as members of committees or as members of departments. Progress was affected
by conflicts and competition among individuals, among
groups, and among conceptions of the ideal and its implementation. Finances and allocation of resources are of major
importance for the historian of university development. The
historian must study carefully the appointment policy of the
university—on what criteria did the president and the fac-

ulty choose men who were to support and to continue their ideals of the role of the university? Here, as in all the cases, the failures are as instructive as the successes. The historian must explore the whole course of President Eliot's leadership —how much he exerted, how he exerted it, and when he exerted it. During Eliot's administration the Faculty of Arts and Sciences grew ten-fold and, in the very nature of the transformation of the college, the president was no longer able to keep abreast of the particulars of intellectual developments throughout the college. The new system of presidential leadership developed during this period constitutes a major part of the story of the transformation of the college. The historian must pursue all these investigations with a firm grasp on what is happening in each department, for it is within each department that the new role of the university is being enacted. There the progression from the general to the probing takes place; there new knowledge is sought. The departments are, in a sense, the exploring arms of a university committed to the exploration of truth, and every decision made by the university administration has reference to the work in one or more departments. And, of course, it is at the departmental level that the historian must begin his examination of how the ideal of searching for truth revitalized the teaching procedures of the university: it is there that he must begin to measure the impact of this teaching on the students.

The essays that follow explore, on the departmental level, some of the intellectual and institutional developments that transformed the college into the university. These essays are selected from papers written for my Seminar in American History which was given in two recent years at Harvard on *Topics in the Intellectual Development of the American University, 1860–1920.* These papers make use of only some of the vast amount of available and well-catalogued material in the Harvard College Archives—the kind of material that is so necessary to any close study of the development of a university. No claim is made for the universality of the Harvard experience—in fact, it is quite clear that in the case of several departments studied here, the Harvard experience was far from typical. Rather, the essays are presented in the belief that studies in depth of universities are needed. Whether studies similar to these carried on elsewhere will uncover parallel developments remains to be seen. It is hoped that such studies, using comparable materials which lie perhaps unorganized and certainly untapped in various universities, will put this Harvard study in broader perspective.

The authors' introduction gives an excellent summary of their findings as to the development of the ideal of searching for truth, of "induction." There is no need for me to add anything to it. Rather, I should like to mention a few ideas these essays suggest to one historian of higher education. First, each author employs a different point of view to attack the problem, and each point of view leads to fruitful results. Second, these essays reinforce the point that the Harvard record in the Eliot administration was not one of uninterrupted progress on all fronts. Third, and most significant, these essays reveal the complexity of the thinking, the events, and the decisions that underlay the development of the modern university. A careful review of the work of any single department reveals not only the immensity of the task that faced the Eliot administration, which had to deal simultaneously with more than thirty departments and schools, but also the immensity of the task that confronts the historian of the modern university.

The author of a scholarly volume knows privately as he proceeds in his work how much his finished book owes to the industry, scholarship, critical wisdom, kindness, and generosity of others—his intellectual forebears, his contemporaries, and his colleagues. He traditionally uses the preface as the platform for a public expression of this indebtedness. A collaboration such as this volume of essays has a dimension beyond monographic work in that a meeting of minds, a uniformity in verbal dress, and a temperamental accommodation must be arranged among the contributors. In this preface the editor and four of the contributors wish to record their gratitude to the first contributor, Robert L. Church, whose intellectual perception, literary style, meticulous labors, and powers of tactful negotiation—all exercised in the common interest—are the cornerstone of this edifice. Robert Church was chosen by the authors to draft their introduction. Such cohesion as this book possesses is to be attributed to his insight and interest, his long sessions with his coauthors, and the invaluable assistance proffered by him to this editor. The editor and all the contributors owe much to the convenience of the archival organization for which Dr. Clifford K. Shipton, Custodian of the University Archives, is responsible. They wish to express their appreciation of the very great kindness of Mr. Kimball C. Elkins, Senior Assistant in the University Archives, and to thank the members of his staff for their guidance, tolerance, encouragement, and patience through all the myriad demands made upon them in the preparation of this collection.

Finally, the editor wishes to express the very profound satisfaction that he has derived from the enthusiasm with which these young scholars have entered as permanent members into the discipline for so many years so close to his heart.

Paul Buck

Widener Library
Cambridge, Massachusetts
May 17, 1965

SOCIAL SCIENCES AT HARVARD
1860–1920

FROM INCULCATION TO THE OPEN MIND

INTRODUCTION

THE IMPULSE to study man and his social life as well as the impulse to improve society are not phenomena unique to late-nineteenth-century American higher education. Gladys Bryson has shown that most subject matter now designated as social science was included in the moral philosophy courses in the pre-Civil War college. Wilson Smith has described the concern for "public ethics" and social reform among antebellum professors. But in the postwar university the study of man and his social life and the impulse to social improvement have unique characteristics only partially explicable in terms of the earlier traditions of the American college. Such outside influences as *The Origin of Species*, positivism, the scholarly, social, and cultural achievements of social science in the German universities, and the growing dislocation in American society after 1860 stimulated a new academic approach to the study of man and society.

This new approach was most often described as the scientific method; in fact, one important change in academic rhetoric between the early and the late nineteenth century was the marked increase in the use of the word "science" in all fields of scholarship. "Science," however, was employed not as a term of precise description but as a term of value or a title of respectability. In the social sciences methodological debate did not center on the substitution of science for philosophy or religion; rather debate occurred among advocates of different conceptions of science. In order to understand the change of emphasis in the social sciences, one must understand the precise nature of the conflicting conceptions of scientific method. Moreover, one should remember that the men debating these issues were more often confused than clear about the nature of the conflict.

Significant debate most often occurred between those who used a predominantly deductive method of reaching "truth" and those who prided themselves on relying on an inductive method. Deductive thinking in the form of the Scottish Common Sense Realism had dominated the American college through the early nineteenth century. The Common Sense philosopher saw no radical dissociation between the forms of human thought and the world outside the mind— between the categories that the mind constructed and the relations among physical phenomena. The Common Sense philosopher dismissed epistemological concerns and relied on "what all people would agree to" as his criterion for establishing the validity of his conceptual patterns. Thus a rational principle of ethics, economics, or psychology to which most men would subscribe must correspond to what existed outside the mind. The Common Sense philosopher reasoned that one could deal with experience only by applying principles thus established to any given body of fact, deducing from them a rule for the specific situation, and testing that rule against experience.

Induction, on the other hand, focused on the epistemological problem of how man can discover the truth about physical reality. Inductive reasoning claimed that the categories of the mind which deductive thinkers imposed on physical reality in the form of general principles falsified that reality. Scholars hailed induction as the means of replacing the distorted picture of reality held by Common Sense thinkers with a perfectly accurate view of reality. In its ideal form inductive reasoning demanded that one confront a body of fact with no preconceptions about how these facts might form a pattern or a generalization. A thorough investigation of the facts was to produce a generalization; reality itself contained the over-all conceptual pattern or principle and all the thinker had to do was to search for, find, and articulate that generalization. Many European and American social scientists attempted to discard all the partial "truths" that the human mind sought to impose on reality in order to find empirically that all-embracing "truth" that lay within reality itself. Ironically, this search for absolute certainty led not to a unified conception of man and society but to a multiplicity of conceptions and to an inability to make meaningful generalizations about any significantly large area of human experience.

Much of the problem lay in the manner in which inductive reasoning was adapted to the needs of social science. Inductive reasoning was seen as the antithesis of deductive reasoning and thus idealized as the goal for all forward-looking disciplines. The history of the social sciences in this period can best be understood as the story of the implementation of the inductive ideal in the methodology of the specific disciplines; and much of the fragmentation of the conceptions of man and society can be attributed, first, to the diverse forms that this implementation took and, second, to an overemphasis by social scientists on the purely observational aspect of inductive reasoning. For, by the close of the nineteenth century, most social scientists had found that an investigation of the facts was just that and no more, that pure empiricism did not lead to meaningful generalizations.

The essays in this volume describe the acceptance and implementation of the inductive ideal in selected areas of the curriculum; and they explore the changes in subject matter, teaching, and institutional structure that followed. This introduction attempts to describe the application of inductive reasoning in the various departments and some of the changes its adoption wrought in the teaching of the social sciences at Harvard.

Since each man and each department had a somewhat different view of what inductive reasoning was and of how it could be applied to the unique methodological requirements of each discipline, no precise pattern of change appeared. Furthermore, the quantity and the pace of change depended in each instance on the presence of men able to effect or to retard significant innovations and on the availability of money with which to finance innovations. Variations in the rate and degree of change are to be expected, of course, in a period marked by the expansion and fragmentation of a once unified college curriculum, but despite the uneven growth and the increasing autonomy of the many disciplines, the development of the social sciences at Harvard does present a meaningful pattern.

The shift of the study of man and society from the realm of philosophy to that of science paralleled and fostered the scholarly, professional, and social aspirations of a new generation of college teachers, who embodied the inductive orientation in their newly independent disciplines. New methods incorporated in the new departments contributed significantly to a fragmentation of knowledge which fundamentally altered the teaching of social science at Harvard: the student no longer received a defined body of social principles; instead he was taught to find such principles for himself. These developments will be discussed under three heads: first, the substitution of induction for deduction as the ideal means to truth in the social sciences; second, the role of induction in the emerging social science disciplines; and third, the substantial alteration in the manner in which students investigated man and society after the introduction of these methodological changes.

The history of the social sciences at Harvard, then, is the story of each discipline's modifying its method in order to find the single principle of order which inhered in reality and the story of the multiplication and fragmentation of knowledge about man and society which resulted from those modifications. Inductive reasoning, or approximations of it, gained acceptance in the University and exerted an important shaping influence on the University because, to many social scientists, it seemed the only way to achieve certainty in their disciplines. *The Origin of Species* had conferred prestige on inductive reasoning, for Darwin's generalization —discovered, many believed, by pure observation—served to equate science and induction. However, American scholars found in Darwin's method only one element of inductive reasoning. The discovery of the principle of evolution by what seemed to be merely the observing, recording, and classifying of data made strict empiricism or pure observation synonymous with inductive reasoning in the minds of many American social scientists.

Spurred by the example of Darwin and by a sense of the inadequacy of older deductive principles, scholars at Harvard, following the tendency of positivistic social thought, seized upon rigid observation as the means to new and significant discovery. They assumed that the workings of nature and the workings of man and society were similar enough that the method used to study the former applied equally well to the latter. Philosophy and the deductive method seemed to present a welter of different interpretations shaped as much by the interpreters as by reality; Darwin seemed to present a monolithic and incontestable generalization grounded in a wealth of empirical data. Those disillusioned with the conflicts of deductive philosophy and eager to discover the single generalization about man and society could not but choose induction, or what they called the "scientific method," as an ideal. Disagreement arose not about the value or usefulness of this method but about just what that method was and how it was to be made applicable to social studies.

Adoption of the rhetoric of science among social scientists did not constitute, as these essays show, a clear break with the traditional methods of studying man and society. A change in rhetoric often disguised an inability or an unwillingness to change method. Because induction challenged an entrenched tradition of deductive reasoning, early manifestations of the "scientific method" in the social sciences most often contained a confusing combination of the deductive and the inductive. The moral philosophy courses, the prewar "social science" courses, were almost invariably taught on the model of Scottish Common Sense Realism, and the social sciences at Harvard, even as they broke away from the moral philosophy course, continued to follow this model. The Social Ethics Department best typifies the continuing dominance of the deductive method at Harvard. Despite his use of the word "inductive" and his introduction of "scientific" methods, Francis G. Peabody sought no new principles from the facts he and his students examined but merely used the facts to reaffirm traditional *a priori* principles. The Economics Department continued to teach students to fit the events of real life to the rigid tenets of early nineteenth-century economics, and only in the nineties did it discuss the possibility that a reexamination of history and contemporary affairs might call into question the universal applicability of those laws. Not until the eighties and nineties did the objective, empirical methodology attributed to Ranke effectively temper the History Department's strict adherence to the Federalist-Whig theory of American history. Albert Bushnell Hart, who imported German standards of objectivity to Harvard, is a major figure in this transition in the Department of History. William James, influenced by the inductive physiological psychologists in Germany, was the first Harvard social scientist to follow the inductive ideal wholeheartedly. His kind of psychology presented such a radical departure from that of the Common Sense School that he in effect founded a new discipline at Harvard, which quickly made a place for itself and its method in the curriculum.

Like James, Paul Hanus set out to reject old principles and methods and to build a new discipline of education. Both men, like so many social scientists, concentrated upon only the purely observational aspect of inductive reasoning when they set out to adapt induction to the materials and problems peculiar to their disciplines. Hanus's efforts, when compared to those of James, illustrate the weakness of strict observation in the social sciences. James introduced the observational method successfully because physiological psychology is a kind of natural science. But, as James himself was to discover in the nineties, the methods and findings of "brass instrument" psychology did not prove very useful in analyzing human emotions or human society. Hanus, attempting to apply the purely observational technique to a purely social science, could not go beyond fact-gathering to the analysis and synthesis of material.

Hanus's failure exemplifies the general failure of inductive reasoning as construed by Harvard social scientists to exert the same kind of influence as moral arbiter or enunciator of certainty that the Scottish Realism had exerted in the prewar University. Attempting to go to the data with an open mind did not produce the synthesizing principle of order that students and scholars sought. On the other hand, the Social Ethics Department's failure to develop a unique set of methodological techniques and a subject matter both academically respectable and departmental in scope suggests that a continuing reliance on the deductive tradition of moral philosophy also failed to meet the challenges that late-nineteenth- and early-twentieth-century thought and society presented to scholarship. Harvard's strongest social science departments after the turn of the century were those like the Economics Department under Frank William Taussig which found ways to combine within the methodology of the discipline the fact-gathering and the theorizing aspects of inductive reasoning.

The application of science to the study of man and society also gained headway at Harvard because it served the professional aspirations of the new generation of social scientists. Because they were becoming increasingly divorced from the ministry and because their number was steadily growing, college teachers began to think of themselves both as members of the new profession of scholarship and as members of more restricted groups made up of scholars who confined their research and teaching to a single field. Professors were beginning after the Civil War to identify as much with their disciplines as they did with their colleges. The profession of scholarship as a whole and the specific single-discipline professions modeled themselves on those found in the German universities, where an increasing number of young American teachers had studied. There Americans had seen scholars with a very high *esprit de corps*, with high salaries, and with a great influence on the social and cultural life of the German nation. American scholars, as the first step in pursuit of similar economic and social prestige, set new goals of scholarly achievement. Adoption of the scientific method promised accomplishments equal to those of German scholars.

Social scientists also tended to emulate the tested strategies of the natural scientists in their drive for professional recognition. The adoption of the aura of science made an independent existence within the university more possible. The pattern had been well established in American and European universities that natural sciences broke away from the core philosophy curriculum most successfully and that, once free, they were allowed to operate within the university quite independently. Furthermore, the utilitarian connotations of the word "science" were very important in an age when the financial support of universities was coming more from businessmen and less from organized religion. Something scientific and thus "useful" was more eligible for endowment support.

An academically respectable and professionally distinct discipline needed the aura of science because "science" meant the most effective means of finding certainty. Thus we find at Harvard scholars as widely divergent as Francis G. Peabody and Albert Bushnell Hart calling their disciplines scientific; or, again, both Charles Everett and William James labeling their psychologies, which were completely antithetical in content and method, scientific. A scientific discipline also needed to mark out an exclusive area of investigation and, if possible, a specific place or at least specific materials for investigation. Thus William James built his famous psychological laboratory; the Social Ethics Department assembled a social museum; and the Division of Education built up its impressive collection of state and municipal educational reports. A professional journal also served to mark out an area of investigation and a place for investigation, as the achievements of Hart in the History Department and of the neoclassicists in the Economics Department demonstrated. The failure of sociology to develop a secure and useful place in the University from 1890 to 1910 can be traced, in part, to its inability to delineate a specific area and specific materials for study.

Adopting the analogy between social science and natural science was one device scholars used to give status to their disciplines and to delimit a special area of competence. In the eighties the scientific method achieved wide acceptance among those social scientists who were concerned with social reform because it provided a means by which they could exercise their social concern while reinforcing their claims to professional capability. Drawing on the traditions of concern for social improvement in the pre-Civil War college and in the German university, these scholars tended to evaluate a discipline in terms of its capacity to judge and criticize the social order. By assuming the important functions of suggesting and assessing changes in the social order and of training students for intelligent participation in society, the disciplines would gain a more important role in the society. Hugh Hawkins, in his study of Johns Hopkins University, has shown that the interest in social reform did not enter the academic disciplines there until the mideighties, and the evidence in the papers that follow proves the applicability of that date to postwar developments at Harvard. Before that date social scientists like Charles F. Dunbar and William James seem to have been motivated toward science as a means of achieving certainty and as a means of establishing the professional discipline rather than toward the application of science to actual social problems. To Dunbar the great advantage of science was its applicability in abstract economics rather than in real experience; it thus prevented the scholar, as scholar, from judging actual social problems. For him, economic science was in a sense a laboratory science requiring rigid control of variables—and no such control could be achieved in real social situations.

After 1880 this point of view began to change quite radically. Many social scientists felt the need to account for an increasing dislocation in society and a widening split between the *ought* and the *is*. Instead of using inductive reasoning simply to discover abstract truth, could not the social scientist apply his science to current social problems, or, better yet, turn all society into his laboratory? Soon several Harvard social scientists were claiming that their inductive method enabled the university teacher to understand, to criticize, and to change the social order. This movement among social scientists paralleled the rise of the Social Gospel Movement and the beginnings of what has become known as "reform Darwinism" in American society as a whole. Many characteristics of the Progressive Movement appear in the social science curriculum at Harvard after 1885.

The public immorality typical of the Gilded Age convinced many scholars that higher education could improve society by training a group of ethically minded, honest, and informed citizens. The Social Ethics Department was one facet of a nationwide attempt to put ethics back into national life. Other scholars were appalled at the growing schism between the rich and the poor, the crowds of immigrants from southern Europe, the great surge of strikes beginning in the eighties and erupting so violently at Chicago in 1886, the social unrest typified by the popularity of Henry George and Edward Bellamy, and the complexity of resolving the conflicting claims of industrialism, urbanism, and social justice. In the face of this growing complexity there was a general turning to science for solutions.

In response social scientists sought solutions by applying their observational techniques to real social problems. One measure of their attempt was the effort they expended on compiling statistics and transmitting them to their students.

Like so many reformers of the Progressive stamp, Harvard's social scientists hoped that once the factual and statistical evidence was assembled, proper solutions would inevitably follow. That very few solutions suggested themselves proved this hope unfounded. Here again pure observation failed to provide significant generalizations. Peabody's ultimately deductive response to the "social question" was initially most productive and effective among students. His empiricism was permeated with the traditional religious and moral principles that could channel the students' natural idealism into the task of improving society. His course did offer some rules for action and thus had an appeal to the student body during the decades of great social unrest. Others at Harvard had less effect on the student body. Men like Edward Cummings and William J. Ashley in the Economics Department were able to apply the empirical aspect of inductive reasoning effectively in disproving older social principles but made only faltering efforts to substitute new criteria of judgment or action.

Part of the value most social scientists saw in applying their inductive method to real social problems was that it reinforced their essentially conservative point-of-view. Almost all social scientists hoped that the inductive method would show them how to bring stability and justice to an increasingly chaotic society. Only one or two at Harvard, however, followed the inductive ideal hoping to secure principles for a radically new social order. Most turned to science because its slow and careful method and its ability to evaluate all sides of a question tended to serve as a brake on hasty or radical theories of reform. Most typical, of course, was the manner in which social science at Harvard arrayed itself against William Jennings Bryan. The inductive method did not provide Harvard's social scientists with any radical systems for social justice; usually the social values and goals the social scientists enunciated were those of an older era.

Despite this appeal to older values, Harvard social scientists did not view modern social problems passively. Harvard scholars and students felt that something must be done and must be done immediately to meet the threats of impending social chaos. They all possessed a faith, an idealism, that this relief was imminent as soon as citizens began working for a better society. Peabody's mixture of Paul's teachings in I Corinthians with the recent findings of social science merely exaggerated the kind of balance of old and new, of past and future, of realism and utopianism that existed in the minds of many progressives and in the Progressive Movement as a whole.

Peabody's outlook fit and shaped the tone of campus life during the Progressive era, but the failure of the Social Ethics Department to maintain its position in the curriculum after the disillusion of World War I indicates that intellectual discipline as well as new modes of thinking were most crucial to the permanent establishment of the social sciences in the University curriculum. Yet the influence of Peabody's variety of idealism on the emergence of the social sciences must not be overlooked. This idealistic attitude toward the "social question" permeated student life in most American universities in the eighties and nineties. The growing attendance at Harvard's social science courses reflected this new student interest, an interest which demanded an ever increasing number of courses taught in the social sciences and which received increasing inspiration from the social science curriculum. Such idealism manifested itself in various student efforts at social service and in various student organizations which dealt with contemporary affairs in debates, lectures, and conferences. That the new courses drew and inspired large numbers of students suggests that the social sciences at the turn of the century were an integral part of the students' college experience just as the moral philosophy course had been before the Civil War.

The study of man and society still played a central role in the University in 1900, but the manner in which the students pursued these studies had altered radically from the prewar pattern of moral philosophy. The student had been expected to master a single, prescribed theory of man and society; by 1900 he was responsible for choosing from a great variety of courses and a great variety of points of view as he studied the social sciences. The inception of the elective system in 1869 manifested the new method of instructing students. But only with the full development of the elective system in the eighties was student responsibility fully realized. In changing to the elective system Harvard was recognizing the increased age of its students and was emulating to some degree the *Lernfreiheit* of the German universities. Harvard was also attempting to improve college education, for free choice was intended to give the well-motivated student a chance to make the most of his years at Harvard and to make the college experience of the less motivated more meaningful; the critical assumption here was that a student learns more from a subject he wants to take than from one he is forced to take. But the elective system, although it provided a structure in which the moral philosophy curriculum could fragment, did not in itself cause this fragmentation.

The major cause of the appearance of conflicting points of view in place of the synthesis once presented by moral philosophy was the introduction of inductive reasoning into the curriculum. The acceptance and pursuit of the inductive ideal was predicated on a faith that the new method would lead to certainty—to the one principle of order inhering in reality. Experience did not bear out this faith. Many individ-

uals found their own answers to specific problems posed by
man and society but no one found the single principle that
would clear away all problems. There followed, then, a subtle
shift in emphasis among teachers—a shift from a faith in the
existence of a single answer to an acceptance of the existence
of a plurality of possible answers. Although scholars themselves were slow to articulate their change in attitude, students were quick to feel it.

The impact of this new attitude toward certainty is best
measured by comparing the over-all appearance of the social
science curriculum in 1900 to the appearance of the moral
philosophy course before the Civil War. From a single textbook a single professor had taught all seniors economics, psychology, political science, social ethics, individual ethics,
family living, and some history. He had included all these
subjects under a single system and had pressed the student
to accept that one system. In 1900 the student studied separately whichever of the subjects he chose, and he studied
each under a different professor. He read a variety of texts.
He no longer memorized a system; he learned methods of
finding truth for himself. The moral philosopher had taught
his students what must be done to improve society. The late-
nineteenth-century social scientist taught his students a
method by which they could judge for themselves what procedures were needed in the face of the social problems of the
day.

Because he used techniques derived from inductive reasoning in judging the social order, the social scientist felt
that he must pass these techniques on to the students, for
every student was to have an important role in society after
graduation. One guiding tenet of the Progressive temperament was the belief that social stability would return when
every intelligent citizen did his part by voting correctly, by
supporting social service, and by participating in the welter

of civic groups or government commissions whenever his influence or competence was needed. To carry out this kind of task in an intelligent and concerned way, the future citizen must be trained to do more than merely accept and memorize principles.

Of course, a student would not have to think for himself if he were merely to participate in bringing to society an order upon whose description all men agreed, but no such description was found in the late nineteenth century. In fact, the most important single factor that determined the University's particular character in these decades was the plethora of conflicting ideas about the nature and direction of society that had replaced the hegemony which Scottish Realism had exercised over the pre-Civil War college. Typical of this new diversity in opinion were the new conceptions of man that entered the Harvard curriculum after the Civil War. In the earlier period, the moral philosophy course had begun each year with a brief definition of man. This definition almost invariably followed the philosophy of William Paley and contained some brief discussion of the differences between mind and matter in the manner of Scottish Realism. Simplicity, rigidity, and full confidence in the uniqueness and individuality of man marked the presentation. After the Civil War scholars questioned this definition of man. Darwin's epoch-making theory suggested that man was not unique, that his mind did not differ from matter, and that man actually exercised no free will. William James carried opposition to the dualism of mind and matter directly into the Harvard Philosophy Department. Positivist social scientists in Europe stressed the possibility that man was merely another form of determined matter. The simple assertion of man's free will could not refute these new doctrines. Positivists who supported the notion of an organic society as well as utopian social reformers forced Harvard social scientists to deal with the conception of man as a collectivist, nonindividualistic creature. Mere affirmations of individualism or Paleyan formulae could not effectively counter these conceptions.

Although few men on the Harvard faculty believed that man was either determined or collectivist, Harvard's scholars became less satisfied with the older definition of man. Each professor arrived at his own substitute, and each at one time or another taught his own conception of man. But no two held the identical conception. No new synthesis emerged to replace the Common Sense philosophers' single definition of man to which all members of the faculty had once been able to adhere. The social scientists had turned to inductive reasoning in an attempt to isolate and prove a single definition of man, but their implementation of induction led instead to more confusion than ever. Any monistic conception of man seemed impossible to substantiate in the face of the overwhelming number of possibilities inherent in experience. The student was encouraged to think for himself because the University no longer had any unified and assured body of knowledge to transmit to him. The University no longer taught the answer; it suggested possible answers. It no longer taught a religion; it stressed ethics. It no longer taught a theory of man and society; it stressed the student's responsibility to make his own judgments and act accordingly.

THE
ECONOMISTS
STUDY SOCIETY

SOCIOLOGY AT HARVARD, 1891–1902

ROBERT L. CHURCH

SOCIOLOGY at Harvard arose out of the conflict of
ideas and methods held by various members of the Economics Department—a conflict at Harvard which reflected
the conceptual and methodological conflict then generally
current in European and American economic thought.
Sociology at its inception embodied a widening of scope and
a significant change of method within academic economics
itself. It served as a forward wing of a great advance in economic thinking at Harvard. In time, however, the whole
Economics Department came to accept the innovations advocated by sociology. Then, because it had not developed a
method or subject matter unique to itself, sociology at

Harvard atrophied. The word "sociology" first appeared in the *Harvard College Catalogue* in 1891 as part of the course title of Economics 3, "The Principles of Sociology—Development of the Modern State, and of its Social Functions." Although the Department of Economics continued to offer this basic course for forty years, no supplementary undergraduate courses in formal sociology appeared. Not until 1931 did Harvard College form an independent Department of Sociology. Only in the first ten of these forty years was sociology a vital and contributing factor in the development of economic thought. This essay, concerned principally with the years from 1891 to 1902, examines the causes and the academic results of the economists' new concern with society.

Sweeping attacks on the dominant system of Manchesterian "laissez faire" economic theory first appeared in Europe in the seventies, and by the eighties and nineties these attacks had grown to be a major challenge to Classical theory. The historical economists with their "inductive" method challenged the "purely deductive" methods of the Classical economists, who, the historians reasoned, produced a set of economic laws that had nothing to do with reality. Thomas E. Cliffe-Leslie began introducing the work of the German historical economists to the English-speaking world in the seventies, and Arnold Toynbee's *Industrial Revolution*, in which this nineteenth-century scholar-reformer argued that modern industrialism invalidated classical economic theories, appeared in 1884. In 1892 William James Ashley, one of England's two leading economic historians and a vociferous opponent of abstract economics, came to teach at Harvard. The theorists and supporters of the deductive method themselves recognized that Ricardo and Mill had oversimplified reality in order to build their great systems. Instead of challenging the Classicists, however, they sought to revivify them by adding to their simplified laws covering supply and demand, rent, wages, and value new concepts and methods capable of reflecting and measuring some of the complexity of actual economic processes. Chief among these new methods was that of marginalism. From 1882 to 1935 Frank William Taussig was Harvard's leading exponent of the theoretical approach and the leading opponent of the historical one.

Adam Smith's "invisible hand" was being questioned on all sides. Nineteenth-century thought and politics had solidified Smith's conceptual tool into a cornerstone for rigid "laissez-faire" policies. When socialists, liberals, and philanthropists rejected laissez-faire, they of necessity challenged current interpretations of *The Wealth of Nations*. In the face of this challenge economists sought to grasp the "invisible hand," to identify it, to define it, actually to go beyond it in order to find a more sophisticated concept with which to study economic processes. Some, like Taussig, sought in psychology a means of arriving at a more precise theoretical definition of social reality. Others, like Ashley, sought in social history a means of arriving at a more precise empirical definition. Both groups, seeking to strengthen economics, turned to a closer analysis of society.

Reality itself intruded upon the University, demanding that the Harvard College student be trained to understand and to decide the many great issues of the day. The greenback and silver controversies, the tariff debate, the problem of monopolies, and the labor question were at the forefront of American thought in the last quarter of the nineteenth century. Furthermore, more successful, and thus much more frightening, trade-union movements, socialist movements, and cooperative movements in Europe preyed on the American mind. Henry George's *Progress and Poverty* was certainly no great contribution to theoretical economics, but its immense popularity insured it a place in the economics course alongside the works of John Stuart Mill and John E. Cairnes. Since problems of economic policy seemed to be part of every public question of the day, the department at Harvard slowly turned from an exclusive study of Classical economic theory to courses analyzing contemporary affairs.

This shift to a concern with society occurred neither quickly nor automatically, for it raised a major conflict among faculty members as to the purpose of academic economics. The prolonged nationwide debate among social scientists as to the role of sociology reflected one aspect of this conflict. Some felt—as Comte—that sociology was the master social science, the one that interpreted and integrated all the findings of the lesser social sciences—history, economics, social welfare, and political science. These latter disciplines were merely parts of a whole, a whole represented by sociology. Other social scientists saw sociology only as another social science, equal in status and importance to economics or political science but incapable of dealing profitably with the findings of economics or history. Still others regarded sociology as an upstart, as unscientific, chaotic, and devoid of unique subject matter. Many economists accused sociologists of trying to invade the field previously reserved for economics in order to appropriate subject matter from the economists. Since academic sociology developed, by and large, within economics departments, the debate waxed most acrimonious between the sociologists and the economists.[1]

The fact that sociology offerings at Harvard remained within the Department of Economics so long indicates that sociology at Harvard had no effective support as the "master" discipline and little support as a "separate but equal" discipline. Debate at Harvard centered largely on the questions of whether sociology had the right to be considered a social science at all, and of whether its academic claims rested on its alliance with theoretical economics or on its own methodology and its own conclusions. In the nineties at Harvard the professors concerned with social study veered away from the peculiar concerns of economic theory and developed an emphasis and a subject matter which might have justified a separate department. After the Economics Department as a whole had come to accept the widened scope of inquiry pioneered by sociology, Harvard sociologists did not pursue an independent course but firmly allied themselves with economics and claimed their academic status on the basis of this alliance.

A more important aspect of the conflict at Harvard involved the definition of the subject matter of economics itself. In the seventies and eighties Harvard economists had been most interested in building their discipline into one that shared the sense of certainty and absolute truth felt to exist in the exact sciences. In order to do so they worked out a system of theorems, equations, and axioms dealing with wealth and distribution. At the same time, in order to protect the universal validity of their theorems, the economists carefully abstracted them from the ever-fluctuating conditions of actual social life. To them economics was the science that dealt with these universal axioms. Sociology and the historical method threatened this conception of economics, for the younger men proposed to turn from the study of these universal rules to the study of individual situations and problems. These younger men wanted sociology to be "scientific," too, but they possessed a much more flexible notion of what constituted a science. Instead of emphasizing economics' parallels with the closed system of mathematics, they stressed its similarities to an open-ended science such as biology where continuing observation of phenomena produced ever-new hypotheses and generalizations.

The representatives of the historical method and of the social application of economics never gained a position of dominance at Harvard, for, although no one after 1900 admitted as openly as the men of the seventies and eighties that they felt that economics was best studied as a closed, theoretical system, the Economics Department at Harvard generally defined economics as a science committed to building an all-embracing system from a few premises.

Sociology, even at its inception, was conceived with a dual nature: some hoped that its concern with observation and individual cases would turn economists away from reliance on deduction and convince them of the fruitfulness of an exclusive concern with observation of facts and testing of hypotheses; others hoped that sociology, by extending the systems of the deductive economists into larger areas of human experience, would give those systems greater universality, wider applicability, and more absolute certainty. In the early years sociology seemed to fulfill the hopes of the first group. The thrust of sociology in the nineties was against the essentially closed system of economics represented first by Charles F. Dunbar and then by Taussig. Its spokesmen delighted in the individual situation and shied away from making simplistic analogies between their work and the exact sciences. They refused to enunciate large premises from which entire systems could be constructed. Chiefly because of this refusal, Harvard sociologists failed to organize their subject into a coherent, teachable "body of knowledge," and thus sociology made no separate place for itself at Harvard. It is indicative that none of the social thinkers with an inductive orientation either wrote a textbook or used one in his courses.

After 1900 the theoretical, deductive approach reasserted itself. When a theoretical economist taught sociology as one part of a closed system of economics, the kind of sociology that Harvard had known in the nineties was forgotten. Instead of serving as an antidote to the abstractness and narrowness of the older economics, sociology became a tool of those who believed that economics was an exact, rigid, deductive science designed to manipulate rules rather than to solve individual problems. Ironically enough, some of the courses in pure economics included more advanced thinking about society and social problems than did the course in formal sociology. By 1910 economics had overtaken sociology in the quest for a thorough understanding of human society.

Political economy, like most of the social sciences at Harvard, was originally part of the moral philosophy curriculum. Until 1879 Harvard's two courses in economics were offered by the Philosophy Department. Until 1871 the only political economy offered had been that taught by Francis Bowen, Alford Professor of Natural Religion, Moral Philosophy, and Civil Polity. Although 1871 marks the Harvard Corporation's official appointment of Dunbar as Harvard's first professor dealing exclusively with political economy,[2] 1868 and 1869 seem to have been the years crucial to the subsequent rapid development of economics at Harvard. In the late sixties a group of Boston businessmen, influential in the affairs of the University, made it clear that Harvard should teach political economy and teach it correctly. Bowen's advocacy of a protective tariff and his theory that the national debt should be repayed below par angered these Boston merchants, and they responded by putting pressure on the Harvard Corporation. In 1868 they donated money to establish an annual course of lectures in political economy, to be filled only by men known for their sound-money views.[3] Apparently by 1869 the University was more impressed with the importance of teaching economics to college students, for in that year Dunbar received his unofficial appointment just before he departed for a two-year period of rest in Europe. Dunbar's only qualification for the chair of political economy, besides the studies he pursued while in Europe, appears to have been the economic orthodoxy of the editorials he had written while editor of the Boston *Daily Advertiser* in the sixties.[4]

After 1871 courses in political economy had grown in attendance and in prestige in the College. At the same time, according to Dunbar, the field became increasingly relevant to American life and to the future security of the United States.

In the coming century an economic blunder in the United States will be a blunder on a far more portentous scale than those of the past, and will work out its consequences among political elements which will admit of no trifling. Already our public men are appalled by the responsibility of answering such a question as is set them by the currency . . . It will . . . no longer be possible for statesmen or scholars to ignore or neglect those economic laws which determine the consequences of our actions . . . The regular course of our development must, at a point not far distant, disclose to us an imperious necessity for investigating the laws of material wealth; and that point being reached, we may confidently expect that the United States will no longer fail to contribute their due share to the advancement of this branch of knowledge.[5]

To facilitate scholarly investigation of the "laws of material wealth" and to give such study a recognized position in academic life, Dunbar organized the Department of Political Economy in 1879 as an area of study distinct from that of philosophy.

The new department offered the same two courses that the Philosophy Department had offered—an elementary course covering Mill's textbook and some financial history and an advanced course which studied Cairnes, Mill's disciple, and America's only economist of stature, Henry C. Carey. (It also offered a third course, a very elementary one for students not well enough prepared for the general introductory course.) The department dealt almost exclusively with Mill, more Mill, and currency. Undergraduate attendance increased from 120 in 1878 to 151 in 1882 and 205 in 1883. Dunbar, accounting for this steady increase in student interest, stated that "the perception of the scope and importance of the questions with which political economy deals . . . turns the popular current so strongly towards it today. It is keenly felt," he continued, "that on the right answer of these questions must depend not only the future progress of society, but also the preservation of much that has been gained by mankind in the past . . ." Furthermore, he stated, people want these problems studied and investigated with the same methods proved so useful in other fields of study, that is, the natural sciences.[6]

Political economy, Dunbar was convinced, consisted of the discovery and study of the laws of material wealth. About just how these laws were to apply to the specific questions upon which the nation's future was felt to rest, he was more hesitant. The first few years of the new department did not see any attempts to relate specific laws to specific problems. Rather, the reverse occurred, for Dunbar, starting from a specific problem like the Bland-Allison Act of 1878, would move to the general laws of currency, monetary expansion, and the wage fund as recorded by Adam Smith, Ricardo, or Mill. No attempt was then made to apply Mill's law of currency in judging the expediency of the Bland-Allison Act. Nor could there be any such attempt:

At this point we must recall the distinction often insisted upon by economists . . . between economic laws and the application of those laws in practical administration and legislation. The economic law, the deduction of pure science, is simply the statement of a causal relation, usually between a small number of forces and their joint effect, possibly between a single force and its effect. For the statement of that relation, the case has been freed from every disturbing element, and with the result . . . of giving a proposition which, however important, is only conditionally true . . . But, when we come to the application of economics to legislation, we enter at once into a region of necessarily confused conditions, and also become conscious of objective ends often having little or no relation to any economic doctrine.[7]

Economic law, Dunbar continued, was within the province of the university, but the university was not to pronounce on questions of legislation and expediency. These questions "involve questions of science, as they involve much else; but their solution is not an act of the scientific judgment." [8] Legislative debate over, and presidential veto of, the Bland-Allison Act raised for Dunbar and for his class not the question of whether the free coinage of silver in the United States in 1878 was a practical policy but rather the questions: What was the nature of money? Why were the precious metals useful as currency?

The Department of Political Economy began expanding in scope in 1883 with the addition of several courses, two of which were very important as forerunners of sociology. In this year Professor Dunbar began teaching "The Economic History of Europe and America since 1763." Dunbar's historical method, however, was certainly not the inductive one that was to be introduced ten years later by Ashley. Dunbar wrote:

Ricardo and his contemporaries naturally spent but little effort in speculating upon industrial and social changes, of which their time showed only the beginnings . . . Inventions, the opening of new continents, the abolition of time and space, the economic rejuvenation of countries by social and political reform, follow each other in a long line and in a certain orderly movement. Reason compels us to reject the vision of perpetual advance; but, for these generations of the world's history at any rate, industrial improvement, or that which tends in the same direction, is not an accidental, but, as nearly as possible, a permanent force, acting with the primary forces of which the economist treats, but constantly masking and for the time, perhaps, reversing their effects. Here, then, has been offered the opportunity for the economist to make useful application of his method, for investigating the movement of society in the ascending part of its orbit, and dealing with a mass of striking phenomena, far too complex for systematic study without the working hypothesis already in his hand.[9]

Dunbar seems to have been looking for another abstract law or formula, which would account for the change brought on by the industrial revolution, a law which was to be discovered through deduction from the Classical laws and which was to take its place beside them. One senses here Dunbar's suspicion that since Ricardo and Mill did not deal with the problems of the eighties their laws might not be relevant. On this premise, of course, the historical school in these very years was declaring the Classicists completely outmoded. Dunbar was far from joining in such a denunciation, but his history course was the first attempt at Harvard to relate the "scientific laws" of Mill's *Principles* to the specific problems of American society. Historical method, according to Dunbar, was not to change political economy into an inductive discipline, but "it would be idle to deny that the verification of conclusions by observation and the selection of new premises for further reasoning—in a word, that the thoroughness of the deductive process and the general scope of the study—have been advanced in a high degree by the improved methods of research and comparison . . ."[10]

If economic history was to verify economic laws by testing them against economic developments over time, the purpose of Political Economy 3—"Investigation and Discussion of Practical Economic Questions"—was to verify economic deductions by testing them against contemporary economic affairs. This course, introduced in 1883 by J. Laurence Laughlin, was described in a departmental bulletin of 1887–88 as giving each student "practice in collecting the facts and in making a simple statement of opposing arguments on some part of a question of the day . . ." Among the questions considered were bimetallism, gold and prices, reciprocity with Canada and Mexico, the advantages of government issues of notes over national bank issues, surplus revenue, cooperation, American shipping and navigation laws, and railroad legislation. The course had three purposes: to teach students to collect facts, to help them understand and interpret economic arguments, and to drill them in comparing these arguments to the laws learned in the introductory course. It constituted the third step in Laughlin's conception of the process of economic investigation: "First, there is observation, then deduction from the basis of established laws, in order to explain the observed facts, and lastly inductive verification, with a severe and exacting standard." [11]

Laughlin, who received his Ph.D. from Harvard in 1876 for research on Anglo-Saxon legal procedure under Henry Adams, adhered to Dunbar's view of the academic place of political economy. He also shared Professor Dunbar's interest in money and banking—writing many articles and books on bimetallism. Although trained in history, Laughlin was so antagonistic to the historical school of economists that he refused to teach the economic history course given in 1883.[12] He opposed the formation of the American Economic Association in 1885, debated hotly for many years with Richard T. Ely, and refused to join the organization until 1904 though his Harvard colleagues, Taussig and Dunbar, had joined the Association in 1886 and 1888 respectively and Dunbar had become its second president in 1892.[13] Laughlin edited a students' edition of Mill in 1884 in which he eliminated Mill's references to social philosophy, "believing . . . that the omission of much that should properly be classed under the head of Sociology, or Social Philosophy, would narrow the field to Political Economy alone, and aid, perhaps, in clearer ideas . . ." [14] Laughlin disliked the lecture system and his students disliked his dogmatic approach to economic questions.[15]

Laughlin's career marks the height of economic conservatism at Harvard in the nineteenth century and his resistance to change was, at times, heroic (including his repeated rejections of the doctrine of marginal utility even in the twenties). Yet his contributions to economic theory and to economic teaching while at Harvard were not insignificant. His widely used textbooks and his belief in political economy's importance as a subject for study influenced college curricula throughout the country. He was one of the first to consider studying applied economics along with economic theory. And his contributions as head of the University of Chicago's Economics Department from 1892 to 1916 were of even greater importance.[16]

With the new courses of 1883 the study of political economy ceased to be merely a study of abstractions, a course in memorizing and trying to understand a set of principles or formulae. One of the most frequently cited advantages of studying economics in the late nineteenth century was that it provided excellent training in abstract reasoning. No matter what its practical value to the student's subsequent career, a course in political economy would have taught him how to think.[17] The ultimate purpose of these new courses was to increase the undergraduate's understanding of abstract formulae by teaching him to manipulate them in light of selected facts taken from a concrete situation.

Only secondarily, and against Dunbar's wishes, did they

give the students some insight into the relation of economic laws to policy decisions. In fact, Dunbar stressed that "the facts, historical, social, psychological, or physical, which create special conditions" around every practical question limit the application of theoretical economic laws in any concrete situation. "This limitation of their [the economic truths] practical effect as supplying a part, but only a part, of the grounds of action, is of special importance, of course, in their bearing upon legislation. Economic laws, in strictness, deal with wealth; but the object of legislation is welfare." [18] Political, social, and ethical as well as economic considerations entered into legislative decisions, but Dunbar was adamant that these other considerations should not enter into the study of economics. Economics must search for truth, not ethics.[19] Dunbar as a teacher refrained from discussing solutions to "current questions of economics and politics," [20] partly because he felt that a teacher should remain completely neutral on all debated questions in order to allow the student to make up his own mind, and partly because he felt that political economy should not confuse its primary scientific function with the much less important function of adjudicating controversies.[21] The economist in the university was to deal with the "questions of the day" only in the most rigorous scientific manner and was to present only those answers which scientific investigation revealed. Such investigation could, in Dunbar's opinion, reveal a good deal, however: "The circle of emotions, hopes, and moral judgments springing from any economic fact, may be boundless;" wrote Dunbar, "but the relation of that fact to its cause and its consequences is as certainly a question to be settled by appropriate scientific methods, as the perturbation of a satellite or a reaction observed by a chemist." [22] But nothing revealed by this scientific analysis enabled the investigator to judge the social usefulness of a course of action.

The introduction of history and contemporary affairs in

the Department of Political Economy in 1883 was intended to widen the economist's experience but did not denote a shift in emphasis from the abstract to the concrete, from the deductive to the inductive, from the natural to the social sciences. Within ten years, however, these two courses, taught by new men, would be the scene of just such a shift in emphasis.

"The Principles of Sociology" grew directly from the course in practical economic questions and replaced it in the curriculum in 1891. Two years before, however, John Graham Brooks, than a minister in Brockton, Massachusetts, had come to lecture on practical economic questions in place of Laughlin. In 1887 the financial impossibility of supporting two assistant professors forced the Economics Department to choose between Laughlin and Taussig. A similar choice had impended in 1883, but Henry Lee's offer to pay Laughlin's salary as an assistant professor for five years put off the decision. At that time Dunbar seemed to favor retaining Laughlin, but by 1887 he had apparently come to agree with Eliot that Taussig was the stronger scholar. Laughlin's opposition to the lecture system that greater and greater student interest in economics was making imperative, his fear that he would be forced to teach economic history, and Eliot's evident preference for Taussig made the latter the obvious choice for advancement. In November 1887 Eliot informed Laughlin that his appointment would not be renewed after September 1, 1888, and two months later Laughlin left Harvard suffering from a nervous breakdown.[23] The loss of one of its two young theorists left the department without any instructor for the problems course. From 1889 until the turn of the century that offering fell, by accident as much as design, into the hands of men of a decided empirical and social reform turn of mind.

The first of these was Brooks, whose career included some study of law at the University of Michigan and a bachelor's degree in 1875 from the Harvard Divinity School. In 1878, while leading the First Religious Society in Roxbury, Brooks had begun his career of countless lectures on economics and history before various groups of workingmen. Many had come to consider his advocacy of "government control of monopolies, voluntary trade unions, and social security legislation" quite radical. Although often accused of being a socialist, Brooks had rejected that doctrine. Brooks had spent the years 1882–1885 at the universities of Berlin, Freiburg, and Jena studying the German social-security system under many of the intellectuals who had helped to implement it. After leaving Harvard and the ministry in 1891 Brooks devoted all his time to lecturing, doing research, and investigating strikes for the Labor Department, for which he wrote his pioneer study, *Compulsory Insurance in Germany* (1893).[24]

Brooks's course offering differed quite radically from Laughlin's, for Brooks drew his subject matter from the "social question," to which he later gave the following definition:

If confined to its economic aspects, the dissatisfaction out of which the social question springs has its origin largely in the growing belief that mechanical science and invention applied to industry are too closely held by private interests. An enormous private ownership of industrial mechanism, especially if coupled with lands and mines, is now clearly seen to carry with it powers and privileges that may easily be turned against every promise of free and democratic society. If it is true that dissatisfaction has gained such headway as to disturb more and more the currents of our social and political life, that of itself makes the problem of our time.[25]

Whereas in the eighties Economics 3 had directed attention to the questions of bimetallism, railroads, currency, and tariff, under Brooks it dealt with labor arbitration, friendly societies in England, German workmen's insurance, trade unions, profit-sharing, and cooperation.

In the departmental bulletin of 1890–91 Brooks promised to give the students "training in simple investigation," which for Brooks meant personal contact, interviews, and first-hand observation.[26] "During six years of weekly economics lectures before a trade-union audience, I learned that any trade-union literature accessible was upon the whole misleading," he wrote in 1903. "An academic student, who has read never so faithfully all the books, has to learn his entire lesson over again by contact with the actual concrete struggles of unions . . ."[27] Such a method, of course, denotes distrust of the abstractions so often relied upon by academic economists and academic social critics. As such it was the first course in the Economics Department at Harvard that stressed observation and inductive reasoning to the exclusion of deduction. Brooks, however, ranks as a reformer, not an academic social scientist; and, as such, he was really out of place in Professor Dunbar's department. Brooks wanted investigation of the concrete reality, not in order to make a generalization about employer-employee relations, but in order to settle a specific strike. His example had little influence upon the style of teaching political economy in the College.

Brooks is important for our purposes, however, in that he was the first to explore the ramifications of Dunbar's identification of the "industrial and social changes" of the nineteenth century as fruitful subject matter for economic investigation. Brooks was the first teacher in the department to suggest that the "social question" or the "economic question" represented something more than a temporary dislocation of a fixed system. He suggested that the industrial revolution had brought about a fundamental change in the economic and social order, a change that necessitated modification of economic and social formulae. He suggested very clearly in his published work, although probably less plainly in his teaching within Professor Dunbar's department, that the machine had created a new kind of wealth and a new kind of laboring class and that a new relation between the two had to be worked out. He was saying that the findings of the Manchester School did not apply to the conditions at the close of the nineteenth century because the appearance of the machine had radically altered the very nature of wealth, labor, and society.[28]

Brooks's concerns paralleled those of society at large. What about this new nature of society, of the labor force? What about this frighteningly rapid alteration of society? Was society progressing or degenerating? How did the economist account for the changes? Socialists, workingmen, even intellectuals and university professors were claiming that the rules of Classical economics no longer applied, that the machine and the capitalist were destroying society, and that the only solution lay in the abolition of capital and private property. On the other hand, many were arguing that the eighties and nineties represented the epitome of human progress, that this progress resulted directly from laissez-faire policy applied to an economy of private property, and that similar progress was guaranteed so long as the individual was left free to operate as he wished.

Such public (as well as academic) debate thrust itself into the Economics Department, for the student body as well as the public at large was eager to hear what the professors had to say. The platform outlined in 1885 in the prospectus for the American Economic Association opened with these words: "We regard the state as an educational and ethical agency whose positive aid is an indispensable condition of human progress. While we recognize the necessity of individual initiative in industrial life, we hold that the doctrine of *laissez-faire* is unsafe in politics and unsound in morals; and that it suggests an inadequate explanation of the relations between the state and the citizens." [29] Many economists disagreed. The public chose sides. The frightened businessman, or his son, wanted to hear a professor say that state control could not work and that free enterprise could. The socialist or workingman wanted to hear just the opposite. The thinkers that rejected laissez-faire and Ricardo flung a challenge at those, like Dunbar and Taussig, who found their authority in the writings of the Manchester School. The challenge had to be answered.

It is important to note that both sides in the public debate sought support for their economic theories in theories of society and in conceptions of man. Which kind of economic system one counted upon to bring social good and human progress was determined by one's definition of the social nature of man. The fundamentals of the debate had finally been identified, an identification that made the study of sociology integral to the study of political economy. Throughout the country courses in and departments of sociology grew up within or sprang from departments of economics or political science.[30] It had become imperative to study society, to compare and select theories of human and social progress, to decide between individualism and collectivism.

The sociology course at Harvard, as outlined in the Department of Political Economy Bulletin for 1891–92, was intended to do just that: the course began "with a theoretical consideration of the relation of the individual to society and to the state . . . [and it dealt] with certain tendencies of the modern state, discussing especially the province and limits of state activity, with some comparison of the Anglo-Saxon and the continental theory and practice in regard to private initiative and state intervention . . ."

Edward Cummings began teaching this course when he returned from a three-year stay in Europe that had included study at the London School of Economics, a year's residence at Toynbee Hall, and briefer stops at, among others, the University of Berlin and *L'Ecole Libre des Sciences Politiques* in Paris. Cummings had received his bachelor's degree from Harvard in 1883 and his master's degree in 1885. In the late eighties he had studied under Francis Greenwood Peabody, who was to found Harvard's Department of Social Ethics, and it was probably Peabody who interested him in social science and study in Europe. Cummings was the first incumbent of the fellowship in social science given to Harvard in 1887 by Robert Treat Paine, Sr., a philanthropist well-known on the local and national level.[31] Cummings left Harvard in 1900 to become associate pastor with Edward Everett Hale at South Church (Unitarian), and after 1910 he devoted most of his time to the World Peace Foundation.[32]

Cummings was one of those fascinating, confused, contradictory conservatives so prominent at the turn of the century. A Social Darwinist, he used rigidly objective standards of social investigation to show that individual initiative and the free operation of natural selection were essential to social progress. Yet he was a social gospeler and headed many, many charity organizations in the Boston area. The only materials preserved from his sociology course are a few examinations and the course description in the department's pamphlet. Cummings wrote no textbooks and his few articles are very limited in scope. However, the themes which ran through his ten years of teaching sociology can be reconstructed from student notes taken in other courses he taught, his examination questions, the course descriptions, his periodical writings, and his career.

Evolution was the primary motif of Cummings' thought and teaching—society develops through the processes of natural selection and the struggle for existence. The evidence points to the fact that he was, however, a very strict evolutionist who used Darwin, rather than Spencer, as the foundation for his thought. Little of the rhetoric of organicism appears in his writings or in his lectures. Economics 3, the department's announcement of 1891–92 stated, "begins with a theoretical consideration of the relation of the individual to society and to the state—with a view to pointing out some theoretical misconceptions and practical errors traceable to an illegitimate use of the fundamental analogies and metaphysical formulas found in Comte, Spencer, P. Leroy-Beaulieu, Schaeffle, and other publicists." The final word of this sentence was changed the following year to the more tactful "writers." The meaning of the sentence hinged, of course, on whether the "theoretical misconceptions and practical errors" or only "the fundamental analogies and metaphysical formulas" were to be found in the named sociologists.

Apparently, Cummings saw many errors, mostly of application, in the writings of the founders of sociology. He could not agree with Leroy-Beaulieu or Spencer that the state should not tamper at all with social processes, nor could he assent to the state socialism and collectivism advocated by Comte and Schäffle. Cummings was caught in the dilemma of the scientific social reformer—on the one hand he posited the inevitable and immutable processes of social development and on the other he desired to change society. "The Principles of Sociology—Development of the Modern State, and of its Social Functions" sought to resolve this conflict.

Unlike such great American professors of his era as Lester Ward, Albion Small, and Simon Patten, Cummings had little interest and less faith in the anthropological speculations of contemporary sociology. As an evolutionist, he of course studied the historical process, but for him history began not with Adam and Eve or the promiscuous horde or the hypothetical matriarchal state of primitive man, but with the beginnings of the industrial revolution. "[The] difference between what we call a tool and what we call a machine sums up the key or the answer to the origin of and the labor questions themselves," was one student's interpretation of Cummings' opening lecture on economic development and social questions in the introductory course of 1898.

This student noted that in later lectures Cummings claimed that the change from the family to the factory system was all important for it caused "a rising standard of living, comfort and intelligence . . . universal suffrage, . . . is due primarily to this increase in use of machinery. It has affected also very principally the social question," for now the workman has lost control over the conditions of labor. A new impersonal relation develops between employer and employee, which in turn fosters the growth of a distinct laboring class. "Trade unionism, profit-sharing [,] cooperation [,] etc [.,] are attempts by workmen to regain control of conditions of industry." [33] What about these attempts? Were they silly? futile? dangerous? necessary? useless because they did not go far enough? Were they standing out against the evolutionary process or were they the next step in the evolutionary development of the human race?

These were serious and unresolved questions in the decades that saw Haymarket and the Pullman strike in America, Fabian Socialism and the birth of the Labour Party in Britain, and compulsory social security in Germany. American and European economists ranged themselves along the whole spectrum of thought—from a Dunbar who saw social conditions as irrelevant to the study of economics to a Spencer who felt evolutionary laws dictated a rigid social policy of laissez-faire to an Ely who advocated studying life in order to discover positive means of shaping the great forces of evolution toward the implementation of the humanitarianism he had found among his German teachers.[34]

Cummings sought to mediate between the conflicting theories of the role of the state by calling on contemporary social-psychological theories of human society. Cummings' period of teaching coincided with the beginnings of the serious study of social psychology—when Weber, Freud, Durkheim, Tarde, and LeBon were initiating the attempt to recover the unconscious.[35] Lecture notes from the nineties show that Cummings used something like a concept of national character when he attributed the failure of unionization and cooperation in America to the American workman's reluctance to make small savings and to the American people's lack of class consciousness. He asked on nearly every examination in his socialism course if the American experiments in communism had failed only for economic reasons, and he clearly expected the student to state that communism thwarted human nature. Cummings criticized Sidney and Beatrice Webb for their naïve faith that the trade-union movement would develop into a great collectivist association legislating for England in a manner free from strife and free from error: "What is true of the psychological outfit of men in general is largely true of trade-unionists . . . society at large may roughly be divided into three psychological groups,—conservatives, individualists, and 'collectivists,' " Cummings wrote in 1899. "And this division holds equally well for the trade union community. These three groups, again, will each have its own peculiar temperamental philosophy of life,—political, industrial, social." The inevitable persistence of these three psychological groupings proved the development of pure collectivism impossible.[36]

Cummings also relied heavily on the social psychology of Gustave LeBon for his critique of socialism. LeBon's La Psychologie des foules was published in 1895 and translated into English in 1896. LeBon's name appears on a final examination in 1899–1900. LeBon, violently antisocialist, argued that the large aggregates of people formed by the urban concentration produced by the industrial revolution, tended to subordinate individual consciousness to a collective subconscious prone to extreme mediocrity and suggestibility. LeBon, a racist and an élitist, claimed that the individual initiative and the national ideals of political laissez faire which prevailed among the Teutonic and Anglo-Saxon peoples assured social progress. The character of the Latin races, on the other hand, drove them to collectivism and revolution.[37] There is no reason to believe that Cummings accepted LeBon's racism, but he did find him useful authority in defending individual free enterprise.

A reference to Gabriel Tarde also appears on the examination of 1900. *Les Lois sociales* was published in 1898 and translated into English the following year. Cummings taught Tarde's fundamental system of repetition, opposition, and adaptation as soon as it was published. Tarde had written that individual inventiveness produced change, that imitation of, or conflict among, ideas diffused inventions through society, and that survival depended on how well each individual adapted himself through imitation to the rest of society, how well, in effect, he socialized himself. Tarde's whole system was psycho-sociological in its definition of the fundamental social processes as mental rather than physical. Thus opposition takes place among ideas and not among material forces; mental adaptation becomes the criterion for survival. Tarde's identification of the principle of imitation as the means by which new ideas take effect built upon earlier theories published by, among others, Josiah Royce and William James, both members of the Harvard Department of Philosophy and Psychology while Cummings studied and taught at Harvard. Tarde taught in Paris during Cummings' stay there. He was the theoretical sociologist most congenial to Cummings, for he claimed that physical conflict was growing less important as psychic forces created an equilibrium. He went on to argue that, although a large state was inevitable since it was needed to insure peace and harmony, the perpetual conflict of ideas and the unceasing imitation of the superior by the inferior would maintain the pace of evolutionary change. The inevitable extension of state activity, moreover, was not to be feared because of the growing effectiveness of popular control over government in the modern world.[38]

For the bulletin of the Departments of History and Government and of Economics for 1896–97 the description of the sociology course was altered to include many concepts of social psychology. Since almost all the course descriptions in the leaflet changed that year, the new description of Economics 3 probably reflected a gradual development in the course since 1891, a change not officially recorded until the bulletin received a general overhaul. Sociology was now to trace the "expansion of social consciousness, and the relative importance of military, economic, and ethical ideas at successive stages of civilization." There was to be "a careful consideration of the attempts to formulate physical and psychological laws of social growth . . ." "Social consciousness" probably refers to Franklin Giddings' "consciousness of kind," first expounded in book form in 1896 in *Principles of Sociology*, and to Emile Durkheim's "collective consciousness." Cummings agreed with Giddings' system and with his empirical method of close scientific observation. Cummings disagreed violently with Durkheim because Durkheim was then an apostle of collectivism.

Assigning the proper function to the state, however, remained the central purpose of the sociology course throughout the nineties. Cummings, addressing a group of Unitarian

ministers in 1897, summed up his theory of the role of the
state. Assuming, as did Tarde, that society and the state
were one, he proceeded to discuss "Charity and Progress."
Was society's philanthropy interfering with natural selection and social progress or was it aiding social progress by
offering the masses an opiate to help them accept the hor-
rors of the struggle? Neither, argued Cummings, for if society performed its philanthropic duties correctly, its philanthropy would recognize natural selection and support it.
Cummings described a pauper thrown into a large tank of
water equipped with a pump with which the pauper could
keep himself from drowning. The "fit" pauper performed
the work and won reinstatement in society; the degenerate
man drowned. Cummings interpreted his allegory:

The tank is a workhouse, run on a reformatory plan, with an
indeterminate sentence and every known device for detecting
germs of virtue and stimulating its growth,—to the end that the
prisoner may be reformed and become fit to re-enter society and
set free from the bonds of his own vices. The pump is the gospel
of work, of opportunity, self-help, and temperance. There are
two exits from these tanks. The one is called improvement, and
stands forever open. The other is death. The medical examination
is the separation of the weak and incapable, that the utmost may
be done for them in hospitals, homes for incurables, asylums, or
retreats for feeble-minded. Within the walls of these tanks is no
marrying or giving in marriage, or breeding of the unfit. They are
the philanthropic monasteries and nunneries of the twentieth century,—that our maxim may be fulfilled, and the unfit either
cease to be produced or cease to reproduce . . .

Thus shall the hereditary burden of pauperism, disease, and
crime grow less, and not greater, from generation to generation.
The tramp shall cease to be a burden, the unemployed shall be
fewer in the land, and charity shall injure no one whom it tries
to help . . .

Thus is the real paradox solved, the sacrifice of the strong to
the weak reconciled with progress, because *intelligent* self-sacrifice
of the strong to the weak makes the strong stronger and the

weak more strong. To him that hath the capacity to receive shall be given the priceless boon of opportunity, and from him that hath not shall be taken away the power of degrading himself and society. The philanthropy of the future will be wise as the serpent and gentle as the dove . . . [thus] the hydra-headed sphinx of evolution satisfied.[39]

This speech, academic enough for publication in the Harvard *Quarterly Journal of Economics,* may be taken as Cummings' resolution of his own dilemma and as his answer to the primary question posed by economists across the Western world.

The decidedly utopian cast of Cummings' resolution must be noted. Cummings was first of all a reformer intent upon meliorating the "tooth and claw" or "dog eat dog" concept of social process so prevalent among the Social Darwinists with an ethics founded on some philosophy other than the struggle for existence. In the realm of psychology he found a social theory which enabled him to view the evolutionary process as a struggle of ideas or states of mind, a struggle for adaptation to a social norm, as Tarde had pointed out, and which allowed him to champion the psychic instinct of sociability, which Giddings had identified, as the norm to which men should adapt.

That sense of fundamental conflict between man and his environment or between man and man over the means of subsistence that Malthus and the Manchester School had posited as their theory of society and that the Spencerians had assumed, was absent from Cummings' thought and from his study of nineteenth-century society. The success of voluntary cooperation and trade unions depended on their being institutions which demanded that a man help others in order to help himself. The social question of 1895 represented a problem, not of food and houses, but of antisocial people who work only for themselves, who do not work at all, or who commit crimes against society. If these people would adapt themselves to the norm of sociability, the social problem would end. Philanthropy, or "the tank," merely aided adaptation. When it had done its work, the social problem would disappear.

But Cummings was always careful to say that the millennium was remote, for society as yet had neither enough sociological data with which to create a truly scientific charity nor the right kind of medical examination with which to separate the fit from the unfit. Nor was human nature sufficiently well-trained to adapt itself to sociability. Cummings' major theoretical emphasis in the course stated that the resolution of the social question would evolve in time and that human intelligence could hasten and could direct that evolution. At the base of this thesis lay two assumptions: human ideas and the human consciousness were forceful and effective in themselves, and human consciousness was not merely a product of material forces, as Marx and Spencer had said, but was independent enough to shape social evolution to some degree. Sociology at Harvard pointed out that man must work for reform within the process of social evolution, a process which he cannot completely control, as the state socialists argued, but by which he is not completely controlled, as the Spencerians claimed.

The millennium lay far in the future because society lacked the knowledge with which to bring it about. Cummings repeatedly stressed this point as he attempted to define the role of sociology in the university and the role of the sociologist in society. His combination of the theories of social psychology with those of evolution suggested some of the mechanisms of social progress and helped him define the desired goal of that progress. None of the theories told him how social changes were to be effected or how to find the best place to start. Faced with the concrete problems of how men were to direct the process of social change, Cummings turned to the inductive method—to a consideration of nineteenth-century social conditions. These investigations, he hoped, would provide him with the knowledge that would guide mankind toward the realization of his ideal of a society which inspired competitive progress within a framework of social harmony.

That he found himself unable to integrate his concrete researches with his generalizations accounts in large part for the failure of sociology to find an important place for itself in the Harvard curriculum. Cummings' approach remained divided—social research did not help him refine his sociological theories nor did his theories help him define significant areas for research. It seems clear that Cummings' primary commitment was to inductive research and that he concerned himself only secondarily with theoretical sociology. Whenever possible he emphasized the need for more research. But his failure to derive either practical plans for action or theoretical tools of analysis from this research doomed his cause in Harvard's Economics Department.

Cummings' desire to combine inductive research with broad generalizations is evident from his evaluation of the contributions of two British sociological projects. He located the most significant sociology in the kind of work done by the Webbs in their *History of Trade Unionism in England* (1894) and their *Industrial Democracy* (1898) and by Charles Booth in his seventeen-volume *Life and Labour of the People in London* (1889–1902). Booth and the Webbs sought, as did Cummings, to evolve scientific generalizations only after intensive empirical research. He greatly respected the Webbs' "fundamental scientific faith in the essential unity and the mutual relevance of political, industrial, and social phenomena. For it is the distinctive feature of the threefold analysis in *Industrial Democracy* that it aims to furnish not only what we have styled a philosophy of Trade Unionism, but incidentally a philosophy of social and industrial organization as well," he wrote in 1899. "It is this which differentiates it from conventional studies, and gives it peculiar interest as an application of broad sociological methods to the examination of seemingly isolated phenomena." [40]

While recounting his impressions of Toynbee Hall, Cummings advised the college-student residents to spend more time gathering facts and less time reading Browning and Burne-Jones.[41]

It is in cities, in East Ends, North Ends, South Coves, that the sociological arena and laboratory are both to be found. It is a happy omen that scientific investigation and popular interest have both felt the need, the opportunity, and the duty at the same moment. The books now publishing [sic] in London under the direction of Mr. Charles Booth show what the best sociological methods, university methods . . . business methods, can do to furnish facts, dispel false prejudices, indicate safe lines of practical work.[42]

Cummings lauded the "thoroughly scientific and comprehensive spirit" of the social-economy section of the Paris Exposition of 1889. "Alongside the great record of industrial progress was to be a parallel study of social and moral progress,—a study sufficiently exhaustive to furnish the data for scientific generalizations" and sufficiently attractive for people to look at it. This latter requirement was the difficult goal, because the students and economists needed only "a library full of statistical reports, brochures, reading-desks, and facilities for critical research . . ." [43]

Had thinkers such as Leroy-Beaulieu and Spencer looked deeply into the sociological data thus collected, they would have seen, Cummings told his class in 1893–94, that "its [sic] behind the times now to argue for or against trades unions; *they are necessary*." Student notes of 1895–96 contain a similar passage:

> The great cities concentrate the great class which are being pushed to the wall. The rate of human wear and tear is dreadful in a great city. The great city draws in the best brains and brawn of the country all about. It is there that the great prizes are won but failure comes there too. Business failure but worse yet the physical failure of bad air, late hours, excitement, bad food, bad amusements, etc. All these tend to destroy mental and moral strength . . . The cities kill off the masses just as the wars of the middle ages.

On the other hand, the state socialists—the Webbs, Schäffle —would notice the ineffectiveness of state action and nonvoluntary social security. Cummings repeatedly stressed that the labor movement could not and did not flourish when it suppressed individual action.

But under what conditions would the labor movement flourish? And what kind of labor movement would contribute most to the ideal society? Since Economics 3 generally stressed principles, theories, and abstractions, Cummings found himself unable to delve into these problems. However, he originated two other courses at Harvard which gave him the chance to apply his rigorous observational method to just these questions. One of these, first taught in 1892–93, dealt with "The Social and Economic Condition of Workingmen in the United States and in Other Countries." The other, begun the next year, examined methods and theories of social reform, from Plato to Marx and Bellamy, concentrating on socialism and communism. It is interesting that both these courses remained in the Economics Department until 1931 although both lost their sociological significance, one turning to the purely economic aspects of labor and the other to a history of utopian economic doctrines. Cummings had conceived them as courses

where inductive sociological methods would be used to find and test solutions to the social questions of the day.

The labor problem resulted, he stated, from the change from tools to machines, which depersonalized the laborer's relation to his work and to his employer, which concentrated great hordes of people into small areas, which created monotonous working conditions and much ill-used leisure time, and which took control of the conditions of labor away from the laborer. As Cummings described the course in the department's pamphlet for 1892–93, it would start with a series of lectures on the history of nineteenth-century labor organizations, especially those in England. Cummings would then trace the laws relating to labor and its organization in various countries. After portraying the social conditions of the laboring classes, he would end with a discussion of "various phases of co-operation and profit-sharing, and . . . the rival claims of other expedients for readjusting the relations of employers and employed." In 1896–97 the description stated that wages, standard of living, housing, disability insurance, convict labor, shorter working days, and migration of workers were all to be considered relative to "experience and . . . economic theory with a view to determining the merits, defects, and possibilities of existing movements."

The methodology of the course reminds us of Cummings' requirements for sociological study expressed in his report on the Paris Exposition—"a library full of statistical reports, brochures . . ." Statistical studies provided the core of the descriptive and theoretical aspects of the course. Cummings' favorite authority was Booth's *Life and Labour of the People*—the result of a five-year statistical study of London, which included house-to-house surveys and exhaustive tables on type of house, number in family, place of birth, hours and kind of work, and so on. Statistics proved the existence of the labor problem, and Cummings used statistics to test the

effectiveness of present "remedies." His students must have felt themselves right in the center of British labor controversy. Of the ten books known to have been assigned in 1896–97, only two dealt with America, one with Germany, and seven with the United Kingdom.[44] The student was expected to know the definitions and advantages of time, task, and piece wages; progressive, collective task, collective piece, and collective progressive wages; of subcontract and contract wages, all outlined in David F. Schloss's *Methods of Industrial Remuneration.* The student was introduced to the conflict between William Hurrell Mallock, a conservative steward of wealth, and the Fabians. Cummings devoted half of each examination to discussions of specific programs or specific statistics. The remaining questions dealt with more theoretical aspects of the labor movement, such as the necessity of labor organization or the effect of class consciousness.

Why did Cummings concentrate on England in a period when there was so much labor unrest in America? First, he had done much research there and had been at Toynbee Hall during part of the Booth survey. Second, despite the efforts of Carroll D. Wright, United States Commissioner of Labor, American production of reliable literature of a descriptive, statistical nature on labor problems compared very unfavorably with that of Great Britain. Third, and most important, Cummings disliked militant labor organization. He favored cooperatives and trade unions which spent at least ninety per cent of their funds upon sickness, old age, and unemployment benefits and no more than ten per cent on strikes. Labor organization provided an acceptable solution to the labor problem only so long as it was voluntary and tended to further social adaptation and social harmo-

Since Cummings favored cooperative trade unionism the British model, cooperation received more weigh'

course than its historical significance or even its contemporary significance justified. The cooperative movement offered the best solution to the labor problem "because of
the element of involuntary thrift, and because every man
must bring in others to help himself, must be a propagandist
to get money himself. The system thus has a profound ethical importance; it makes it, so to speak, pay to be good. This
is in contrast to principles of Pol[itical] Econ[omy] as we
studied them during [the] first half-year," Cummings told
the introductory economics course in 1896. "The Labor
Question" proved to be Cummings' most popular course. In
its first year it drew only seven per cent of the number of students that attended the introductory course, already one of
the University's largest, but by 1898–99 it was drawing
twenty-nine per cent of the Economics 1 population. For the
five years, 1894–1898, when the American economic history
course was not offered, the labor course outdrew every economics course except Economics 1.

The course on the utopian movements was never popular
while Cummings taught it, drawing five per cent or less of
the number attending the introductory course. "Ideal Social
Reconstructions, from Plato's Republic to the present time"
was described in the bulletin of 1893–94 as a course dealing
"not only with those romantic criticisms of society which are
avowedly Utopian, but with the constructive efforts at reform, offered as practical guides for economists, statesmen,
and political parties." Cummings intended to compare these
utopian ideas with "actual historical evolution" to see if they
effected any changes and thus to judge "how far they must
be regarded simply as protests against existing phases of social evolution; and how far they may be said to embody a
sane philosophy of social and political organization." Analysis of these schemes was to give the students the chance to
discuss the thematic questions of both the labor and the

sociology course—the relation of the state to the individual, the ethical and historical values of institutions, and the sociological, political, and economic "bearing" of communism, collectivism, and current socialistic theories. In 1895 Cummings cut the course to a half year's length while narrowing its scope to socialism and communism. Plato, Bellamy, and Theodor Hertzka remained on the reading list, but Marx, Lassalle, the Webbs, Bernstein, and other contemporary socialists received most of the lecturer's attention. Cummings saw Marx as no more important than Lassalle, and as less important than the English "evolutionary socialists." No notes from this course remain, but it is safe to say that its emphasis and its conclusions were similar to those of Cummings' other courses—collectivism when nonvoluntary and unevolutionary was unviable, and cooperation stood in the vanguard of social progress. On the examination of 1899–1900 the students answered questions on Plato and Rousseau, related the thought of Gustave LeBon, Henry Sidgwick, and Anton Menger to socialistic theories, and related Christian teachings to the development of our economic laws. Finally, all students were to know the causes and results of socialist experiments and socialist party activities in Europe and America. And they were to know that cooperation, not socialism, was the best plan for social reconstruction.

In 1896–97 the department's pamphlet stated that the work of the social-reform course "is especially adapted to students who have had some introductory training in Ethics as well as in Economics." This statement was directed at those students who had taken ethics with Professor George Herbert Palmer or social ethics with Professor Peabody in the Department of Philosophy. At the same time that Cummings and the Department of Economics were developing sociology courses, the Department of Philosophy had introduced instruction in social ethics under Peabody's tutelage. The Department of Social Ethics grew out of this single course and existed side-by-side with the sociology offering of the Economics Department until the forming of the Sociology Department in 1931.

Why did they remain apart so long? Some causes of the conflict that lasted until 1930 lay in the different approaches and points of view of Cummings and Peabody. In the rhetoric of the time theirs was a conflict over identification of the "primary social unit"—whether the sociologist was to start with the individual or with a much larger group as the focus of his investigation. Cummings had been Peabody's student and was a Unitarian minister soon to take an assistant pastorship with Peabody's close friend, Edward Everett Hale. Yet Cummings tended, at least in the academic world, to look to the broad picture of society in an effort to find generalizations applicable in over-all social reconstruction while Peabody tended to look at the individual social unit, the person, and to work out ways for improving that individual's lot.

The split in the nineties did not come because Cummings refused to mix economics and ethics, but because he approached the social question as if it were a problem relatively unrelated to any individual person's problem. There is no record of Cummings' talking about child labor or individual suffering; the poor so often in his lectures are "the poor" or "the masses," not individual people. Peabody was embarking on the casework methodology which proved so important to all social science after its introduction in social work and in the work of social psychologists. He stressed the ideals of ethical idealism and human service which were to express themselves in individual action.[45] Cummings, although no less convinced of the need of ethical idealism, disregarded the hortatory approach of Peabody and sought to analyze social ideals more dispassionately. Not individual action, but rigorous empirical study followed by organized group or state action was the key to social reconstruction.

Edward Cummings' contribution to sociology at Harvard might have been great, for he was much more conversant with social theory than any of his predecessors or immediate followers in the Economics Department and was a thinker receptive to new ideas. He exerted some influence by helping to introduce observation, statistics, and inductive reasoning into the Economics Department, and thus he was instrumental in the revitalizing of economics at Harvard. But it is impossible to call Cummings a transitional figure. His replacement, Thomas Nixon Carver, had taken one course in sociology at Cornell in 1894 and had taught sociology and anthropology at Oberlin for two years when he came to Harvard in 1900. Carver's primary interest lay in economic theory. He first offered the sociology course on a temporary basis but taught it for thirty years. The positivism of Comte and Spencer was the keystone for his sociology in 1900 and in 1930.[46] Carver was no follower of Cummings or of Cummings' tradition. Cummings left very little mark on Harvard or on Harvard sociology. He wrote no books, he directed only two doctoral dissertations in sociology, and he does not seem to have left any tradition—only three course names and numbers.

Cummings was ultimately unsuccessful in establishing sociology at Harvard because he could not mold his inductive reasoning and his observational and statistical techniques into a coherent methodology which could lead to generalizations of predictive value. His courses remained largely descriptive, and when he turned to the social theories of Tarde and Giddings, his discussions were eclectic and incomplete. His analyses of socialization and imitation remained tentative. They suggested ideals, but did not provide analytic tools for understanding actual social processes. Instead he turned to a purely descriptive analysis of social conditions. He treated of the "what happened" but did not probe very deeply into the "why or how it happened." Thus his ideal solution to the social question and his methodology remained divided. He failed to pursue his theoretical ideas, yet his inductive methodology produced no results or hypotheses large enough to require the extensive study that might justify a separate discipline.

Cummings in a way fell victim to his circumstances. There is little reason to believe that most of the American sociologists who built separate departments in this decade experienced any more success than Cummings in finding significant generalizations. But Cummings taught in an economics department of unusually perceptive men who quickly adapted his specific techniques to economics as a whole, thus giving sociology no reason for breaking from economics on purely methodological grounds. Furthermore, since theory and abstraction were more important in the Harvard Economics Department than in similar departments at other universities, Cummings' fundamentally descriptive offerings were not well-regarded by the powerful men in the department. His failure to generalize and systematize meant his contributions did not advance "economic science" or social science as Dunbar and Taussig defined those sciences. The Economics Department recognized Cummings' investigational techniques as useful if not overwhelmingly important, and the department came to include these techniques as a minor part of its own thinking. But Harvard's theorists found Cummings' few conclusions inconsequential to their quest for a general understanding of how society works. Cummings' elucidations of specific situations did not provide the economists with any generalizations about the mechanisms of social action.

Cummings' assistant professorship was terminated rather abruptly in 1900,[47] and although the records do not specify the reason, it can be assumed that Cummings had been compared to Dunbar's ideal pattern of the economic theorist and found wanting. Thomas Nixon Carver did not emphasize the techniques of observation or experiment but immediately presented a complete, abstract theory of society. Carver received tenure within two years of his arrival at Harvard. Cummings' foundation for vital, exploratory, and experimental sociology instruction at Harvard lay unused. He had been unable to build a systematic academic discipline on this foundation; his successor did not try.

Edward Cummings' brother John came to Harvard in 1895 and taught "The Theory of Statistics—Application to Social and Economic Problems—Studies in Movements in Population, etc.," as a half-course in 1895 and as a full course thereafter. Attendance averaged around eighteen students per year in a department whose introductory course attracted approximately 420 students per year. Little student demand for statistics courses was the rule for another ten years until economic theory's reliance upon sound statistical knowledge became an accepted fact. The nineties saw great expansion in the scope and prestige of both theoretical and applied statistics. The Booth survey is typical of the applied uses of statistics in the decade. Two pioneer works on the theoretical aspects of statistics appeared in this decade—Emile Levasseur, *La Population française: Histoire de la population avant 1789 et démographie de la France comparée à celle des autres nations au XIXe siècle*, 3 vols. (1889–1892) and Columbia University's Richmond Mayo-Smith, *Science of Statistics*, vol. I (1895). The census of 1890 was the first to show results from Francis A. Walker's twenty-year effort to make the census a useful and valid statistical source.

John Cummings had received his A.B. and A.M. at Harvard in 1891 and 1892, respectively, and his Ph.D. in Political Economy from the University of Chicago two years later for a thesis on "The Poor Laws of Massachusetts and New York." After leaving Harvard with his brother in 1900, he took a newspaper job in New York. Two years later he received appointment to the University of Chicago, but in 1910 he left college teaching to join the federal government as an expert statistician and economist. His course at Harvard was the first in the University to consider statistical theory, statistical validity, and "the scope of statistical inductions" and their importance to the proper study of economics and sociology. Cummings also dealt, according to the course description of 1895–96, with practical applications of statistical method to political, fiscal, and vital statistics, to population growth and migration, to urban growth, to pauperism and crime, to capital formation, and to the production and distribution of wealth. The course was not, however, dry or dull. Half the questions on the examinations of 1900, for example, dealt with life tables, methods of interpolation, methods of smoothing graph lines, and ways of questioning statistical evidence. But some quite philosophical questions appeared: "How far is it possible to give to moral and social facts a quantitative statement?" "The growth of cities and social election?" Do statistical laws preclude free will? In other years Cummings asked questions on the increased crime rate as an index of social degeneration, questions on the Malthusian problem of population growth and food supply, and one to which we wish we had Cummings' answer—the causes of urban migration. What evidence remains of this course offering indicates that John Cummings was teaching in large measure the methodology for his brother's kind of sociology and that he was attempting to prove that statistical studies constituted the first step in the inductive study of the development of society.

In the spring of 1899 John Cummings offered "an historical and descriptive account of European population and its movement in the nineteenth century," variously entitled "Ethnology—Race Migrations and Problems of Population" or "Ethnology in its Application to Economic and Social Problems." Notice how limiting "nineteenth century" was in a period when social thinkers argued vehemently whether each race had a separate creation or whether all people had originally descended from the one couple in the Garden of Eden and had then divided into races as a result of multiple environmentally produced mutations. Lester Ward was advancing his sociological system, which rested on the assumption that the races had all separated from one root, wandered over the earth, come into conflict, conquered each other, and through miscegenation begun a universal racial amalgamation that was ultimately to create social harmony. The eugenics movement in the United States was growing with great impetus during these years. Much of Carver's sociology was to rest on this kind of anthropological guesswork.

The description of the ethnology course in the department's announcement shows that Cummings focused entirely on the nineteenth century, discussing ethnic stratification and selection, ethnic and anthropological factors in crime and dependence, immigration and the Negro problem in the United States. In this course, as in John Cummings' other offerings (he also taught parts of the introductory economics course and parts of the course on labor problems), statistics were the fundamental facts that the student had to master, just as they formed the core of Cummings' study, *Negro Population, 1790–1815* (1918).

One of the two questions on the ethnology final examination (in an era at Harvard when any examination of less than eight questions was rare) asked: What does the cephalic index prove, and Cummings added slyly, "if anything?" This question leads us to an article in which Cummings proves quite rightly and quite bluntly that the cephalic index proves nothing.[48] His attack focused on the writings of William Z. Ripley, who, ironically enough, was to replace John Cummings in 1901. Physical anthropologists had summarily divided Europe into three racial groups: those with blond hair, light skin, high foreheads, thin lips, and a certain cephalic index formed one group; those with dark hair and skin, low foreheads, and so forth, formed another. Approximately two to five per cent of the European population fitted any one of the three racial categories. Anthropologists began to pare down the qualifications, many of them coming to depend exclusively on the cephalic index for racial identification. Others tallied each qualification separately, in that they counted the hair colorings and forehead sizes of a population and if the plurality of hair were blond and the plurality of foreheads high, the whole population was identified with that group. Cummings pointed out that statistically this process was invalid because the investigators took no account of how many times blond hair appeared with high foreheads in individuals.

Cummings reserved his special scorn, however, for those who relied only on the cephalic index. The index meant absolutely nothing, he said. It bore no relation to brain size and had no discovered relation to character. And worst of all, he added, the description of populations by head shape and size revealed nothing—no country, region, or even village showed any decided trend toward any cephalic type. And yet, he concluded, the physical anthropologist like Ripley was attempting, with his crude and meaningless criteria, to identify the social characteristics of people. The physical anthropologist concentrated completely on heredity and paid no attention to environment, by far the most important factor.[49]

Anthropology has undertaken to interpret those movements [of population in the nineteenth century] in terms of ethnic generation and selection in face of the obvious fact that those movements have been almost entirely an economic consequence, and that economic development during this period has tended, and tends more and more, not to dissociate, select, and establish ethnic factors, but, on the contrary, to break down all natural differentiations, to break up and obliterate ethnic stratification, and to substitute a classification and hierarchy of social groups dependent upon economic efficiency and function.[50]

The importance of Cummings' rejection of physical anthropology's physical classification of social character-istics lies in its implied rejection of the racism prescribed by Arthur de Gobineau, Ludwig Gumplowicz, and Gustav Ratzenhofer, who founded their theories on the assumption that present social conflict derived in large measure from prehistoric racial differences. Edward Cummings evidently shared his brother's attitude when he lectured in the sociol-ogy course on racism, the implied dangers of immigration, and what he called in 1896–97 "the dangers which threaten civilization"—probably racial degeneration. One question on Edward Cummings' examination of 1894 asked the students to describe the anthropological concept of the primitive promiscuous horde and to explain why it was an unscientific theory. We know today that it is unscientific, simply because there is no evidence of its ever having existed, but many race theorists of that era postulated the promiscuous horde as a starting point for their surveys of cultural development.

These two teachers were destroying the groundwork for the description of the new floods of immigrants from eastern and southern Europe as racially inferior and supporting the view that environmental factors did and could rapidly change the character of these people. John Cummings con-stantly repeated that environmentally produced changes in each generation were more important than inherited conti-nuities. Rejecting the amalgamation of physical and social science that Ripley was attempting, he remarked: "Anthropologists do not present any data to justify the assumption that the cephalic index carries any mental attribute or any character with it; nor can any such contention be maintained in the face of modern psychology . . . the sort of racial phrenology with which modern anthropologists are engaged is bound to go to the same limbo. Sociology may then breathe again naturally." [51]

A conscious rejection of the equation of social science with natural science and an increasing reliance on psychology are themes, not only of John Cummings' course in ethnology, but of courses in sociology in general at Harvard in the nineties. Yet there was no total rejection of Spencerian positivism nor any complete embracing of social psychology. Both these men were more effective in questioning older deductive systems than in providing equally viable alternatives. The Cummings brothers did significantly alter the teaching of economics at Harvard by demonstrating a method different from that of the absolute, deductive economics that Dunbar favored. Their work had an important effect on Harvard economics as a whole; ironically, it did little to further the teaching of sociology as a separate discipline. The Cummings brothers were able to introduce some methodological techniques; they were unable to construct an academic subject.

In the nineties another area within the Economics Department developed an antiabsolute, observational point of view which was to have more important ramifications for the expansion of the scope of academic economics. William James Ashley introduced the inductive method of German historicism to Harvard's economic history courses in 1892. The "deductive-inductive" battle was the most significant point of conflict among economists from 1885 to 1905. It served as the major point of disagreement between the Harvard economists and the American Economic Association from 1885 to 1892, and when Ashley came to represent the inductive method on the Harvard staff, it became a "bone of contention" at Harvard for the nine years of Ashley's professorship.

Ranged against Ashley were Dunbar and Taussig. Ely could never have said of Taussig, as he once did of Dunbar, that Taussig did not understand the real difference between the theoreticians and the historians.[52] Taussig, always conversant with the literature, understood the difference perfectly and was a formidable antagonist. Ashley seems to have been his match, however, and a decade of strain, intellectual and social, inside the department followed Ashley's appointment. Although he was surely a student of German historicism and the inductive method, Edward Cummings took little part in the methodological arguments among Dunbar, Taussig, and Ashley. Since Cummings, unlike the other men, had no academic tenure, he apparently felt some hesitancy in openly challenging those above him.

Ashley felt no such restraints. He did not come to Harvard to continue teaching the kind of economic history Dunbar established in 1883. Ashley's conception of academic economics involved a complete repudiation of the classical economists. Because they supported laissez faire and opposed trade unions and because they advocated a kind of political economy that occupied no "very dignified or useful" position, classical economists had, Ashley thought, rightly drawn the hatred of intellectuals and workingmen.[53] Nor had the classical economists' "neat little body of compendious 'laws' and maxims" any relevance to the social problems of the eighties.[54]

It was just this confidence in neat dogmas that was the main fault of the average economist of the old school . . . I should . . . even accept most of the so-called 'laws' of rent, wages, profits, and price, as hypothetically true,—that is, true under certain conditions, of which the existence of complete competition is the most important . . . The method of investigation, in my opinion, most fruitful I would call the *historical* . . . the method of direct observation and generalisation from facts, whether past or present; a method you can call 'inductive' . . .[55]

These words of 1888 are far different from Dunbar's statement that the science of economics should work with laws abstracted from reality. Or compare Dunbar's insistence that economics dealt only with wealth and not with welfare to Ashley's view of the economist's role: "Having got to certain conclusions on a particular economic question, it seems to me, it is then the duty of the economist to point out the evils or dangers, if any, that may be present, and to suggest means for their removal." Economists must not refrain from making value judgments because they consider economics to be a science.[56] "All the studies of this course," he continued, "are concerned ultimately with society in its organised form as the State; and in all of them, accordingly, the final test in any matter must be the welfare of the State." [57]

In his inaugural lecture at Harvard, much tempered by the presence of Dunbar and Taussig in the audience, Ashley made only a few gibes at the expense of the deductive economists:

[Economic history] has changed the whole mental attitude of economists towards their own teaching. The acceptance of the two great principles,—which are but different forms of the same idea,—that economic conclusions are *relative* to given conditions, and that they possess only *hypothetical* validity, is at last a part of the mental habit of economists. The same is true of the conviction that economic considerations are not the only ones of which we must take account in judging of social phenomena, and that economic forces are not the only forces which move men. It need hardly be said that all this was recognized *in word* long ago; but it may be left to the verdict of those who are conversant with the literature of the last generation whether these convictions were really underlying and fruitful parts of daily thought, as they are now tending to be.[58]

Nor was Ashley convinced that the Harvard economists had genuinely posited the conditional nature of abstractions as an underlying part of their thought.

In a letter to his fiancée in 1886, Ashley defined the goals of economics as "the investigation of economic history—no facts are too remote to be without significance for the present, . . . and the examination of modern industrial life *in the piece*. We can leave to the Cambridge people hair-splitting analysis of abstract doctrine." [59] Taussig seemed to reply to that very letter when he wrote in 1888, "No one will deny the advantages of a careful description of industry and investigation of economic history, though it may be doubted whether as much time should be given to each of these as to economic theory itself." [60] For Dunbar economics was an exact science, a battery of the laws of "what was" and "what is"; for Ashley economics was a historical study, a record of the unique and conditional and ever-changing development of the "what is." The result of economic study should be, thought Ashley, a picture and not a law.[61]

Ashley had been born in a small English village in 1860, educated in the British private-school system and sent to Oxford, where after much snubbing he received a degree in 1880. He struggled against the stigma of his background for five years until Lincoln College awarded him a fellowship in 1885. In those five years he made three short trips to Germany where he met some of the greatest proponents of German historical economics. While living as a private tutor at Oxford, Ashley read William Cunningham's pioneer *Growth of English Industry and Commerce* (1882) and Frederic Seebohm's *The English Village Community* (1883), "a vivid picture of the daily life of the agricultural population, which has for the first time imparted to

Mr. [Thorold] Rogers's facts a true significance." [62] Since 1879 he had eagerly been reading Cliffe-Leslie's essays on the German historical school.

Ashley, in the eighties, worked closely with Arnold Toynbee while the latter was writing *The Industrial Revolution*, the "chief value" of which Ashley later identified as "its showing how impartial investigation of the past could be combined with ardent enthusiasm for social improvement." [63] The contact with Toynbee convinced Ashley that his future lay with economic history, and he wrote his great *Introduction to English Economic History and Theory: The Middle Ages* in 1886. When the book was finally published in 1888, Ashley immediately took first rank with Cunningham among economic historians in the English-speaking world. In 1888 he moved to the new Department of Political Science at the University of Toronto and in 1892 came to Harvard.

Ashley combined his eminent scholarship with a belief in socialism of the Fabian variety.

In the first place I [he wrote in 1886] am a bit of a fatalist. It is *possible* that some discovery *may* transform society in ways we cannot anticipate—but this possibility is so small that it may almost be disregarded. Now just as in the way in which in the past certain transitions have been prepared by events and have gone through stages, which can be clearly traced, so that after a certain time they became inevitable, and in some cases were seen then to be inevitable, so I think it is with Socialism. Over the history of the last century the development of individualism to its furthest point in industry may be traced, and then the counter movement setting in, both in philosophic thought and in actual fact. I feel, at the point to which we have got, that the principal branches of production and exchange will ultimately be organized socially is as certain as the rising of to-morrow's sun.[64]

His daughter states that "when he was over sixty [he] still described himself as an 'evolutionary Socialist.' " [65]

Since his historical method and his socialism were so interwoven, it is doubtful that Ashley could have kept his social viewpoint out of the classroom, especially in light of the fact that, for him, the economist's duty was to determine matters of welfare and to suggest means for the implementation of reform. He certainly did not keep such views from the public. In an 1881 review, he remarked, "Though Trade-Unionism in itself may not be the ideally best means of remedying social inequalities, yet it is really the only means towards that end." [66] Ashley often spoke at labor-union meetings and spoke favorably of trade unions at public occasions while at Oxford, Toronto, and Birmingham. He curtailed his activity somewhat while at Harvard although he was a member of the Church Social Union of Cambridge, chairing its Publication Committee. He was very interested in the Consumer's League of Boston, an organization which attempted to develop a citizens' boycott on goods produced under unfair labor conditions. Ashley had a great deal of contact with the Reverend Charles H. Brent and with John Graham Brooks, both often considered quite radical and both champions of labor. Sidney and Beatrice Webb were his guests when they stayed in Boston on their American tour of 1898, and Ashley had extensive contact with the Webbs before and after his sojourn in America. [67]

Ashley was more radical than Edward Cummings in advocating the trade unionism explicated by the Webbs as the complete solution to the social question and in openly advocating collectivism. Yet the two men were similar in that their interest in sociology, or in what Ashley preferred to call the study of society, had both an academic and a reformist impulse. The revival of the study of economics resulted from "the growing interest in what are called 'social questions,' and, combined with this, a perception of the need for more systematic training for that work of municipal and political administration which is every day embracing a larger part of the national activity," Ashley wrote.[68] Cummings would have agreed. Both carried into the classroom the desire to make subject matter practical and immediately useful in affecting the social problems of the late nineteenth century. Both respected the German concept of college education as a means of training civil servants.

Why, then, did the Economics Department, which wished to emphasize theoretical economics, choose an outspoken champion of the historical method and of state social action? The case of Edward Cummings does not offer a useful parallel, for Cummings was far from radical and was content to allow deductive economics and inductive sociology to follow their separate paths. Furthermore, Cummings had been trained at Harvard and had been sent to Europe with a Harvard fellowship. Dunbar and Taussig knew that Ashley, on the other hand, would certainly carry the methodological debate right into the heart of the department and that he would take issue with Dunbar's scientific pretensions. The historical or inductive approach never represented just another approach to the study of economics for Ashley; it was the only approach.

If Ashley's appointment is to be understood, it must be viewed within three contexts. First, more than coincidence seems to be involved in the fact that 1892 saw Ashley move to Harvard and Dunbar become president of the American Economic Association. The choosing of an eminent economic historian and an outspoken opponent of laissez faire in 1892 may be seen as Harvard's gesture of good faith to the American Economic Association, which in the same year had attempted to deemphasize the conflict out of which it had been formed by electing Dunbar president. All the members of the Harvard department refused to join the Association in 1885 because the statement of principles attached to its constitution represented too closely, they felt, the views of the German-trained economists gathered around Richard T. Ely. In 1888, in an effort to widen the membership of the American Economic Association, the leaders dropped the statement of principles, with its offending clauses on the belief in the use of the state as a positive social force.[69] Special invitations were sent to Dunbar as well as to men at Yale and Princeton.[70]

Taussig had joined somewhat tentatively in 1886 and Dunbar followed in 1888 (Laughlin remained outside until 1904), but Taussig wrote in 1890 that "the first step" in making the Association a center of common interest for all economists "seems to me a change in the officers . . ." [71] The maneuvers that produced the changes of 1892 formed a part of the general effort of economists to smooth over or even hide from the methodological debate that had raged among them since 1885.[72] Dunbar's elevation also represented the Eastern conservatives' quiet reassertion of power in the organization.[73] And, after the appointment of Ashley, Harvard's economists could argue that the catholicity of their department's approach qualified them to lead all economists.

Demonstrating the catholicity of its approach signified not only reconciliation with the American Economic Association but also Harvard's attempt to draw abreast of other colleges in the teaching of economics. The second context, then, involves the fact that the battle with the Economic Association endangered the appeal of the Harvard department in that Harvard's opposition was too easily equated with that of dogmatists like William Graham Sumner and Harvard's own J. Laurence Laughlin.[74] Harvard's department was too small to risk being typed as a bastion of old-line ideas. Ever since 1888 Eliot had attempted to widen its appeal by widening its offerings in practical economics—in railroads, in corporations, in labor problems, and in business. In 1889

Dunbar and Eliot reviewed the qualifications of Bernard Moses for a post at Harvard. The following year Eliot entered into more serious negotiations with Edwin A. Seligman of Columbia and Edmund J. James of the Wharton School at the University of Pennsylvania. These negotiations came to naught, however.[75]

Although part of the urgency in the efforts of 1889 and 1890 derived from the fact that Dunbar's health forced him to take a two-year vacation in Europe, Eliot's desire to have the department teach more practical aspects of economics remained, as evidenced by the appointment of Cummings in 1891. Furthermore, Eliot pressed upon the department the necessity of offering courses relevant to the future needs of undergraduates, so many of whom were going into business. Eliot undoubtedly understood that Ashley's interest in the history of economic institutions denoted an interest in the teaching of practical economics, and he may have pressed Ashley's appointment for that reason. Ashley left Harvard in 1901 to set up a school of commerce at the University of Birmingham. Higher education in business was one of his lifelong interests. In 1903 he wrote Seligman that his Harvard colleagues had thwarted his desires to teach practical economics:

To a large degree it [his work at Birmingham] is work which I always desired to do, and in part it is work of a kind in which I came to take more interest during the last two or three years of my stay in America. I never wanted to be a medievalist for medievalism's sake but with the strong masterful personality of my kind friend Taussig on one side, and Cummings taking another group of subjects on the other side, it was not easy for me, as a foreigner intending to remain a foreigner, to go far outside the groove into which I fell.[76]

Ashley's letter reveals the tension in the Economics Department between those who wished to maintain the dominance of theoretical economics and those who wished to see inductive methods of approaching economic questions applied to present conditions. Ashley's description lends support to the argument that Eliot pushed Ashley upon a department that was not especially eager to have his kind of economics taught.

A third context that suggests reasons for Ashley's appointment concerns the pressures put upon Harvard by influential alumni to have protection as amply advocated as free trade. In 1889 the Board of Overseers' Committee on Political Science returned a scathing attack on the free-trade orientation of the Economics Department. In the conflict between free trade and protection, the committee felt, "Harvard College has . . . practically taken sides as decidedly as if she constituted a political body instead of an educational institution. To such criticism two replies have been made. First, that no competent person can be found to set forth protectionist doctrines. In view of the evenness with which the intelligence and ability of the country is divided upon the great question of Protection, these gentlemen of the Committee respectfully allege that they are incredulous concerning this excuse." [77] Despite the committee's incredulity, this "excuse" seems to have been a valid one. There are literally scores of letters in the Eliot Papers concerning attempts to find men of protectionist views to lecture at Harvard. One reason that Eliot sought to appoint Edmund J. James was that he was one of the few academic protectionists in America in this period.

No issue of academic freedom arose in this case since the Overseers' report was easily brushed aside. Dunbar's reaction to reading the report was fairly typical:

My cheeks burned a little at first but before it was half read through I was saying to myself in amusement "Johnie M.[orse, the author of the report] is the same boyish amateur that he was when I used to correct his articles for the [Boston] Daily [Advertiser] twenty-five years ago." He never wrote anything that showed the firm hand of a man and if the protectionists can stand such advocacy they are tough.[78]

And Charles Francis Adams, president of the Board of Overseers, suggested that in the future the committee could be packed with men favorable to free trade.[79] Nonetheless, the volume of correspondence that Eliot handled in relation to this matter indicates that it proved a constant headache for the administration. Eliot may well have viewed Ashley's appointment as a means of balancing the free-trade emphasis of the Economics Department. Ashley, a disciple of the *Katheder-Sozialisten* and their kind of national economy, was in the process of becoming an avowed supporter of a protectionist policy for Canada and England. Although he did not openly campaign for protectionism while in America, his open support of Joseph Chamberlain's policies after 1903 [80] came as no surprise to his former colleagues. It is not surprising that Harvard's ardent free traders in the Economics Department regarded Ashley with some distrust.

While at Harvard Ashley offered only two courses of his own—an annual course that alternated between medieval and modern European economic history and a course in advanced economic theory—and he gave five weeks of lectures on economic development in the introductory course. One must wonder that so eminent an economic historian never taught American economic history, which from 1893 to 1897 was not offered at all.

Detailed notes from Ashley's lectures in Economics 1, the only ones preserved from any of his courses, give us an overall idea of his teaching. A full account of the purposes of the historical method began each of his offerings. Students may be drawn to the study of economic history by "the hope that they may thereby arrive at a more satisfying and intelligible conception of the evolution of human society," Ashley suggested. "Just as in biological and physical science the investigator is buoyed up by the conviction that every isolated fact, could he but learn how, has its own place in a sequence, its own significance and appropriateness," he continued, "so in the history of man we can never be content until we have found it a connected and consecutive whole, or until we know of a surety that it is but a chaos of meaningless fragments." Economic history offered the method with which to achieve this "connected and consecutive whole," and German scholars like Schmoller and Georg Knapp were in the process of finding that unity.

[Their researches and conclusions] will not be mere corrections or amplifications of current economic doctrines: they will rather be conclusions as to the character and sequence of the stages in economic development. The point of view is here no longer that of a bargain between individuals in given social conditions, but of the life and movement of whole industries and classes, of the creation and modification of social mechanism, of the parallel progress and interaction of economic phenomena and economic thought. The studies of the school are no longer individualist and psychological, but collectivist and institutional . . . Our first requirement is to understand, far more precisely than we do at present, what has been the institutional framework of society at the several periods, what has been the constitution of the various social classes, and their relation to one another.[81]

According to his syllabus for 1895–96, Ashley used five of his fifteen lectures in Economics 1 to describe various manifestations of historicism in the nineteenth century. Ashley attributed the expanding application of that method to the romantic movement, the evolutionary philosophy of Hegel, Comte, and Spencer, the evolutionary biology of Darwin, and the anthropology of Edward B. Tylor. Among the results of the new approach were the interest in the Middle Ages; the sense of uniformatism, as opposed to catastrophism; the sense of relativism; and the view that regarded the present, the past, and the future as parts of a single development. Ashley mentioned that the historical movement had affected the study of law, of theology, and of economics.

He then discussed the changes that had occurred within the historical school of economics—the changes that had taken place between the publication of the work of Wilhelm Roscher and the publishing of those of Gustav Schmoller. Economic history was valuable for its own sake, for a right estimate of current economic theory, and for insight into modern economic facts. "In tracing Economic History we must start out with [the] conception of stages or epochs . . . [The] whole of Economic History can not be viewed from one stand point," Ashley told his students in 1893. He attacked Friedrich List and Bruno Hildebrand because they had taken only one point of view. He outlined very briefly some anthropological theories as to the primitive development of the concept of property and the primitive development of industrial arts. He then described European economic development since early medieval times, using the conflict between industry and agriculture as his particular focus in 1893–94, and traced industrial development through the family, the gild, the domestic, and the factory systems. In 1896 his lectures related European economic development to the growth of individual liberty, moving from the manor and the village through the period of "Town Dominance" to the period of "National Economy," the age of individual liberty. His final lecture asked whether the beginnings of a "Period of International or World Economy" were discernible. After lecturing for five weeks on the evolution of the modern industrial order, he turned the students over to Edward Cummings who would discuss "various recent movements towards the reconstruction of a stable industrial organisation, and the solution thereby of the 'Labor Question' . . ." Reading assignments consisted of parts of Schmoller's *Mercantile System,* Lewis Henry Morgan's *Ancient Society,* Richard Jones's *Peasant Rents,* and Book Two of Mill's *Principles.*

Throughout the course Ashley stressed that economic conditions had changed and that Smith's laws fit the nineties no better than they fit the conditions of the English manor system. He stressed the relativity of economic "laws" —that Mill provided a point of view applicable to one stage of economic development, the early nineteenth century, but that other points of view had to be applied to other stages. He, like Edward Cummings, stressed the importance of the change from tool to machine and argued that the resulting dislocation must be bridged by some sort of cooperation. The very shortness of his Economics 1 offering—Professor Ashley covered at least two centuries a week—emphasized evolutionary development and the sense of crisis that Ashley felt when he viewed modern society.

Ashley felt it was just as important to stress the methodological problems in his more advanced courses. In fact, his "The Scope and Method in Economic Theory and Investigation" was described in the departmental bulletin of 1897–98 as a discussion of the advantages of a "wider or narrower scope" of investigation and of the historical school's influence. The five students, including one sophomore, read definitions of method by Mill, Cairnes, John Neville Keynes, and Wagner and Schmoller in German, and answered Ashley's favorite examination questions—discussions of the historical method as against the deductive method and of economics as an art against economics as a science. There is no doubt about what the correct answers were to have been.

When Professor Ashley journeyed to England on his sabbatical leave in 1898–99, Professor Cunningham from Cambridge University visited Harvard to teach courses in economic history. In his medieval history course almost one hundred students heard him give one of the earliest explanations of the relation of religion to the rise of capitalism. A student noted that Cunningham apologized for going "into rather deep questions of philosophy and religion, seemingly very far from our economic purpose." But two new ideas, "the importance of individual human life" and all souls being "responsible to God," caused "great divergences" between Roman and medieval civilization, subtle "differences rather in the character and spirit of the civilization." Religion was the dominant trait of medieval civilization; it was both the "force that kept society together" and "the foundation of medieval society." It created a new spirit in medieval society.

More specifically this spirit in the new civilization works out into the doctrine of gain, which was wrong at another's expense; the greater respect for labor; and the greater responsibility of the wealthy. The tone of the new society is thus seen to be different from that of ancient Rome . . . We must therefore examine the influences which gave rise to social conditions and order to a definite system of society . . . [Among them are] physical, geographical conditions . . . [and] a great army . . . Moral authority [however, is the] cause for . . . the development of greater security in the enjoyment of landed property.

Max Weber, Ernst Troeltsch, Friedrich Schulze-Gävernitz, and Cunningham in his *Christianity and Economic Science* [82] were, of course, to pursue the study of the power of an irrational, unconscious emotion over material reality, and Weber's *The Protestant Ethic and the Spirit of Capitalism* (1904) has often been considered as marking the beginning of modern social science. The kind of methodology to which Ashley and Cunningham exposed Harvard students in the nineties was to prove the most fruitful for modern social science. Although we cannot contend that students of economic history at Harvard were ready to grasp the subtleties of the new hypotheses about social psychology, we can safely say that they did, because Ashley was so vitally concerned with teaching method, carry away some sense of the dynamic possibilities of the new point of view.

Guy Stevens Callender, one of Ashley's graduate students, employed this point of view in the American economic history course which he taught from 1897 to 1900. Callender, graduated from Oberlin College in 1891, received an A.B. from Harvard in 1893, an A.M. in 1894, and a doctorate in 1897. He moved to Bowdoin in 1900 and to Yale in 1903, where he died in 1915. Callender's course, always drawing at least twenty-five per cent of the Economics 1 population, combined social history with economic history long before social history came to be regarded as a field of study. The syllabus of 1899–1900 shows that one group of lectures outlined "Economic and Social Changes in the United States, 1763–1815." The course considered many value questions such as trust and railroad legislation and the labor problem. Demography, the subject of so much of the sociological investigation of the era, received repeated study, as did the social effects of immigration. The Know-Nothing Movement found a place in this economic history course. Callender stressed the fact that, although the North made the mistake of viewing emancipation as a political problem, it was a social problem, with effects on the Negro's health, morals, and industrial efficiency. In an effort to test comparatively economic and social results of American emancipation, Callender discussed emancipation in Russia and in the West Indies.

Callender's final lectures, as outlined in one set of notes of 1898–99, focused on "The Economic Influences in American Political and Social Development" and argued that democracy flourished because of economic conditions. Before the Civil War the frontier and rapid expansion caused a movement toward greater equality, but since the War "economic opportunities for great wealth have changed the structure of society without changing its spirit" and have caused a growing inequality and separation of social classes. His final examinations asked about the Negro problem, immigration, population increase, and the social and political effects of the frontier. Turner's essay on the frontier in American history was assigned reading.

Ashley's influence is evident when we compare Callender's offering to the economic history courses that preceded and followed. In these courses the subject matter involved tracing money and banking theories and their operation through time and examining tariff-rate fluctuations. The approach of these courses recalls Dunbar's idea of applying economic theory through time in order to prove that the Classical laws did work. These economic history courses, clearly appendages to the theory courses, supported what Cunningham had called "The Perversion of Economic History"—the belief that economic causes could be scientifically determined and the belief that, when so determined, they held true for all time.[83] Because it included social history Callender's course emphasized that economic theories had to change because social conditions always changed.

For Ashley, economic history was the only kind of sociology worth having. He was suspicious of the name "sociology" largely because it was so closely linked with the name of Herbert Spencer. The American concern with sociology of the Spencerian type derived from American curiosity and American fondness for generalizations and quick results, Ashley wrote. In Europe other disciplines were more adequately providing fields for the interest that Americans could express only in sociology. Historical jurisprudence in Europe was a large and challenging field; in America only a professional-school course. Ancient and medieval history were in "lamentable condition" in the United States. And the Europeans taught historical economics while Americans learned only abstract formulae. American sociology was a reaction to this limited academic offering in the more traditional fields.[84]

When sociology attempts to "arrive at and teach a general theory of 'social development, structure, and function' " it tries to do too much and succeeds in doing nothing, Ashley felt.

But [sociology's] value has lain not in the positive results of professed sociologists, but in the influence of such a conception upon students of history and political economy. It has raised before them the hope that they may be able to make out some sort of rational development in the life of humanity . . . if our economists are no longer content to give exclusive attention to the workings of individual self-interest in the pursuit of wealth, it is due largely to the prophets of sociology. But while we agree with them in thinking that we must try to get our heads above the turmoil of isolated facts, and arrive at generalizations as to the meaning of facts, we cannot but feel the dangers of a too soaring ambition . . . [It is] wise to limit our view to smaller and more manageable groups of phenomena than the whole experience of the race.[85]

A similar distrust of closed systems and absolute theories governed Edward Cummings' teaching of "The Principles of Sociology" with its concentration on the facts of nineteenth-century society. Such a conception of sociology constituted the first step in social science's fruitful rejection of the system builders and their analogies to physics and biology.

Sociology or the study of social development was, at Harvard in the nineties, dynamic, vital, and in close contact and accord with those European lines of thinking that were redirecting the study of sociology. After 1900 this vitality and the contact with Europe disappeared from formal sociology at Harvard, to be replaced either by rigid deduction or by indifference. The nineties stand alone as a sort of fertile oasis in the midst of the relatively barren desert of sociology's growth at Harvard. The most important reason for sociology's atrophy was its failure to find and exploit methods and theories of its own that would serve to label it as a discipline in its own right. Three other reasons help account for the rapid waning of sociological creativity in Harvard's Economics Department.

First, the abilities, interests, and personalities of the professors involved determined the growth of sociology. Professor Carver, who replaced Cummings in 1900, was trained wholly in the United States in the "hard-knocks school," working and attending a small Kansas religious college, then dry-farming in Southern California. He worked his way through the University of Southern California (graduating first in his class of three), moved to Johns Hopkins, and took his Ph.D. at Cornell. Carver's conservatism seems to have developed from the experiences of his youth as it has done in the case of so many "self-made" men. He had taken one course in sociology in his whole career but felt competent to teach sociology and anthropology at Oberlin.

He was chosen for his Harvard position on the strength of two articles published in the *Quarterly Journal of Economics* on the theory of marginal utility applied to interest and wages.[86] These two articles received deservedly high praise from Dunbar. Carver's first interest was in economic theory, his second in agricultural economics, and his third in Carverian sociology, the epitome of Social Darwinism. "In either case that which will be, will be," he wrote. "Instead of saying, therefore, that whatever is, is right, which would carry with it the conclusion that whatever was, was right, we should say that whatever inevitably tends to be is right, for the right is that which inevitably tends to be under the laws of variation and selection." [87] Carver devoted his trips abroad almost exclusively to the study of agricultural methods on the Continent. He had little contact with European or American sociologists and his dislike of reading in foreign languages kept him from contact with the important current foreign scholarship in sociology.[88] Spencer and Comte were for him, all his life, the foundations for his sociology, and despite the very dynamic and significant advances in sociological and anthropological thinking from 1900 to 1930, Carver's "Principles of Sociology" changed very little. He built a great system in a period when the very idea of great systems was being demolished by scholars. Modern sociology paid little attention to him and he paid even less attention to it.

Edwin Gay, on the other hand, may be called one of the leaders in the development of the modern social sciences, but his influence was felt only indirectly at the college level. Gay, trained under Dewey at Michigan and men like Schmoller and Wagner in Germany, all his life fought for the integration and furthering of the social sciences. But he led this fight on the national, nonuniversity level. He played major roles in the creation of the National Bureau of Economic Research, in the founding of the Council on Foreign Relations, and in the publishing of the *Encyclopedia of the Social Sciences,* and he helped launch many interdisciplinary and international research projects as a charter member of the Social Science Research Council's Committee on Problems and Policy.[89]

In 1914 he and Taussig were invited to serve on an exploratory committee investigating the feasibility of a social science research group under the Rockefeller Foundation. Taussig was cool to the project for he thought it should be carried out on the university level; Gay chaired the committee. Gay was an influential member of the faculty committee which finally created the Department of Sociology at

Harvard. He was an astute and eminently successful committee man. He learned how to raise money while setting up the Harvard Business School and was a master at obtaining money from the Rockefeller Foundation. Throughout his life he campaigned for Schmoller's belief that history, economics, political science, sociology, ethics, and psychology should all be brought together to form one science of society.

Gay resembled Ashley in this respect, and, like Ashley, he believed in a cyclical theory of history in which society was said to oscillate between epochs of individualism and epochs of collectivism. Yet as teachers the two men were very dissimilar. For all his regard for individual facts, Ashley never lost sight of the forest and he never allowed his students to do so. Gay seldom saw the forest although he was sure that it was there, and his students apparently never saw it. Illustrative of Gay's whole scholarly problem is the fact that he spent twelve years in Europe working for his Ph.D. under Gustav Schmoller and still needed two extensions in order to get his thesis in on time. Similarly, all his life Gay wanted to write a book covering the Industrial Revolution. The only way he could do this correctly, he felt, was to read every book in the Widener Library, in the Kress Library (at the Harvard Business School), and in the Huntington Library that dealt with Europe from 1600 to 1730. He read most of the books but never got his own book written. In his early years at Harvard he spent half the night preparing formal lectures for classes of ten to eighteen students. Gay always seemed to be afraid to generalize until he had every single fact in mind. This fear cut his scholarly production to a trickle and made his lectures too often mere chronicles of events. In the classroom he was not the social or economic historian Ashley was nor did he ever produce the social insights that Ashley did.

Upon Dunbar's death in 1900 Frank William Taussig assumed the intellectual and administrative leadership of the department. For the next thirty years Taussig molded the tone and the *esprit de corps* of the teaching of economics at Harvard. Although he shared Dunbar's emphasis on theoretical economics, Taussig's influence was somewhat different. Taussig was at once more catholic than Dunbar and yet more dogmatic. He shared Dunbar's aversion to economic historians and sociologists who tried to impose their method upon all economic investigation, yet he recognized and respected the merits of the study of society. He, like Dunbar, quoted the Classics as his authorities, but he understood that the Classics did not cover all the conditions of reality and that theoretical economists should make every effort to expand their abstractions to include as many real conditions as possible. Taussig was, thus, very receptive to the theory of marginal utility and to the neoclassicism of Alfred Marshall. He became one of America's leading exponents of these doctrines, even in the decade of the nineties.

Taussig's was far from being a closed mind. In his long career he explored innovations in economic thought from all over the world and from all disciplines, and he accepted many of them. After receiving his B.A. (1879), his Ph.D. (1883), and his LL.B. (1886), all from Harvard, Taussig began his fifty-three-year teaching career there in 1882. Although he spent but one year studying in Europe, his upbringing in the intensely German village of Carondolet (soon to be incorporated into the city of St. Louis) had instilled a love of German thought and culture which was to keep him as up to date in German scholarship as if he, like Gay, had spent twelve years there as a student.

Moreover, Taussig was not circumscribed as Dunbar had been by a belief that academic economists should refrain from taking part in policy controversy or policy making. The theoretical economist with his principle of free trade must go out into the world and apply that theory, Taussig wrote in 1904. "But its application is not so easy and simple as was thought by the economists of half-a-century ago," he continued. "A principle can be stated in clear cut terms, and an answer of yes or no can be given with regard to it. The mode of its application, however, raises questions of *pro* and *con*, and often involves a balancing of conflicting principles. The question of principle is none the less important, and important for practical purposes." [90] Like Dunbar, Taussig realized that abstract principles had to be flexible to fit a real problem. But Taussig refused to remain aloof from real problems in order to protect the universality of his principles. Instead, he felt that the economist must apply his principle, unless the opposition can prove that it does not apply. But the burden of proof rests with the opposition.[91] The note of defensiveness, so often assumed by the theoreticians in the face of criticisms from men like Ely and Ashley, never appears in Taussig's work.

While at Harvard Taussig demonstrated that the theoretician could and should act in practical matters; he served as the first Chairman of the Federal Tariff Commission, traveled to Paris and wrote the tariff clauses of the Treaty of Versailles, and worked for many years on the President's Industrial Conference and on the Sugar Equalization Board.[92] Taussig represented, in a way, the economist that neither Ashley nor Dunbar believed could exist—the master theoretician who could and did act with assurance in the realm of practical affairs. He had the confidence to state what Dunbar never could—that economic "laws" were useful in predicting economic phenomena—and set out to prove it. This kind of fusion of the theoretical with the practical destroyed much of the basis for the criticism of abstract economics that had arisen in the eighties and the nineties and thus destroyed much of the vitality behind the impulse toward social study as a separate field within the Economics Department.

Note must be taken of the fact that 1900–1902 saw an almost complete break of continuity in the Economics Department. Taussig was the only tenured member who remained, and he was critically ill from 1901 to 1903. Dunbar died in 1900, both Edward and John Cummings left in 1900, Ashley resigned in 1901. Three instructors, all Harvard doctorates, held over and did receive assistant professorships before leaving the University. The faculty that was to be the backbone of the department for the next thirty years, however, was recruited from outside the University: Charles Jesse Bullock from Wisconsin, Gay from Berlin, Ripley from Columbia, and Carver from Cornell. Not one of these men had been at Harvard before. This break accounts for the small influence the teachings of Cummings and Ashley were to have after 1900.

The second reason for sociology's loss of vitality after 1900 is symbolized by the transition from the term "political economy" to the common juxtaposition, "economics and business." By 1900 the distinction that Dunbar had made between the science of wealth and the art of applying that science to welfare seemed irrelevant. Sociology grew out of the attempt to apply economic laws to human welfare—out of concern with the practical social questions of the day. In the nineties economics as it concerned contemporary social problems was considered important enough for inclusion in the introductory course. In those years Economics 1 included a half-year of lectures by Taussig on theoretical economics and a half-year of lectures by Ashley and Edward and John Cummings on the application of economics in social analysis. After 1900 Economics 1 became devoted solely to economic theory.

Cummings and Ashley had both been concerned, as the

German economic historians had been, with developing general laws of society so that they could learn how best to effect social reform, probably the most important problem facing political economists in this era. After 1900 the sense of the urgency of the "social question" had somehow disappeared. With the growth of a business orientation in the Harvard Economics Department after 1900 and especially in those years (1908–1913) when the Business School took many of its classes with the College, the practical economic questions of the day became those of maximizing profits, double-entry bookkeeping, and industrial organization. Even Taussig's practical work in policy-making concerned the technical business of governing rather than the furthering of social welfare. The "Labor Question" became a study of how to avoid or how to arbitrate strikes instead of an examination of the social conditions of the laborer. Carver's course in social reform became a course in learning how to refute socialist arguments. The practical or applied part of the economics offerings became geared to the potential businessman rather than to the potential political leader.

The third reason for sociology's loss of vitality was that economic theory itself had developed enough by 1900 to fill the gaps in its picturing of reality that the historians had pointed out. Men like Ashley attacked the Manchester School's conceptions of the economic man who always acted in a rational way to gain additional wealth with the least sacrifice and of the "invisible hand" that controlled and balanced supply and demand. Economic theorists, especially men like Taussig, knew that the historians had a point.

Taussig was also very familiar with the new theories being worked out in the last thirty years of the nineteenth century by the Marginalists, W. S. Jevons in England, Carl Menger in Austria, and Léon Walras in France. The Marginalists started with two laws: "The amount of one and the same enjoyment diminishes continuously as we proceed with that enjoyment without interruption, until satiety is reached"; and "In order to obtain the maximum sum of enjoyment, an individual who has a choice between a number of enjoyments, but insufficient time to procure all completely, is obliged . . . to procure all partially, even before he has completed the greatest of them. The relation between them must be such that at the moment when they are discontinued, the amounts of all enjoyments are equal." [93] These concepts greatly increased the precision of economic thought when they were added to the general doctrine of utility, which states that a person buys not what is cheapest, but rather that from which he thinks he can derive the most pleasure relative to its price. In 1907 Ashley had a few characteristically trenchant remarks to make on the theory of marginal utility.

[Marginal utility is] quite true, so far as it goes . . . It puts an elementary bit of psychology in a way calculated to make the youthful beginner do a little thinking . . . I cannot help thinking that it takes us a very short way indeed. Instead of leading us to the very heart of the problem, the doctrine of marginal value seems to me to remain entirely on the surface: it is not much more than a verbal description of the superficial facts at a particular point of time . . . But *why* do people demand just those things? On what does the rapidity of satiation depend? . . . The problem is, in a wide sense of the term, an *historical* one; or, if you prefer the phrase, a *sociological* one . . . Behind the workman's wife making up her mind on Saturday night whether to buy another loaf or a scrap more of meat stand the whole of human nature and the whole of social history. And this is what, I suspect, the deeper thinkers among the Marginalists are obscurely realising.[94]

Actually the deeper thinkers had realized it for quite some time.

Taussig was one of those who saw that marginal utility

had opened a vast field for psychological research into economic motivation and that the fruits of this research would sophisticate economic theory enough to bring it into useful relation with reality. Take note of his presidential address to the American Economic Association in 1905:

The topics on which I propose to touch this evening lie in the borderland between economics, politics, and psychology. This sounds formidable; but my subject is after all of a very simple sort . . . human nature, we find, works with no single motive force, but with a curious assortment of inconsistent impulses . . . In economics, much as the science has gained by the Ricardian method of analyzing the bare working of fundamental forces, we feel the imperative need of bearing in mind the complexities of real life, the interaction of opposing or converging causes. And so we are not content with the acceptance of a simple desire for additional wealth as the one human motive that deserves the attention of the economist. Why always additional wealth? and why additional wealth only? and is it not possible that further examination of the apparently simple desire for wealth may open new inquiries and point the way to new conclusions? . . . The desire for wealth . . . is . . . not a simple motive, but a very complex one, made up of all sorts of differing passions and instincts.[95]

Taussig was here pointing out the fruitful approach that social science was to use more and more in the twentieth century and identifying two of his own most important interests—human motivation, to be pursued in *Inventors and Moneymakers* (1915), and the development of human character, to be pursued in *Social Origins of American Business Leaders* (with C. S. Joslyn—1931).[96] His speech also identified the only fruitful contributions that the study of the science of wealth at Harvard was to make to the study of sociology from 1900 to 1925.

Taussig's point of view consistently informed his teaching of economic theory. Even in the nineties, when marginal utility was not taught in the introductory course, Taussig raised the point that human motivation was complex and that the "effective desire to save" was not the automatic reaction that Mill and Ricardo had assumed. Rather, it depended, Taussig explained, as one student recorded it, on stability of property, thrift, foresight, and the desire for distinction. "The desire for distinction and for distinction for your children is the immediate [?] cause of saving. The accumulation of wealth is a necessary feature in rising in the social plain [?]." He also raised the question as to what caused differences in earning capacity, mentioning social conditions and inherited gifts as possible answers and arguing for the importance of the latter. But these points were only slight detours in the explanation of John Stuart Mill and students in the nineties probably did not notice them, for these questions of motivation never appeared on examinations.

It was in Taussig's advanced course in economic theory that his point of view had its greatest effect on the teaching of economics at Harvard in the twentieth century. Economics 11 was required of all graduate students, and it was from these students that Harvard recruited its host of tutors, instructors, and section men from whom—in turn—Harvard selected most of its future senior faculty. Students explored the writings of the Austrian Marginalists in the advanced-theory course after 1890, and to their insights Taussig added his own comments on the need for a closer relation between economics and psychology. In notes for this course headed "Some Applications of Psychology to Economics" Taussig stated his position.

It may be objected that for the economist it is not material *why* men have the love of wealth—whether for expenditure on "unlimited wants," or from instinct of domination, or from instinct of accumulation, or because in obeying instinct of workmanship they can't help making money,—the complex love of wealth (preference of more for less) exists and impels them. This remains the simple [cannot read the next word] force for the economist.

Answers: various things are explained by the psychological point of view, as for example:

(a) Trusts and consolidations,—why made? Because of economics? or is this only a pretext, an unconscious self-deception? Real motive force the instinct of domination?—How explain cut-throat competition, "getting competitors," dominating the industry (done by men already millionaires) except on ground of instinct of pugnacity (domination)?

(b) Employers and trade-unions—making work—instinct of contrivance (workmanship) violated.

(c) Invention and Patents—instinct of contrivance.

For a dynamic account of economics, Taussig told the graduate students, the economist must ask why man loves wealth.

Sociology's vitality in the Economics Department depended on its contribution to economics in general and to the department's academic goals. In the nineties sociology under Cummings and Ashley made a very necessary contribution to economic thought and helped carry out the academic goals of "political economy." After 1900 sociology and history as taught by Carver and Gay did not make such a contribution and found little academic function in a department that was teaching economics and business. Cummings and Ashley were men to whom, and they taught the kind of course to which, all economists had to pay attention whether they agreed or not; the same cannot be said of Gay or Carver or the courses they taught. These two men quickly floated out of the mainstream of the development of economic thought, yet they were unable to define a field of their own. The Department of Economics did not lose its interest in the study of social reality, but it did, in Taussig, turn in a new direction.

Sociology, under Carver, refused to make this change. Carver was to write that "the ultimate basis of all social conflict is found in economic scarcity of one form or another. Around this fact of economic scarcity with its inevitable conflict of interests are grouped practically all our moral ideals, our social, political, and legal institutions. Moreover, it is the basis of all real values whether they be classified as economic, moral or aesthetic." [97] Carver's system contained no directions that sociology could explore as an independent discipline; in fact, he repeatedly stated that sociology did not differ from economics in subject matter or in method. Yet Carver's system would not go very far in explaining the "complex love of wealth" that constituted a major focus for the economic theorists. The intellectual content and the underlying assumptions of Carver's sociology prevented it from contributing to the new developments in economic thought. The wheel had come full circle: Harvard's economists were eager to probe the complexities of reality; Harvard's sociologist was content with oversimplified and rigidified general principles.

SOCIAL ETHICS

AT HARVARD,

1881-1931

A STUDY IN ACADEMIC ACTIVISM

DAVID B. POTTS

FRANCIS GREENWOOD PEABODY, founder of social ethics instruction at Harvard, was trained as a theologian rather than a social scientist. Within the Harvard curriculum Peabody's courses occupied a half-way station between the Divinity School and the psychological laboratory of his colleague, William James. Peabody and his successors in social ethics sought to develop and hold a middle ground between the dominant concern for religion and ethics characterizing the nineteenth-century denominational college and the quest for pure, inductive scholarship embodied in the rising American university. The major task of social ethics at

Harvard from 1881 to 1931 was to establish a meaningful and active relation between the *ought* and the *is*.[1]

Efforts in the same direction can be seen in all the emerging social sciences. In 1885 Franklin B. Sanborn noted that many members of the newly organized American Economic Association were directing their scholarly investigation toward the ultimate purpose of reform. As General Secretary of the American Social Science Association, Sanborn went on to state, "Methinks this expresses very well what our association has been doing in its broader field and with more miscellaneous activity, for the last twenty years. To learn patiently what *is*—to promote diligently what *should be*—this is the double duty of all the social sciences." As late as 1902 Lester Frank Ward found the prevailing public concept of sociology to be "sociology as philanthropy." "More than nine-tenths of the papers that are read before the American Social Science Association," Ward said, "proceed from that idea of social science." [2]

A major portion of this reform impulse was embodied in the late-nineteenth-century Social Gospel movement. Many leading figures in the social sciences such as Albion W. Small and Richard T. Ely were also social gospelers. Striving to overcome the currently assumed conflict between religion and science,[3] Small directed his sociological investigations toward ethical as well as scientific ends. Ely was a member of the "new" or "ethical" school in American economics, and his career as a social scientist was permeated with religious commitment.[4]

Extremist viewpoints ranged on either side of these mediators. William Graham Sumner's use of Herbert Spencer's *Study of Sociology* as a textbook at Yale in 1880 brought sharp exchanges from both sides. Some members of the religious press deplored the exposure of students to writings such as Spencer's chapter on "the theological bias."

Advocates of a pure science approach to the study of society rallied to Sumner's defense. *Popular Science Monthly* asserted that "human society is a part of Nature to be studied by observation and induction, like the other parts of Nature, and to be pursued in conformity with established scientific method." The magazine went on to assert that scientific truth should be allowed to emerge unimpeded by religious considerations.[5]

Viewing such struggles with philosophical detachment, one scholar defined the problem of the social sciences as follows:

If we efface the distinction between the sociological and the ethical points of view, we are led either to regard the results of development as such as ideally right, or to suppose that the ideally right as such must have an existence. In the first place, sociology masters ethics; in the second, ethics masters sociology.[6]

In the late nineteenth century the distinctions between sociology and ethics were more often blurred than effaced, and neither subject attained a position of mastery. A poll taken in 1894 asked more than forty teachers of sociology in American colleges a wide range of questions about their discipline. The author's major conclusion was that replies to his questions clearly revealed "the chaotic condition of sociological thought." [7]

Desire for a more ordered and productive relation between the *ought* and the *is*, or ethics and social science, permeates the intellectual biography of Francis Greenwood Peabody, who began teaching social ethics at Harvard in 1881. Peabody graduated from Harvard in 1869 and received his B.D. from the Harvard Divinity School in 1872. Repulsed by the "arid rationalism" of conservative Unitarianism, attracted to the transcendentalism of Emerson, and confused by the trend toward relativism in science in the thought of Charles Sanders Peirce, Peabody took his intellectual problems to

Germany. In the lectures of Professor Friedrich Tholuck at the University of Halle, Peabody found a "mediating theology" which "stressed the compatibility of a spiritualized Christian faith with the demands of unfettered, independent scholarship." From the writings of Otto Pfleiderer, professor of theology at the University of Berlin, Peabody learned that the inductive study of human nature and ethical activity rather than the common-sense realism of current American theology might provide a more scientifically respectable foundation for the philosophy of religion.[8] Peabody returned to the United States in 1873 armed with an academic theology which claimed the *ought* and the *is* to be inseparable partners.

Most of the time from his return until he became a lecturer on ethics and homiletics at the Harvard Divinity School in 1880 was spent as minister of the First Parish Church (Unitarian) in Cambridge. In 1881 Peabody was appointed Parkman Professor of Theology and offered a course in "Practical Ethics" at the Divinity School. Starting in 1883 this course, now entitled "Ethical Theories and Moral Reform," was opened to undergraduates. For the next thirty years Peabody was to divide his teaching time between the Divinity School and the Yard.[9]

Social ethics was offered within the Philosophy Department until the fall of 1905. The number and title of the course were altered several times, but the subject matter remained relatively unchanged. In 1890 Peabody settled on the permanent title, "The Ethics of the Social Questions." Undergraduate enrollment increased from eight in the academic year 1883–84 to 112 in 1902–03. With the formation of the Social Ethics Department in 1906 "Ethics of the Social Questions" assumed the role of an introductory course and enrollment continued to increase. An all-time high for the Peabody era, 146 undergraduates, was achieved in 1906–07. This represented over seven per cent of the undergraduate enrollment at Harvard for that year.

Starting in 1895–96 a second social ethics course was offered. Peabody called this one a "Sociological Seminary," and its topic for the next five years was "The Christian Doctrine of the Social Order." This offering was designed primarily for divinity and other graduate students and will not concern us further in this paper. Only one other course in social ethics preceded the creation of the department. In 1904–05 Dr. Jeffrey Brackett, a professional social worker, taught "Practical Problems of Charity, Public Aid, and Correction" to a class of 33 students. Prior to the 1905–06 school year, therefore, social ethics at Harvard centered primarily in a single course, the undergraduate lecture course offered by Peabody.

When Peabody retired in 1913, course offerings within the Department of Social Ethics included Peabody's and Brackett's courses plus "Criminology and Penology," "Selected Topics in Social Ethics," "Moral Responsibilities of the Modern State," "Social Amelioration in Europe," "Rural Social Development," several research seminars, and the School for Social Workers operated jointly with Simmons College. Evidence of just what was taught in each of these courses is lacking, but catalogue descriptions and enrollment figures indicate that Peabody's course was the most distinctive, popular, and significant course in the department. The other courses usually attracted only graduate students preparing for either social work or the ministry and the handful of undergraduates concentrating in social ethics. For the key to social ethics at Harvard one must look to Peabody's course.

"Ethics of the Social Questions" was more commonly known to undergraduates as "Peabo's drainage, drunkenness, and divorce." This epithet was probably uttered with varying degrees of affection and respect. Many no doubt enrolled because Peabody had the reputation of offering a "snap course." Yet many others probably studied social ethics with more serious intentions. President Eliot, in the words of one faculty member, viewed his college as "not a nursery of tradition but a seminary of service." Many students supported this concept by assisting in the various local charities of Boston and Cambridge. In 1894 the Student Volunteer Committee was formed to coordinate all these charitable impulses and act as "a sort of employment bureau in the interests of charity." By 1902 almost four hundred students were engaged in volunteer social work.[10]

Peabody regarded his course very hopefully but probably with few pretensions. He realized that he could only give a somewhat superficial survey of a few questions of social reform. In such a new subject lectures formed the core of the course and in these lectures Peabody humbly claimed "not to be original or interesting, but simply to be sound and just." [11] A letter from Peabody to Franklin Sanborn in 1886 is worth quoting extensively, for it offers the best introduction to Peabody's attitude, approach, and aspirations:

I was led to my subject by a somewhat different road from most of those who deal with it. As a teacher of ethics I became aware of the chasm which exists between such abstract study and the practical application of moral ideals; and it seemed to me possible to approach the theory of ethics inductively, through the analyses of great moral movements, which could be easily characterized and from which principles could be deduced. I studied thus with my class the problems of Charity, Divorce, the Indians, the Labor Question, Intemperance, with results of surprising interest. My class, under our elective method, grew from ten to fifty and was made up from five departments of the university. Each student made written reports of personal observation of some institution of charity or reform; and from the data thus collected I endeavored in each case to draw out the ethical principles involved. The results of the examination showed that the students felt a living interest in the subjects treated; and I think they will be more public-spirited as citizens and more discreet as reformers by even this slight opportunity for research. There is in this department a new opportunity in university instruction. With us it has been quite without precedent. It summons the young men who have been imbued with the principles of political economy and of philosophy to the practical application of those studies. It ought to do what college work rarely does—bring a young man's studies near to problems of an American's life.[12]

Despite its humble origins, social ethics in Peabody's estimation had a bright future.

Yet social ethics at Harvard can be best understood with an eye to the past. The general nature of Peabody's course, the type of professorship he held, and his educational philosophy clearly indicate that social ethics at Harvard during the Peabody era was primarily an extension of the moral philosophy tradition which had once dominated American higher education. At a time when sociology at other universities was beginning to shed its moral philosophy origins and was becoming increasingly concerned with developing new techniques for scientific investigation of social phenomena,[13] Peabody retained the early-nineteenth-century emphasis on character-building. The social sciences in the hands of his academic contemporaries were being increasingly directed toward the discovery of new scientific truths. Peabody was using these disciplines to reaffirm traditional ethical and religious truths.

Compared to other courses at Harvard during the presidency of Eliot, Peabody's lectures attracted an unusually large number of upperclassmen. At the turn of the century "Ethics of the Social Questions" was outnumbered in terms of senior enrollment only by Charles Eliot Norton's courses in fine arts and several offered in the booming Economics Department. Whatever the reasons for the popularity of his course, Peabody at least had an opportunity to influence about one out of every four undergraduates during the twenty-year span, 1890–1910. Peabody's lectures did not hold the keystone position which the required senior course in moral philosophy occupied in earlier days. Under Eliot's elective system, however, "The Ethics of the Social Questions" was about the closest possible approximation to moral philosophy in terms of size and nature of enrollment.

A practical and system-building approach to his subject matter also placed Peabody closer to the old-time college president than to his Harvard colleagues in similar and related subjects. Professor George Herbert Palmer's course in ethics operated on a more abstract and critical level. Sociology as first taught in the Department of Economics by Edward Cummings in the nineties was more statistical than systematic. Other attempts at development of sociology within this department were weak and were restricted by the belief that sociology should be used only as the servant of economics.[14] In the tradition of earlier teachers of moral philosophy, Peabody meanwhile traversed the provinces of almost all the social sciences. He constructed a philosophy which urged practical social action in the interest of improved ethical relations among men.

In its early years, Peabody's course probably contained a more balanced combination of social theory and practical reform than similar offerings at other colleges and universities. Some institutions employed outside authorities on a part-time basis to give a series of lectures on social problems. President Andrew D. White, for example, invited Franklin Sanborn to lecture at Cornell in the spring of 1885. Sanborn combined his attacks on "the chimera of non-interference by government—the Franco-Britannic specter of laissez-faire," with visits to asylums, prisons, and poorhouses in a rather haphazard manner. In the eighties lectures on social problems were also given at the University of Michigan and the University of Pennsylvania. Many colleges concentrated on the theoretical, with courses in theory of property, production and distribution of wealth, and theory of government. Few combined such instruction with reform-minded analysis of practical problems such as temperance and charity. While most social science courses were breaking away from moral philosophy in either theoretical or practical directions, Peabody was building an ethical system to restore the balance between ideals and realities which had formerly been maintained by moral philosophy.[15]

The professorship which Peabody held also placed him within the moral philosophy tradition. After serving five years as Parkman Professor of Theology, Peabody was appointed Plummer Professor of Christian Morals in 1886.[16] This professorship was established in 1855 and relieved Harvard's president of his obligation to provide instruction in religion and Christian ethics for freshmen and seniors. Such instruction usually resided in philosophy courses. By 1879–80 the elective system had grown to such proportions that all prescribed work in philosophy disappeared. When Peabody assumed the Plummer Professorship, its functions had decreased sufficiently for him to teach both in the Divinity School and the College, yet the charge remained to provide instruction in Christian ethics and religion.[17]

Peabody was fully conscious of the tradition in which he stood and vigorously assumed the duty of reviving moral philosophy. In the mideighties he began to argue that the old "deductive, introspective, and psychological" approach had turned ethics into "a dull study." "What moral philosophy needs," Peabody claimed, "is a new method of approach." The new method he advocated was "inductive ethics . . . that study which reaches the principles of ethics through the observation and analysis of moral facts." With such an approach Peabody thought that "the idealism which the scientific method seemed to displace" could be "restored to moral philosophy again." [18]

Like those of the old-time college president, Peabody's ultimate goals in teaching moral philosophy were religious. "There is no study," he asserted, "which more manifestly shows the spirit of God in the affairs of men, or the blessing of the Christian position, than the study of social reforms. They exhibit both the need and the inspiration of the religious impulse." Under the new title of social ethics, moral philosophy while studying reform movements could at the same time "strengthen religious aims." [19] On the competitive menu of the elective system Peabody offered moral philosophy garnished with the rhetoric of modern science.

In addition to his specifically religious efforts Peabody sought to revive an educational philosophy held by the old-time college. Universities and churches should not just be guardians of the Christian faith, according to Peabody, but also should cultivate the highest standards of ethical idealism. "A liberal education," he asserted, "has failed of its main intention if it does not prolong and justify the natural idealism of healthy-minded youth." The teacher should serve as a system-builder for such young men and by properly channeling their idealism give them "the capacity to look on the facts of life not excitedly and passionately, but sanely and steadily, and to see them, not as fragments, but as parts of a comprehensive whole." In its updated form, moral philosophy might thus become "a new department of liberal study" and perhaps even reoccupy its former position of influence in the curriculum. [20]

Although Peabody was consciously responding to the moral-philosophy tradition of the past, he was also significantly influenced by the era in which he taught. His courses focused on the "burning problems of the time" in order that more college graduates would be able to control and alleviate the growing, "startling gospel of discontent." The threat of violent class conflicts worried Peabody. Between 1881 and 1900 over eighteen hundred strikes and

lockouts occurred in Massachusetts. Yet Peabody optimisti-
cally believed that he lived in the "age of social service"
which included a "movement of passionate fraternity and
social justice" as well as immigration and labor problems.[21]

Peabody's response to his times flowed into quite traditional channels. The specific approach and content of his
course indicate most clearly his affinity to the moral philosophy tradition. This affinity is best seen by noting the resem-
blances between "Ethics of the Social Questions" and the
usual pattern followed by moral philosophy courses earlier in
the century. While reviewing Peabody's course within this
context, we can also take a detailed look at its content.

Gladys Bryson's historical analysis of the relation between
moral philosophy and the social sciences suggests that most
antebellum moral philosophy followed a similar pattern or
approach. A discussion of methodology usually was held at
the beginning of the course. Next came an exploration into
human nature and its "drives." This was followed by the
construction of a general ethical system based on a central
moral law. Finally, these tools were employed in a wide-
ranging investigation of various social institutions and relations.[22]

Surviving lecture outlines and student notes reveal that
after a few opening remarks about the purpose of his course
Peabody always discussed in detail the methods he would
employ. The course would take its cue from the recent developments in the social sciences and in Christian social
thought. Whereas the individual once reigned supreme, now
the focus had shifted to the problems of society. Such a
change was "as important as that from Ptolemaic to Coper-
nican theory."

The approach to society, Peabody announced, would be
both philosophical and scientific. Reflection should precede
reform since "there are no immediate panaceas." A science

of life "should frankly take its start from the data and the problems of life and should proceed inductively to analyze and classify these data and to discover what may be their law." With the aid of scientific research, "our object is to see the principle running beneath the facts."

Peabody also defined his approach in more specific terms by comparing it to that of the social sciences and ethics. Social science in general contributed the proper spirit of inquiry, but its specific divisions were of only limited use in solving social problems. Sociology, for example, was not yet even properly defined. "Sociology for us must either be limited to the study of primitive types, or must be regarded as the metaphysics of society." In the first instance Peabody found sociology too narrow and in the other too broad for anyone except "a genius like Comte or Spencer" to handle. At best this latter type of sociology offered a noble but unattainable ideal.

If social science in general provided the proper spirit of inquiry and sociology the ideal, then economics could be called on to supply the mechanism. Peabody always advised political economy to "remain a pure science." Economics alone would not be effective in dealing with present social problems, Peabody asserted, because it was too often associated in the minds of the poor with harsh laissez-faire doctrines. In trying to apply his ideas among the poor, the economist would probably meet with resistance and even open hostility. Economics should be content with supplying the "pure and unbiased truths" to be used in social reform. Peabody's usual dictum at this point was drawn from the German philosopher, Rudolph Hermann Lotze: "Mechanism is everywhere essential, yet everywhere subordinate."

Economics, in other words, should be subordinate to "the impulse to reform." Revolutionized by the inductive and case methods, ethics now could and must provide the energy or "moral dynamic" for the machinery of economics. Without ethics, economics would be "hard-headed" and, in the hands of radicals, perhaps even dangerous; without economics, ethics tended toward "soft-headedness and sentimentality." Here Peabody in addition to concluding his argument for "going slow" in social reform would soar to generalizations which reflected contemporary tendencies within the social sciences to blur distinctions between the realms of the *ought* and the *is*. Since ethics dealt with man as a part of society, he concluded, it may be termed a "sociological science." "Ethics is finally social science and social science is ethics. Ethics is the end of sociology."

Peabody usually summed up his method as involving three steps: "1. observation, 2. generalization, 3. correlation." Somewhere between the second and third steps "science passes into philosophy," from the mere aggregation and grouping of facts to "the principle which includes and explains them all." At this point Peabody passed from the first stage defined by Bryson to the second and third stages, but he presented them in reversed order.

The popular concept of "social organism" was used by Peabody to construct his ethical system. Employing Thomas Hobbes as a foil, Peabody offered the prolongation of infancy theory of John Fiske as proof of human sociality and interdependence. Such a conclusion, Peabody usually pointed out, reaffirmed the teaching of Paul in I Corinthians that "they are many members, but one body." Peabody admitted that social organism was not a completely accurate term when compared to the realities of society, but he did not go to the other extreme of regarding it as merely a useful fiction. He used this concept in the Spencerian sense of evolutionary progress but also gave it the non-Spencerian emphasis on governmental as well as individual responsibility for human welfare. The social organism for Peabody was both a reality and an ethical imperative. The reality was that social problems had an effect on all segments of society, especially if allowed to grow to revolutionary proportions. The moral imperative was that each individual should seek self-development and fulfillment through self-surrender and helping others. From the concept of social organism Peabody reaffirmed the Christian law of love and the biblical paradox that one must lose his life in order to gain it.

Human nature was the final subject discussed by Peabody in the introductory portion of his course. Standards of moral conduct were not as important as motivation, Peabody declared, and therefore they would not be discussed in detail. By quickly launching a search for the sources of social action, he avoided the pitfalls of relativism.

The key to a correct assessment of human nature, according to Peabody, was "the moral hero." Careful study of heroic actions would reveal that moral heroes were motivated not by self-interest, determinism, or prudentialism, but "loyalty to an ideal." A similar capacity for idealistic action, Peabody argued, resided in all men. At this point he usually quoted the British philosopher, John Grote: "Man is an ideal-forming animal." "That is the same as to say," Peabody continued, "that man is a rational animal." Thus rational idealism must be recognized as a powerful motivating force in human nature.

Moral idealism was the key to the philosophy of the social questions, Peabody concluded, and all the social questions to be studied would be variations on this one theme. Having used ten or eleven lectures to acquaint students with his methods and system, Peabody was ready to apply his principles to "the problems of our time" through a study "of people trying to do good." The deck had been carefully stacked to the point where one student remarked in his notes: "Peabody's 'generalizations' depend on uncriticised and specious assumptions—this method is dogmatic deduction." Despite this rather deductive beginning to "inductive ethics," Peabody now sought empirical support for his system in studies of the family, charity, labor, and temperance.

The fourth segment of "Ethics of the Social Questions" closely resembled that which Bryson describes as the fourth stage in moral philosophy. Beginning with a history of the family, Peabody used anthropological data to prove that the family was "the basic unit of civilization." He then made extensive use of divorce statistics to show the startling dimensions of the current problem in America. The divorce problem offered a challenge to his belief in gradual evolutionary progress. "In the instability of the family," he admitted, "we perceive a set-back, a reversion of type, a repudiation of the benefits of evolution." But Peabody's idealistic meliorism was more Fichtean than Hegelian. The human will must play a role through reformers working for better housing and offering increased religious assistance to decaying families. Idealism, working through reform efforts, was the answer to this problem. It must be a realistic idealism, however, and seek to correct this "set-back" by environmental as well as spiritual means.

In the area of charity Peabody seemed more at ease. The various charitable organizations provided ample evidence for the power and importance of idealism. Even though charity often paid monetary dividends to builders of model tenements, for example, the basic motivational force always was "moral intent." Peabody's task here was not so much to exhort as to counsel discretion. One should never assume that charity cures, but one should be encouraged by the fact that it does ameliorate. Peabody thus occupied a middle ground between what he termed "the sentimentalists" and William Graham Sumner. Charity should be regarded realistically but not pessimistically. Peabody argued that Sumner erred in not perceiving that society is an organism, and that "some poverty is not its own fault." Sumner was right in criticizing overly sentimental charity, but he "would have us retreat to an uncivilized state."

Peabody assumed that his students would be most likely to err in the direction of sentimentalism. He counseled them in the art of becoming "discreet reformers," emphasizing that science must be used to restrain emotion. Charles Booth's investigation of poverty in London [23] was often cited by Peabody as an example of enlightened and scientific charity. Frequent descriptions and analyses of European efforts such as Booth's were used by Peabody to expose the comparative lack of a scientific and systematic approach to charity in America.

Modern labor problems were interpreted by Peabody as signs of progress. Since strikes were basically "moral protests," they indicated an increase of idealism within the American working class. Statements such as this one suggest that Peabody's idealism operated on at least three levels. Idealism meant a tendency to govern one's actions by ideals, an epistemological belief that ideas are the most significant elements of reality, and an evolutionary optimism which saw in human history a gradual progress toward spiritual perfection, with some important help from man.

Political answers to economic problems were next discussed. Anarchism, Communism, and Socialism were each systematically explained, analyzed, and found to be inadequate. Anarchism and Communism were rejected by Peabody because they both unrealistically regarded government as intrinsically bad. The key question for Peabody was: "Which system, if any, will elevate character?" His answer was that systems are mere tools and only as good as the spirit with which they are used. Because of its attitude toward religion, socialism would mean more than just a change of system and probably would have an adverse effect, if any, upon character. Peabody presented Christianity and socialism as parallel lines of thought moving in the same direction. He taught that they were probably irreconcilable because one found the other too materialistic and the other thought its counterpart too other-worldly. Once these possible political systems were eliminated, gradual modification and improvement of the *status quo* was offered as the wisest course of action.

To emphasize further his interdisciplinary approach, Peabody occasionally invited faculty members from other departments to give one or two lectures in his course. Edward Cummings of the Economics Department gave several lectures on trade unions and cooperative enterprises. "Changes in Social Ideals During the Last One Hundred Years" was the subject of two lectures given by Professor Palmer of the Philosophy Department. In 1904 President Eliot, Peabody's brother-in-law and close friend, spoke to Peabody's class on "The Labor Questions." Most of Eliot's lecture was devoted to the problem of lower-class workers failing to find pleasure in work during an age of increasing specialization. He offered the Protestant ethic of hard work as one solution to this problem and as advice to the students. "Honest, faithful, enthusiastic work elevates one's standards," he concluded, "and shiftless work degrades. Labor that improves, gives satisfaction."

After outside information and advice had been offered, Peabody concluded this segment of the course with a hopeful look at profit-sharing, arbitration, and cooperatives. These were offered as modifications of the *status quo* which could greatly alleviate social problems. Their success, however, would depend on the spirit with which they were pursued. All roads led back to idealism.

Temperance was the final area in which Peabody attempted to prepare his students for "good citizenship." A variety of arguments for abstinence was offered. The "drink bill" was compared to other municipal expenditures and shown to be a shocking and "useless expense." Liquor was cited as a cause of disease, poverty, and early death. Insurance tables were employed to demonstrate this last point. Referring to testimonies from scholars, Peabody warned his students that alcoholic stimulation offered no assistance to intellectual life. Drinking often limited job opportunities. "To keep in the pink of condition," Peabody asserted, "one ought to be a total abstainer."

Pragmatic considerations, however, were only a prelude to the moral imperative of the social organism. Like all the other problems discussed, temperance was defined as ultimately an ethical question. Prevention of the evils emanating from drinking would depend not on legislation, but on the spirit of the community. Each individual should contribute to improving this moral spirit through the influence of personal example. Peabody urged his students to recognize "the hereditary transmission of qualities" and resolve not to be a weak link. As a part of the social organism, one should follow the maxim, "As I become strong, others are made so."

Summarizing the purpose of his course, Peabody said that he had attempted to combine "science with sentiment," to blend the scientific aspect of mind with ethical passion. He hoped that he had provided "an introductory course to life" which would open questions, not close them. His final words were usually an exhortation varying from "Make a life as well as a living," to "Putting to practical service the principles here laid down is the happiest result that could be wished for by your instructor or the university that sends you out."

While systematically presenting his personal mixture of ideals, theories, and scientific investigation, Peabody followed very closely the pattern Bryson describes as typical of moral philosophy. Like the old-time college president he constructed a religiously based system and assumed a unified science of man. Peabody's wide-ranging lectures were both an attempt to integrate knowledge which students had gained from previous courses in other disciplines and an effort toward preparing them for life.

Although Peabody's lectures stressed the ideal rather than the real, other elements of the course work supplied a complementary emphasis. Field trips and assigned readings were primarily designed to provide the students with empirical data. Students went on field trips to observe hospitals, asylums, industrial schools, labor organizations, cooperative and profit-sharing enterprises, temperance movements, and socialist political campaigns. Peabody's syllabus included substantial readings in such books as Charles Booth's massive *Life and Labour of the People in London,* and Evelyn Fanshawe's *Liquor Legislation in the United States.* Both works assumed an objective approach and contained extensive charts and statistical tables. Praising Booth as the "first authority in the scientific approach to the social problem," Peabody even used the prospect of an honorary degree in an unsuccessful attempt to lure him to Harvard in the spring of 1905 as a visiting lecturer.[24]

Examination questions in "Ethics of the Social Questions" show a similar concern for the factual and the sociological rather than the ethical. In the early years of his course Peabody sometimes asked what might be termed a "confessional" type question: "State, *briefly,* what general results you have gained from this course of study." Occasionally an evaluative question appeared on a topic such as "the ethical importance of infancy." A large majority of questions during the Peabody era, however, were not even theoretical, but demanded specific details from the assigned readings.

Student research papers handed in at the end of each semester reflect a strong concern for the empirical approach. If the research had been done primarily in books, extensive footnoting pervaded the text. Most contained much more exposition than analysis or evaluation. An example of this heavily-footnoted and expository type of paper is "Two Christian Socialists—Maurice and Kingsley" written in 1893 by a member of the senior class. This student spent most of the paper writing biographies of his two subjects. His only conclusion was a vague prediction that because of its "ethical impulse," Christian Socialism would be "realized in a few generations."

Only one of the quite generous sampling of student themes available from Peabody's course extracted ethical conclusions from exposition and analysis. Entitled "Recreation for Employees," this paper compared the efforts of three companies. The student combined data obtained from observation and interviews to construct four general principles to guide future programs of this nature for employees. He then moved from the practical to the ethical and concluded that intelligently administered recreation for employees will improve their characters by giving them "a purer and higher perception of American citizenship, American life, and American ideals."

Many of the papers are copiously illustrated with pictures and diagrams. Everything from pictures of employee housing to charts on infant mortality was offered as evidence of the authors' empirical and inductive approach. One student even presents a chemical analysis of "Alcohol in the Body." The author carefully explains that he would approach this problem "not from the standpoint of a student of sociology

or reformer, but from that of a student of physiology merely
searching for scientific data." He further assures the reader
that no attempt will be made to discuss "the question as to
whether alcoholic liquors are a blessing or a curse to mankind." After pages of chemical symbols and formulas the
student cautiously concludes that from a "scientific point of
view" alcohol is at least potentially "harmful" to the body.

The type of research which Peabody considered most
valuable was probably that which today is termed functional
analysis. An example of this type of investigation can be
found in the work of one of Peabody's students, Raymond
Calkins. In 1895 Calkins wrote a paper entitled "Recreation
of the Poor." At Peabody's request he expanded this paper
by making a detailed survey of the Boston area that summer.
Calkins' findings were subsequently published in book form
in 1901 under the title *Substitutes for the Saloon.*

Calkins' initial aim was "not at an abstract statement of
the principles involved nor at a possible ideal to be attained;
but rather at a description of what already exists." As a student researcher he visited the "clubs" of juvenile gangs,
saloons, and even theatres where "dancing girls contort
themselves suggestively." In the interest of scientific knowledge Calkins dutifully sampled a new kind of beer with low
alcoholic content. He then visited and compared the drawing power of these establishments to "dry" lunch rooms and
mission reading rooms. The results indicate that the saloon
is merely a more attractive "social center." A partial solution
to temperance and morals problems would thus be to provide attractive substitutes for these evil influences. Those
who desire to elevate the poor, Calkins concludes, must use
"rational amusements" which will allow them to express or
release their natural "social instincts."

Calkins' combination of empiricism and meliorism was
probably encouraging to Peabody. Here was a student who

did not lose himself in irrelevant description or draw hasty conclusions. His ethics were assumed, yet his research was carefully and scientifically pursued. Inductive methods were used to suggest a practical solution to an ethical problem. Induction was primarily used not to discover ethics but to serve ethics. Calkins perceived what Peabody really meant by "inductive ethics."

The Social Museum in Emerson Hall was an embodiment of Peabody's inductive efforts. He began collecting material for the Museum in 1903 and enlisted three of his former students as agents. Stanley Lubin spent most of the summer of 1903 visiting industrial and charitable organizations in the New York City area and arranging for gifts and purchases of charts and pictures illustrating their welfare activities. An example of such material might be pictures showing a machine before and after a shield had been affixed to protect the operator from an exposed flywheel. Edwin Bechtel was awarded a fellowship for study in Europe with the agreement that he too would acquire data for the Museum on such topics as workingmen's insurance in Germany. The largest single source of museum material probably was the St. Louis World's Fair of 1904. Many European countries displayed evidence of their welfare activities at the Fair. Peabody and his course assistant, David Rogers, engaged in a long but quite successful series of negotiations to obtain these exhibits once the Fair was over.[25]

Assembling and displaying the elements of a social museum proved to be a rather large financial undertaking, but Peabody, as will be shown shortly, had an ample supply of funds. By 1920 his Social Museum had grown to more than ten thousand charts, maps, photographs, and models illustrating social conditions in Europe and America and the institutions and methods devised to alleviate these conditions. The Museum was housed and displayed on the second floor of Emerson Hall. When Peabody retired in 1913, the Museum and a library of over three thousand volumes provided the Social Ethics Department with extensive research facilities.

Practicality and idealism coexisted in the purpose of the Social Museum just as they did in all of Peabody's social thought. As a social scientist, Peabody hoped that the Museum would promote inductive investigations analogous to those pursued in the natural sciences. "To interpret nature," he asserted, "one must, first of all, see, touch, scrutinize and analyze. The laboratory, the dissecting table, the clinic, the microscope, the museum, are the instruments of sound learning." Peabody based his Museum on the assumption that "the most immediate need of students concerned with the social question is, not merely enthusiasm or sympathy or self-sacrifice or money, but wisdom, discretion, the scientific interpretation and comparison of facts." [26]

Yet the Museum was to serve as a source of inspiration as well as induction. Peabody as an ethicist believed that the students using the Museum would be "inevitably led" to see in all its exhibits "the working of a social motive quite distinguishable from the desire for industrial advantage or the hope of economic gain." The Museum would give the students a sense of "companionship," "sympathy," and "patience" by showing them that they were part of worldwide "social evolution." In short, the Museum would "verify the faith of ethical idealists." [27]

Methods employed by Peabody to promote ethical idealism received a rather cold reception from several of his faculty colleagues. When Professor Hugo Münsterberg, Chairman of the Philosophy Department, first saw the exhibits of the Social Museum displayed on the walls of Emerson Hall, he laughed. He said that these pictures, charts, and diagrams might just as well be in a book. Münsterberg, whose department occupied the first floor of the new building, was more disturbed than amused by the Museum and seemed to hold little respect for any of Peabody's activities on the second floor. As early as 1903 he had tactfully informed Peabody that his "special department" was "certainly very pleasant company," but "from the standpoint of pure philosophy, it lies of course somewhat on the periphery of the field and . . . we should regret, therefore, if it should give too much the real stamp to the whole building." By 1906 Münsterberg's worries were even more specific: he feared that the noise of public and student visitors to the Museum might disturb the meditations of the philosophers below. Peabody was not present to hear Münsterberg's laughter or complaints, but he wrote to one of his assistants that the "relation with Prof. Münsterberg is one which I have always feared would occur, and which I must deal with gently when I return." [28]

One observer of the academic scene in 1905 indicated that Peabody's efforts were also not likely to meet with the endorsement of sociologists and economists. It seems likely that sociologists might object to his "Sociological Seminary," in which the topic for 1902 was "The Ethics of Jesus Christ." If so, the lack of respect between Peabody and academic sociology was mutual. In 1909 he stated that "Sociology, like dirigible ballooning, may easily become a passion for inventive minds, but it is still involved in great difficulties of balance and steering, and remains for the present very much in air." [29]

Friction between Peabody and the economists on the faculty is more evident. In the midnineties Professor Frank W. Taussig of the Economics Department suggested to Peabody "an enlargement of instruction in the general direction which we call Sociology." Peabody's reply was to propose that, "if new teaching were to be introduced, it might be in

the direction of prison reform." Taussig later charged that
the "halting and unsatisfactory" development of sociology
at Harvard was "due in some part to the way in which the
Department of Social Ethics grew up." The continued
"hortatory flavor" of social ethics, "supposedly alien to the
cold dry atmosphere of science," discouraged Harvard's social scientists from making a coordinated effort, under the
banner of sociology, "to meet a wide public need for sound
advice and guidance." [30]

In the face of such opposition and in the context of the
developing social sciences at other universities, why did
social ethics linger so long at Harvard? One reason may have
been Peabody's tactfulness. Although "sensitive to the skepticism he sometimes met among his colleagues," Peabody, as
in the case of Münsterberg, dealt with such skepticism
"gently." Another factor to be considered is Peabody's persistence. While "charitable in his judgment of his critics,"
he was "dogged in his opposition to any merger of his department with other divisions of the University such as
might reduce its freedom to deal with the moral problems of
our social and industrial order." Another, minor reason for
the longevity of social ethics may have been his refusal to
carry his character-building to the point where it lost all
academic respectability. The aura of science which he cast
over his activities may have rendered him somewhat less vul-
nerable to criticism.[31]

Continued and extensive financial support from a source
outside the University, however, appears to be the primary
reason for the long reign of social ethics at Harvard. Alfred
Tredway White, a New York philanthropist engaged in
charity administration and low-cost housing projects in
Brooklyn, provided the funds to "perpetuate, expand, and
dignify" social ethics at Harvard. Starting in 1903, White
supplied a "continuous stream of benefactions" for almost

twenty years. His gift of fifty thousand dollars toward the construction of Emerson Hall carried the stipulation that *pro rata* space in this building should be given to social ethics. Successive gifts included two one hundred thousand dollar endowment funds for the Social Ethics Department and smaller sums used for furnishings, publications, and material for the Social Museum. The total of his contributions to Peabody's department reached almost three hundred thousand dollars.[32]

White was carefully advised by Peabody as to the form which his contributions should assume. Peabody even drafted statements concerning the conditions to be placed on each endowment and in doing so gave himself the sole right, as long as he taught, to direct the expenditures of income. White's contributions freed social ethics from dependence on the University treasury. Writing to a friend in late 1903, Peabody claimed that this new source of funds put "the study of the Social Questions in a more stable position than any other department of the University, except the newly endowed School of Architecture." [33]

In addition to problems of finance and faculty politics, Peabody had to deal with the broader intellectual challenges of his times. Abundant evidence that Peabody clearly sensed the problems of relativism can be found in one of his two major books, *The Approach to the Social Question*, published in 1909. Peabody admits that life is complex and that "the Social Question" is "as fluid and changeful, and often as turbid and violent as a rushing stream." Yet he affirms "an underlying unity in nature" and a meaningful evolution in human history which justify "a practical and constructive faith in ethical idealism." The scholar in perceiving and identifying this process can be "a priest of Truth." But he must use his will as well as his reason—"the will leads and the reason and feelings follow." [34]

Having thus denied relativism and side-stepped one of its primary arguments, the fallibility of reason, Peabody confronts the more immediate challenge of philosophical pragmatism. Emphasis on the will is common to both philosophies, he observed, but ethical idealism does not "take up the path of philosophy now so warmly defended and condemned under the name of Pragmatism." Such a path would lead to "empiricism, experimentalism, probabilism, [and] the confession of bankruptcy for the faith of idealism." "Pragmatism . . . has failed to observe the process of experience which the dedication of the will initiates. The will is, in fact, a medium to insight and the dedication of the will to spiritual ends is a path to spiritual certainty." What counts most for Peabody is not the "will to believe" but the "will to help." [35]

Confronted with the epistemological challenge of Pragmatism,[36] Peabody, like many other social and religious philosophers of his time, found a refuge in activism. He also, of course, fell back upon his religious faith. Complete realization of the kingdom of God on earth was, in Peabody's estimation, "not . . . likely," yet a very relevant and compelling ideal. One week of his seminar was usually devoted to "Utopias in Literature" and he was an "avid collector" of such books. Peabody's Christian activism led him to play "a leading rôle in the Social Gospel movement of his time." [37]

To implement the social philosophy and ideals of his introductory course, Peabody guided the rest of the department toward professional social work. Jeffrey R. Brackett, the first appointment to his staff other than course assistants, had been a director of public and private charities in Baltimore. "Social Ethics 2—Practical Problems of Charity, Public Aid, and Correction" was first offered by Brackett in 1905. A strong indication of how the course was taught can be found in Brackett's statement, "Work in applied social ethics should approach as nearly as possible to the 'case work' which is doing so much in the study of law and medicine." The two men chosen by Peabody to be his successors, Robert F. Foerster and James Ford, combined social work with legislative efforts at reform.[38] They had both studied under Peabody and were appointed instructors in 1909.

By the time Peabody became emeritus in 1913 the emphasis in social ethics was shifting from values to techniques. Except for the introductory course, most offerings in the Social Ethics Department resembled those of a professional school. Fewer undergraduates were electing even the introductory lectures. Despite Peabody's assertions that action would lead to belief, Pragmatism and the scientific spirit in general had taken their toll. An all-encompassing moral philosophy had become irrelevant.

Between 1913 and 1920 the Department of Social Ethics under the chairmanship of Foerster had no tenure-holding faculty members. Ford and Foerster taught Peabody's introductory course. Brackett's course in the practical application of social ethics was now entitled "Administration of Agencies for Poor Relief and Neighborhood Welfare." Foerster also taught "Social Amelioration in Europe" in addition to continuing a course in his specialty, problems of race and immigration, which was first offered during the last year of Peabody's chairmanship. Ford's other courses were "The Housing Problem," "Rural Social Development," and a seminar on "The Alcohol Problem." The one entirely new course added was "Child-Helping Agencies," taught from 1913 to 1916 by Dr. C. C. Carstens, General Agent of the Massachusetts Society for the Prevention of Cruelty to Children. Graduate courses in the School for Social Workers were no longer offered after 1916, but the general emphasis on methods of social work remained strong in the undergraduate courses.

Professionalism even invaded the introductory course, now entitled "Social Problems and Social Policy." The announced purpose of this course was "to train the student in the scientific investigation of social problems through careful personal observation, deliberate judgment, and systematic presentation of results." Divorce, for example, was no longer considered in the light of Christian teachings or in accordance with the concept of the social organism but in terms of strategies for eliminating prostitution. Temperance became a purely pathological, physiological, and legislative problem. Discussions of anarchism, communism, and socialism were replaced by investigation and treatment of feeblemindedness, insanity, industrial accidents, and adult recreation. Ethical considerations were largely left to one of the assigned readings, *Ethics*, by John Dewey and James Tufts. Values were still stressed, but, unlike Peabody's students who observed the construction of one all-embracing system, students using this textbook studied many ethical systems, and from an eclectic and analytical, rather than religious, point of view.[39]

Emphasis on professional social work and the retirement of Peabody seemed to signal the end of the moral-philosophy tradition at Harvard. Rather than integrating all the sciences of man, the Social Ethics Department was now more interested in pursuing and developing its own professional interests. Since 1890 all the social sciences had been "expanding so rapidly that they utterly refused to be bound or restricted in their development by any considerations of unity." This process of fragmentation had finally penetrated the walls of Emerson Hall. Comtean, Spencerian, and even "Peabodian" attempts at the unification of all science were rendered futile.[40]

During the period 1913–1920 no one, apparently, knew just what to do with the Social Ethics Department. Many were not even sure what the department was doing. The

Economics Department, for example, prior to 1913 had listed most of the social ethics courses under the subdivision "Sociology." From 1913 to 1921 the only heading they could think of for social ethics courses was "Social Sciences." There is evidence that President Lowell would have liked to transfer the whole department to the Divinity School. He had to be reminded by the generous benefactor, White, to "keep in mind the interests of that large body of undergraduates who, as likely to become men of affairs, should realize the fundamentally ethical nature of many of our social problems." [41] By 1918 Lowell had developed a compromise position in which social ethics would be split along two lines: general undergraduate instruction and professional instruction under the auspices of the Divinity School. He wrote to James Ford:

> For the more general and undergraduate instruction, it is our plan to search for a man, rare and difficult to find, who would, by his personality, attainments and reputation, impress the students to an unusual degree. We have no immediate expectation of finding such a man, but hope to do so, and shall certainly secure him whenever found.[42]

The following year Lowell found this charismatic figure in the person of Richard Clarke Cabot.

With the arrival of Cabot in 1920 the Department of Social Ethics was extensively reorganized. An increased emphasis on the *ought*, reminiscent of the Peabody era, appeared in several new undergraduate offerings. The *is* of social work remained in a few undergraduate courses but was centered primarily in a separate group of graduate courses administered by Ford and listed as "Professional Courses in Social Ethics."

Cabot, professor of clinical medicine at the Harvard Medical School, had recently returned from active duty in

World War I when offered the chair in social ethics in 1919. The war had convinced him that a "non-ethical education was just as apt to be a curse as a blessing." Without a moral foundation, education enabled many men to be "smarter villains and livelier crooks." Cabot accepted the chairmanship of the Social Ethics Department "with enthusiasm," for it gave him a chance to "put ethics on the map." It also provided him with an opportunity to counteract those educators advocating "pure science" and "art for art's sake." Although the "pedagogic fashion" of his time was "against the attempt to influence anybody in any direction," Cabot pledged himself to "trying to make men better themselves." This would be "the most unfashionable attempt," he supposed, "in all the modern educational world." [43]

Implementation of this educational philosophy appeared in the form of several new courses. The most important of these was Social Ethics A—"Human Relations," which enrolled 317 students in 1920–21. This course dealt with the ethics of veracity, property, sex, freedom and restraint, and punishment. Cabot's major purpose was to stimulate student thinking on ethical problems. He used the case method extensively and often brought handicapped people into class. A man whose eyes and hands were destroyed by an explosion of dynamite, for example, told the class the story of his accident and of his courageous rehabilitation efforts. Biographies of other heroic men were read and discussed. "The contagion of these great personalities," Cabot asserted, "is the most effective teaching of ethics that I know." [44]

Here was Peabody's "moral hero" used for an ethical yet quite different purpose. Surviving student lecture notes indicate that Cabot's primary goal, as compared to Peabody's, was not to induce from this phenomenon of human heroism the first principle (ethical idealism) of a systematic philosophy of social reform, but to stimulate students to work out a philosophy of personal conduct based on such principles as honesty, growth, and "supermorality." Where Peabody emphasized the social organism, Cabot lectured on Emersonian self-reliance. Where Peabody started with an ethical system, Cabot merely stated, "We are going to assume that right and wrong, the universe, and man all exist," before going on "to discuss concrete ethical problems." [45]

Cabot's courses were almost entirely, as he intended them to be, a function of his own personality. The frequent changes in the titles and descriptions of his courses suggest that the only constant elements were the case method and Cabot himself. A typical student reaction was that his introductory course had "no unity, no coherence or order." The *Harvard Crimson* commented in 1929, "An introduction to Social Ethics A is primarily an introduction to Dr. R. C. Cabot" and "is subject to change on a moment's notice according to the whim of the man at its head." By discarding the systematic and more socially oriented approach used by Peabody and concentrating almost exclusively on situational and personal ethics, Cabot had adapted the aims of moral philosophy to the climate of the nineteen-twenties.

The members of his faculty found it more difficult to establish themselves as social ethicists. Unable to move up, Foerster moved out to become Professor of Economics at Princeton in 1922. After 1924 Ford spent most of his time in Washington as director of Better Homes in America. He retained his associate professorship until his death in 1944, teaching a handful of graduate students preparing for social work or the ministry and an occasional course in the Sociology Department. Niles Carpenter and Gordon Allport, two of Cabot's young instructors, also left to accept positions which better suited their academic interests. Carpenter became professor of sociology at the University of Buffalo in 1924, and two years later Allport accepted an assistant professorship in the Psychology Department at Dartmouth. Allport subsequently returned to Harvard as assistant professor of psychology in 1930.[46] That these men left the Social Ethics Department suggests that despite the revitalization efforts of Cabot, social ethics at Harvard had no academic future.

One young teacher in the department identified the basic problem of social ethics—it had increasingly fewer academic reasons for existence. He found that the method of "treating particular problems from the ethical point of view would seem to lead to all sorts of logical difficulties" and "to jurisdictional disputes with other social sciences." In planning a course on labor problems this teacher found himself duplicating the subject matter of a similar course in the Economics Department. He found his methods indistinguishable from those of "Sociology-as-it-is-taught-elsewhere." [47] A modern version of moral philosophy might be successful in one course taught by a powerful personality, but it lacked the distinctive methods and subject matter to construct a completely new and necessary academic department.

Cabot reacted to this dilemma by attempting to break down departmental barriers so that social ethics could draw freely upon the resources of the other social sciences. An effort in the same direction had been made by Peabody in 1911 but resulted only in the publication of *A Guide to Reading in Social Ethics and Allied Subjects* containing sections compiled by various faculty members.[48] Cabot seems to have desired integration of a broad range of social science courses under the heading of social ethics. This approach probably did not assume the philosophical unity of all science as Peabody's ideas did, but was a problem-centered approach.

A field of concentration in sociology and social ethics was established by Faculty vote in 1927 and opened to undergraduate concentrators in 1928. The field was administered by a special Committee on Sociology and Social Ethics appointed by President Lowell. Members of the Committee were drawn from the Departments of History (A. M. Schlesinger and, for part of this period, E. A. Whitney), Government (W. Y. Elliott), Economics (E. F. Gay, later joined by T. N. Carver), Anthropology (E. A. Hooton), Philosophy and Psychology (R. B. Perry, chairman of the Committee until the arrival of Sorokin, and G. W. Allport, who joined in 1930), and Social Ethics (R. C. Cabot). The theory behind this new field of concentration was that both social ethics and sociology, lacking unique methods of their own, should be supervised by representatives of those social sciences from which methods were borrowed.[49]

The history of concentration in Sociology and Social Ethics, 1928–1931, reveals a steady reduction in the position of social ethics in relation to the other participating social sciences. An early draft for the pamphlet describing this field of concentration outlined four subdivisions: society, its structure and development; social history; social standards and values; and social problems. The final printed copy substitutes the word "theory" for "values" and eliminates social problems as a distinct subdivision, thus undermining the major area in which social ethicists could claim to be specialists.[50]

A second step toward pure sociology was the appointment in 1930 of Pitirim Sorokin as professor of sociology and Chairman of the Committee on Concentration in Sociology and Social Ethics. Sorokin, who came to Harvard from the University of Minnesota, was a promoter of sociology as a distinct social science with certain unique methods and functions. Hailing his arrival, the *Crimson* sensed the current critique of social ethics which such an appointment implied. "In the past," the *Crimson* editorialized, "the Social

Ethics Department has been a neglected makeshift composed of men from various allied fields without unity or central control." It was hoped that Sorokin would "bring about a centralization and unity of purpose hitherto impossible," so that Harvard could "make contributions to the science of social development." [51]

By the fall of 1930 social ethics was fighting for survival. The struggle focused on the issue of whether social ethics and a new group of sociology courses set up by Sorokin would be joined in the same department or lead separate departmental existences within the same division. Beneath this issue lay various strategies for either eliminating or perpetuating social ethics. Supporters of social ethics included Cabot, Ford, Allport, and R. B. Perry. A majority of the faculty committee set up to resolve the issue was interested primarily in the establishment of sociology. Cabot even noted "the hostility of certain members of the Department of Economics to the very existence of our Department and its courses." Important members of the Administration also saw little reason for the continuation of Cabot's department and cited rank lists to show that many social ethics courses were heavily populated with poor students. [52]

Two more specific issues were finances and the ethical tradition in social ethics established during the Peabody era. Cabot feared "the rapacity of the Administration in case they want to take some money previously given to us and use it to pay for sociology work." The carefully restricted endowment fund given by A. T. White was the chief weapon of the social-ethics supporters, but their defense was also ideological. Allport prepared a memorandum to inform Sorokin on the Peabody tradition in social ethics and convince him that training students "for an intelligent participation in public and private social enterprises" was a worthy academic endeavor. [53]

Sorokin was willing to let the Department of Social Ethics go its own way but was opposed to combining it with sociology within a single department. He thought that such an arrangement would promise "incessant troubles in the future, since the dualism is put at the foundation of the proposed department." Cabot had the feeling that neither arrangement would permanently protect social ethics, but he also favored separate departments. On February 10, 1931, the Faculty Committee on Instruction accepted the recommendation of the Committee on Sociology and Social Ethics that "the present Department of Social Ethics be unified with the new Department of Sociology to form a single department which shall be called the Department of Sociology." [54] Most of the social-ethics courses were offered in this new department the following fall, but in a few years they were abandoned, or altered and absorbed.

When viewed within the context of American collegiate history, social ethics at Harvard is a special case. Social sciences at other universities were beginning to outgrow their moral philosophy origins by the first decade of the twentieth century. A similar development at Harvard was impeded first by the ethical idealism of Francis Greenwood Peabody, next by the sidetrack of professional social work, and finally by an updated combination of both under the chairmanship of Richard Clarke Cabot. The financial contributions of Alfred Tredway White provided the necessary support for all these diversions. Parallel developments within the Department of Economics also subordinated sociology to other interests. Sociology at Harvard was finally forced to establish itself by revolution rather than evolution.

Although it is a special case, the history of social ethics at Harvard offers some insights into the growing pains of the social sciences and the character of the emerging American university. Peabody's unsuccessful intellectual efforts to bridge the gap between the *ought* and the *is* with "inductive ethics" suggest that induction was an especially elusive and perhaps unrealistic method for his area of study. For all the emerging social sciences, induction initially proved to be more an abstract principle or general procedure than a specific method immediately applicable to all their intellectual endeavors. Unlike most social scientists, Peabody failed to move from a vague and general use of the inductive method to the development of a more specific and elaborate set of methods appropriate and unique to his area of study.

Peabody chose to concentrate on ethical ends rather than scholarly means. Systematic ethics and creation of certain reform-minded attitudes toward society and its problems were his chief concerns. The relatively disinterested stance which contributed to the growth of distinct and elaborate sets of methods in other social sciences was absent in social ethics at Harvard. Promotion of a primarily academic attitude toward society and pursuit of a discipline largely for its own sake were antithetical to Peabody's ethical activism. This activism achieved considerable initial success in terms of interesting and influencing Harvard students during the Progressive Era. But reformist zeal also prevented social ethics from finally meeting the crucial test of academic permanence—the possession of a distinctive and respectable method and sphere of study.

The ultimate failure of Peabody and his successors to provide for and insure the permanency of undergraduate social-ethics instruction at Harvard when compared to the success of contemporaries in other social sciences, however, must be viewed as a matter of degree. The career of social ethics is merely an exaggerated case of tensions present in all the social sciences. Even today, it can hardly be said that any of the social sciences completely measures up to the ideal of scientific rigor, precision, and objectivity.

That such a criterion should be applied to determine the fate of social ethics reveals how far the ideal of induction had carried the late nineteenth- and early twentieth-century university. Induction had hastened the fragmentation of the academic world into clusters of technique specialists, each playing a variation on the theme of objectivity. Critical thinking and intellectual honesty had replaced orthodox religious faith and traditional systems of ethical conduct as the prime objectives of higher education. Some concern for a broader range of values remained, and in this context social ethics may be regarded as a stage in the transition from moral philosophy to current ideas about the liberal arts, the humanities, and general education, rather than a mere impediment to the development of sociology at Harvard. In its attempt to justify itself as a social science, however, social ethics lacked the academic credentials necessary for survival within an altered framework of university priorities which elevated intellectual and professional above ethical development.

ALBERT
BUSHNELL HART

THE RISE OF THE PROFESSIONAL
HISTORIAN

CAROL F. BAIRD

THE ASTOUNDING energy of Albert Bushnell Hart, professor first of history and then of government at Harvard from 1883 to 1926, involved him in almost all phases of the growth of a profession practically nonexistent at the time he began to teach.[1] His work makes an excellent focal point for an examination of the activities of American historians during this period.

Albert Bushnell Hart was born on July 1, 1854, in Clarksville, Pennsylvania. In 1860 his family moved to Hartford County, Ohio, and in 1864 to Cleveland, or as Hart liked to say, they moved West.[2] His father, both a doctor and a dentist, was trained at the Jefferson Medical College in Philadelphia "to make a blue pill, and to draw teeth, and to cure fevers." He also owned a gristmill and a sawmill, and had a part interest in a local coal-oil business. Hart never refers to his parents' financial status, and it is unclear whether or not they contributed to his Harvard education. During his last two years he did have a scholarship which paid $300 of the $400 that Harvard estimated as minimally necessary in those years.[3]

There is not very much known about the family's cultural background. They were Congregationalists and strongly imbued with ideas of goodness and morality. Such ideas were to become more sophisticated in Hart but were never lost. He liked to refer to himself as the "descendant of Abolitionists"[4] (his father had been a surgeon in the Union army), and a strong tinge of morality is reflected in his high-school valedictory address, titled "American Progress." Its theme was that for a time after the Civil War people had forgotten their high ideals and had lost the spirit of reform; wealth had become more important. But now, "right has triumphed." He discussed great men and the evils of liquor, and he ended his speech with the optimistic statement that material progress and spiritual progress must and could be harmonized:

So we must press on. One false step may lose us all that we have gained, but each step toward the truth, toward the right, is a step upward. If we study successful national reforms, we shall find them operating through and toward moral improvement.[5]

Hart attended the district and public high schools in Cleveland, and after his graduation in 1870 he worked as a bookkeeper. During this time a young Harvard graduate, a minister, acquainted him with the existence of "a place called Cambridge," where Hart decided he wanted to study. He was tutored to make up for some of the gaps in his education, took the entrance examinations for Harvard, and entered with the freshman class in the fall of 1876.

Hart's years at Harvard coincided with the final extension of the elective system, a change that did not affect his early studies (primarily classical, with German, geology, and mathematics as additions); by his junior year, however, he was free to concentrate on his historical interests. Samuel Eliot Morison has implied that Hart was one of Henry Adams' pupils and that it was from Adams that Hart received the inspiration which led him into history.[6] But Hart himself corrects this statement:

> I count myself fortunate in having, rather by chance direction than by deliberate intent, steered into a profession where the opportunities were great and trained men were few. By the inspiration of several of my professors—notably Emerton, Torrey, Dunbar, Nat Shaler and more than anybody else, Norton—I was led to enter the field of history. Henry Adams and Cabot Lodge lectured while we were there, but I knew them not.[7]

Oswald Garrison Villard has recalled Norton's "priceless and caustic comments on men and affairs in our public life" and a possible influence on Hart:

> Professor Norton deliberately included in his lectures discussions of events of the day, of every phase of manners and morals and social happenings, called politicians by their right names . . . [He] upheld the theory that the university teacher was profoundly concerned with public affairs.[8]

Whatever the source of the inspiration, Hart, graduating *summa cum laude* in 1880, stayed on in Cambridge on a three-year fellowship as a special student of modern constitutional history, and read particularly in the history of England and America. His fellowship provided for a year of study in Cambridge and two years of further study abroad. Hence, in 1881 Hart joined the pilgrimage of American students to Germany.

Hart studied language at Eisenach, the German constitution and nineteenth-century history at the University of Berlin, and after traveling in Austria, settled down in Freiburg to study American history with Hermann von Holst, who was both a constitutional authority and a historian of the Civil War. Hart did not stay in Freiburg without a break, however, for he went first to Italy and then to Paris and *L'Ecole Libre des Sciences Politiques,* where he not only studied but spent time observing political behavior at rallies and meetings around Paris. Receiving his doctorate in 1883 from the University of Freiburg, he then returned home.[9] Later he was to refer only rarely to his academic experiences abroad and he never became an apostle of German scholarship as did some of his contemporaries. Yet his two years abroad must have made a profound impression on him, if only because the German schools were so sophisticated and mature, especially when they were compared to the very provincial American colleges.

In 1883 Hart was appointed an instructor at Harvard to teach the only course in American history offered. This was in spite of the fact that Edward Channing, then an assistant in European history, had wanted to teach the course himself.[10] Hart's appointment might have resulted from the prestige of his German training, especially since President Eliot was very much impressed with German educational advances.

Hart was to remain at Harvard for the rest of his life; he became an assistant professor in 1887, a full professor in 1897, the Eaton Professor of the Science of Government in 1910, and Professor Emeritus in 1926, but he possessed none of the characteristics of the cloistered scholar. He served on many committees inside and outside the University, gave speeches to countless groups, and pursued a singularly active professional career. During his years abroad he developed a love for travel which he indulged at every opportunity. He spent his sabbatical of 1908–09 traveling around the world; he made several trips to the West coast, took two extensive trips to the South, and boasted that he had been to every state in the Union, most of the important cities, and almost all the countries of Europe.[11] He had an overriding interest in contemporary affairs, especially politics; in later years he gave enthusiastic support to Theodore Roosevelt. His concept of history was dominated by the idea that an understanding of the past would enlighten the present; he viewed the enlightenment of the present as the historian's duty. He thought of himself as a worker and organizer, a performer of needed tasks in a growing professional field, and not primarily as a scholar.

Of his personal life not a great deal is published. He was married to Mary Putnam in 1889, and his relationship to her was always close. To their great sorrow they had no children of their own and in 1897 they adopted twin boys. Unfortunately these children did not share the intellectual abilities of their father; relations between the children and their parents seem never to have been very good, growing worse as the years wore on. Hart himself did not seem to reflect undue sorrow over the difficult situation; or perhaps it only increased the seemingly unflagging energy of a naturally outgoing and active person.[12]

His accomplishments are impressive. According to one article written at the time of his death, "the bound file of his pamphlets, articles, books, and edited works in his study amounted to about two hundred and fifty volumes." [13] His books and articles made him widely known, and since the name he had made for himself was highly respected, he was in great demand as a speaker and honored guest on many occasions. He was an excellent and conscientious teacher, interested as much in improving the methods of teaching as in expanding course content; his suggestions and developments of teaching methods were among his most significant contributions. He was greatly concerned with the professional problems of his colleagues and the needs of the organized group of whose growth he was so proud. He was a born committee man and served in this capacity as an early and active member of the American Historical Association, an originator and for many years an editor of the *American Historical Review,* and a member of committees on methods of teaching history. He edited several volumes of source materials in American history and did a great deal of work in the bibliography of American history; the best known of these efforts was the epoch-making *Guide to American History* (1896), which he edited with Edward Channing. Through his many interests, we can trace the growth of a coherent school of American history, in which Hart served as scholar, teacher, and professional organizer. Because of the wide scope of his work he, more than other individuals, introduces an investigator to the field itself.

The origin of history as an academic discipline lies within philosophy and theology, and only shortly before (and in some places during) Hart's time was differentiated from its traditional intellectual associates.[14] However, recognition as a discipline made little difference to the prestige of history as a study, for it was regarded merely as an unimportant frill, something that might be added to a man's accomplishments after he had been taught the important things. At Harvard it was merely an "adjunct of other studies," Ephraim Emerton recalled.[15]

History was regarded in this light not only at Harvard but also at other institutions. Charles K. Adams, of the University of Michigan, wrote in the introduction to his *Manual of Historical Literature,* published in 1882, that until recently

history . . . was condemned to receive only such charitable attention as could be given it by some benevolent professor after his energies had already been too much exhausted by absolute necessities of what was thought to be more important instruction.[16]

In 1883 a professor from Nebraska State University wrote to Herbert Baxter Adams at Johns Hopkins:

It is painful to realize the condition of historic study in the multitude of so-called colleges and universities in the United States, particularly in the West . . . When a chair of History was established here, grave professors, educated under the old order of things, regarded it as an unwarranted expenditure of time and money. History should, they thought, be made auxiliary to some other department.[17]

In 1880 there were only eleven professors of history in the country,[18] and President Eliot of Harvard reported in 1884 that if men asked his advice about the possibility of teaching history for a livelihood, he was forced to advise them that "it would be the height of imprudence on their part." [19] There was little demand for the teaching of American history:

Any "cultivated gentleman" could teach European history; and as for America, one might suppose a knowledge of its history to form a part of those innate ideas some philosophers tell us about, for all the effort visible to compass it by way of education.[20]

Thus when Channing wrote to Eliot in 1880 asking for a chance to teach American history, Eliot replied:

Your desire to teach American history is a laudable one; but you of course recognize the practical necessity of having other strings to your bow. There are only two colleges in this country within my knowledge where much is made of American history, and you know how elementary the teaching on that subject is in American schools.[21]

As history was regarded as part of another aspect of "humane letters" so the writing of history in the eighties was the "avocation of lawyers, clergy or businessmen" [22] and not in any sense a profession. Those who taught history seldom wrote it; those who wrote it viewed it as one of the arts, a branch of literature. In the next twenty years great changes were to occur. History by 1900 was written primarily by university-trained professors who sometimes felt a sense of superiority to the older generation,[23] by men who considered their discipline a "science." Henry Adams had sensed the coming changes and had written to Francis Parkman in 1884 that "before long a new school of history . . . will leave us antiquated." [24]

This is exactly what happened. Even by the nineties there was a small but enlarging group of people who grew proud of their increased specialization and more exacting standards. As their sense of *esprit de corps* mounted, the members of this group became concerned with achieving the status and recognition accorded to other professions [25] and with defining their own role. For this reason, and because they had many things to say to each other and, they hoped, to a wider audience, they formed the American Historical Association and began the *American Historical Review*. They were concerned about each other's problems, especially those related to bibliography and possible increased opportunities for publication, not merely from common generosity, but because they faced the same problems, some of which could be solved through cooperation. As the number of monographs and monograph writers grew, as the number of teachers in various colleges increased, and as the number of students multiplied, there emerged a class of professors who took over the teaching of a now-recognized academic discipline. These men began to write for professional purposes.[26]

Many factors contributed to the increased self-consciousness of historians as a professional group. In the first place, these men were of similar backgrounds and age, sharing attitudes about their society, about democracy and progress, and about the Anglo-Saxon heritage. They were all Northerners, strongly impressed by the Civil War (Hart recalled that at the age of eleven he had been taken, in Cleveland, to see the open coffin of Lincoln as the mournful train moved west for burial) [27] and even more strongly impressed by the concept of national union. This idea possessed Hart, just as it did his colleague at Harvard, Edward Channing, who wrote in the preface to his multivolume history:

I have also thought that the most important single fact in our development has been the victory of the forces of union over those of particularism . . . for it is the triumph of these which has determined the fate of the nation.[28]

In the second place, many of the oldest members of this generation of American historians had studied in Germany after their undergraduate training, and they returned with certain attitudes which they shared and which they transmitted to their students. Hart, Herbert Baxter Adams, John Burgess, Henry Adams, and C. K. Adams were deeply influenced by the greater freedom and stimulation of the German methods of study and individual work, all the more so because they had experienced the provincialism and rigidity of the American approach. They were also influenced by the German techniques of study and German attitudes toward history, and they believed, if uncritically, that history could be science. [29]

This belief was a third and by far the most important factor uniting these men, for whatever their disagreements, they agreed in this basic concept. In an age impressed by the achievements of scientific thinking, and specifically by the ideas of Charles Darwin, historians were eager to discover the laws of the universe, usually less in the predictive than in the descriptive sense. They shared fundamental beliefs about the operation of society and the institutions within it, especially the beliefs that institutions were not static and permanent but had an origin and a development (seen usually as progress) and that it was the duty of the historian to trace this development.

The historian could do so only if he were trained, as a scientist was trained, to be expert in the use of those techniques peculiar to his discipline. In the case of the European historians this meant paleography and languages and philology; the process of studying documents led them to formulate the goal of finding out what really happened, of telling about things "as they really were." Even those who began to study American history, in which many of the techniques of European study lost immediate relevance, were permanently convinced that by assembling facts, literally by "digging them out" as Henry Adams urged his students to do,[30] they would find truth. It is not to be assumed (nor did they assume) that earlier American historians had been inaccurate.

What scientific methodology contributed at this time was less the kind of factual accuracy which the best of the earlier historians took for granted, but a mystique about historical data in which the facts would yield meaning to the impartial historian provided his researches were sufficiently painstaking.[31]

This concept of history as a science is worth examining in some detail. Rarely was the concept itself examined; it was taken on simple faith that the great progress of the natural sciences, especially biology, held lessons for the historian, the student of society.[32] Nevertheless this belief held all of the powerful influence on their work of a consciously realized philosophy of history. The prestige of science in the late nineteenth century had strongly impressed these men, and since they felt that its success had come from its method, that method must be applied to their own work. In his presidential address to the American Historical Association in 1910 Hart said:

What we need is a genuinely scientific school of history, which shall remorselessly examine the sources and separate the wheat from the chaff; which shall critically balance evidence; which shall dispassionately and moderately set forth results. For such a process we have the fortunate analogy of the physical sciences: did not Darwin spend twenty years in accumulating data, and in selecting typical phenomena, before he so much as ventured a generalization? History, too, has its inductive method, its relentless concentration of the grain in its narrow spout, till by its own weight it seeks the only outlet. In history, too, scattered and apparently unrelated data fall together in harmonious wholes; the mind is led to the discovery of laws; and the explorer into scientific truth is at last able to formulate some of those unsuspected generalizations which explain the whole framework of the universe. That is the way in which Darwin came upon his universally guiding principle of natural selection; is it not the way in which historians must work? [33]

J. F. Jameson, in his speech "The Influence of Universities upon Historical Writing," referred to our "science," meaning history.[34] Emerton, in discussing the importance of a good library, said that

what the laboratory is to physical science, that the library must be to moral science . . . Books must exist not so much to be read as to be studied, compared, digested, made to serve in the development of new truth by the method of practice with them.[35]

The document, like the laboratory animal, could be dissected for the greater revelation of truth.

As W. Stull Holt has pointed out, two points of view were possible on the question of history as a science.[36] On the one hand it was possible to say that, like science, history would yield laws and generalizations, but on the other hand one could reject philosophy and say that science in history was a method, a search for objective fact, impartially described and reported. The American historians of the period, said Holt, uncritically did both. They did not examine the difference between the two meanings of the statement that history could be scientific; such analysis remained for a later period and men like Charles Beard. It is certainly doubtful that Hart ever followed the thought of the "New History" which came to make a distinction between objectivity in fact and objectivity in interpretation.

Holt cites Hart as an example of "the widespread misconception" of the way in which facts, when assembled, might produce general laws. In fact, he uses Hart's statements quoted above.[37] Though it is true that Hart believed that the assembling of the facts themselves would lead to truth, his position was not so simple. The gap between fact and generalization was not bridged automatically by some sort of electric spark; it was bridged only by the person and thought of the historian. "It was all very well for Ranke to begin his lectures: 'I will simply tell you how it was,'" said Hart, but "did not his student really get 'how it was' as seen through the mind of Ranke?" [38]

In the introduction to one of his volumes for the American Nation series, Hart said:

This conception of history as including conditions and standards requires a constructive mind to see connection, causation, and development; to apply the standards of each age to its own problems; to compare the achievements of one race and one century with those of another.[39]

He was well aware that no final answers could be given, for he said to the American Historical Association:

Still the analogy of natural sciences may be pushed too far: we use terms like "research" and "investigation" as though history could be prepared in a laboratory with all the accidental causes shut away, with the phenomena which we wish to examine dissected out from the vast body of material; we speak of libraries as "laboratories of history"; but the ultimate material of history is neither books nor records but mind . . . Science does not need, like history, philosophers to ascertain the laws of the mind before generalizations can safely be made and laws deduced.

Nor would all historians agree on the causal explanations in history:

The application of these themes is easy—anyone may arrive at the causes in history; but the process is subject to the same difficulty as reading the Hittite inscriptions; various people decipher them, but the readings are all different. Critical historians are more or less cannibals: they live by destroying each others' conclusions . . .[40]

History was indeed the careful assembly of sources: "As in pure science also the scientific pursuit of history includes a verification of the materials: every assertion must rest upon a source, as every scientific result rests upon experiment." [41] Nevertheless, the process of generalizing from facts required a peculiar talent, and this, Hart said repeatedly, was trained judgment, which could come only from the mind of the historian.[42]

History was scientific in its accurate and objective treatment of source material; that is, it was scientific in method. It was also scientific because, like science, it generalized from an accumulation of data. Hart considered the possibility that judgment might not be objective enough to convey truth; he merely set himself, first, the task of classifying and gathering the sources of American history as accurately as possible, and second, the extremely important task of using his own faculty of judgment and developing that of his students. It was because he believed that the goal of historical study and inquiry was generalization and judgment that he developed his teaching methods. Judgment was vital because it allowed historical generalization, and historical investigation and generalization would allow men to make assessments of the present and probable future of United States action. Hence historical study was more than scientific in an abstract sense; it was also of utilitarian value. Hart's ideas about the role of historical study in general and of American history in particular can be taken as fairly typical of the attitudes of the profession.[43] Without constant reference to these attitudes, especially in a consideration of method, we can hardly hope to understand completely the work of Hart and of his contemporaries.

Hart was not a great scholar; he has always been accorded much more credit for his work as an organizer and editor than for anything he wrote.[44] Nevertheless, he had many sound ideas about America's past and—more particularly—its present, and he published an incredible number of articles in his professional lifetime, the vast majority of them in popular and not scholarly journals. From 1883 to 1910 he published 330 articles (including letters and articles for various newspapers, and minor as well as major articles), and until the time of his retirement from teaching in 1926 he published, at his own count, 930 articles in 218 different publications. Or to put it another way, he published roughly one article every two weeks, including summers and sabbaticals, from the time he began to teach at the age of twenty-nine until the day he retired at the age of seventy. Not all of his articles were by any means "popular" efforts. At least eighteen appeared in two journals of scholarship, nine in the *American Historical Review* and nine in the *Annals of the American Academy of Political and Social Science*; roughly, one appeared every two years.

Articles were not his only means of expression. At the time of his death, it was reported that he had written or edited about one hundred books.[45] Although this estimate is accurate, it must be said that of these about a fourth were written by him; the other three-fourths he edited. Of strictly original works, omitting the bibliographical guides and students' manuals, original in their own way, he published three volumes of collected essays, at least four textbooks (each quite different), and eight book-length studies; or roughly one book every three years and, counting the books he edited, two and a half books a year!

The great majority of these writings dealt with contemporary affairs; this emphasis was not inconsistent with Hart's philosophy of history but was a consequence of it. If the function of history was to train judgment, then the historian should have lessons to teach his fellow Americans about the present meaning of past events. The lessons of history *should* be applied to current events. He once said, in criticizing the faults of American historical education:

That the people of the United States are fond of history is shown by their eagerness to make it, rather than by any habit of turning to the past as furnishing precedents for guidance in times of uncertainty or peril.[46]

It would be impossible here to examine with any kind of completeness Hart's views on America, past and present. However, his answers to a few of the questions he considered important reveal his concept of the role of the scholar in public life, as well as his reasoning about historical questions.

One major area of his interest was diplomacy and foreign affairs. In 1905 he wrote that

the Spanish War left many questions interesting to the student of American politics, and I have given much attention to questions of colonial and foreign policy, especially the Philippines, the Monroe Doctrine, and the question of an Isthmus Canal.[47]

Hart himself was opposed to imperialism. He entered into public controversy with Roosevelt on the subject and wrote him on

the question of the best foreign policy for our country. On that I have long differed from you and shall always differ. I believe that the best thing for the happiness of American and of other people [*sic*] is for us to remain within our present boundaries, and give our strength to governing ourselves well. I don't want Hawaii nor Cuba nor Mexico nor Canada as a free and peaceable gift.[48]

Hart's reasoning did not depend solely on his belief that American energy could well be devoted to improving the state of its own government and civil service. He had a more fundamental objection to imperialism: imperialism, as formulated by many of his contemporaries, was a contradiction to the basic meaning of American democracy. America had always had colonies, he contended; all the western territory that had been held by the United States as a preparation for statehood had been "colonial." It was the peculiar characteristic of the new territorial acquisitions that these were unlikely to become states, and therefore America was not, as in the past, preparing to extend democracy to new areas through a migration of Anglo-Saxon peoples. The new colonies differed because they held in subjection a people who would not become Americans and for whose treatment American experience and constitutional history furnished little guidance.[49] The lesson of the American past lay in the glories of the extension of democracy; he was concerned lest Americans forget that idea and its benefits and lest their own democracy suffer by compromising its ideals.

Another of Hart's concerns was the rise of the city and the problems of democracy within it. He was aware that because of the problems peculiar to the increased population in cities, it had been necessary for governments to take on powers that they had not previously exercised. These powers had grown more complex as government had become more complex, and he observed that it was necessary to have trained people to wield them. Centers and concentrations of power were necessary, even in a democracy:

> The boss has come to the front, not simply because he offers rewards and punishments, but because experience shows that in the whirlpool of contrary interests and desires, nothing can be accomplished except through a small body of persons to whom democracy intrusts power.[50]

It was not the immigrants who had created the problems in city government:

> The most turbulent period of city government, the greatest dominion of mobs and the greatest lawlessness in American communities came in the thirties and forties, before the foreign elements had become dominant.[51]

Rather it was the American belief, stemming from the days of Jackson, that any intelligent man was qualified to act as a public servant and that democracy was best served by simple and frequent rotation in office.

> Why should the public service, in efficiency, in interest in its performance, be so far below the usual standards for the management of corporations? Perhaps one explanation is the national tradition that the affairs of government can be directed by any intelligent man, which is the transfer of the ideals of the town meeting and the county convention to the affairs of a nation. To admit that life long experience makes a man a better legislator or governor seems to be a denial of the doctrine of equality. Therefore American democracy is fairly open to the charge of an indulgence of, if not a preference for, mediocre men in public life.[52]

To solve the problem Americans must realize the difference between past and present, understand the meaning of historical development, and see that old ideas were no longer applicable to new situations. What was needed, most of all, was a "respect for trained expert opinion which is so difficult to secure for a democratic republic like ours." [53]

As another example of Hart's interests we may consider briefly his view of the Southern problem, to which he devoted so much interest and attention. To explain the origins of the Civil War and the defeat of the South, he made a detailed examination of Southern geography, resources, economy, and leadership. Looking for the basic cause, he said that the fault lay with slavery itself, which had weakened the Confederacy by discouraging immigration and by stimulating the method of agriculture which had impoverished the South. The inferiority of railroads, shipping, and transportation was due to the lesser business training of the South, which had deliberately chosen slavery while the North had chosen freedom. "Slavery had enfeebled the defenders of slavery, and they and the institution which they strove to protect fell together." [54]

The lesson that the war held for the South could be seen clearly when Hart looked for answers to the Negro problem facing the South after Reconstruction. There was no doubt in his mind that "the average of the Negro race is much below that of the white race." [55] But there was also no doubt in his mind that just as Negro and white had been inseparably bound in the outcome of the Civil War, so they would be bound in determining the possibilities for the future of the South. He noted the growing economic progress of the South, the violence between the races, and the whites' attempt to prevent the Negro from receiving any education or improving his situation. He was liberal enough to believe in civil rights for their own sake, but he also felt that if for no other reason than self-interest, the Southerners should be taught to allow the Negro to improve himself as best he could and thus increase the prosperity of the whole section. The white man was dependent upon Negro labor, and as the character of that labor improved, there "would be more business for everybody" and therefore greater racial harmony. If the South did not now learn the lesson taught by the Civil War, racial strife and poverty would be its reward. [56]

That man could learn from the past and apply its lessons to the future implied a definite doctrine of progress. Hart did indeed believe in progress as he believed in democracy, and he possessed a faith in the American people which strengthened his sense that the duty of the historian was to interpret the implications of the past to the decision-makers of the present. His views can be inferred from Theodore Roosevelt's reply to a letter from Hart about Hart's book *National Ideals,* which had been dedicated to Roosevelt, "Practicer of American Ideals."

> I believe it is true, as you say, that in the midst of all that is sordid and self-seeking in public life and in the field of high finance, there remain the wholesome, right-minded standards of the average man, of Lincoln's plain people, the masters of us all and the arbiters of our destinies.[57]

As the belief that man could learn from history implied a belief in progress, so the fact that there were lessons in the past determined the historian's obligation to teach. It was the historian's function to see that the public was taught whatever lessons were to be learned from the past. It was thus important that more American history be given in the schools, for such education was a preparation for citizenship. Hart contributed no truly original ideas to the study of history; he made no brilliant and lasting synthesis of the material at his command. In this sense he was not a great scholar. However, he did fulfill one standard of scholarship as he viewed it: he united the historian with the public, presumably to the public's benefit. Some men have devoted themselves to a narrow and brilliant monograph written for a specialized audience; Hart wrote a great deal that was, if not brilliant, usually sound and widely read. In this way he was close to an older school of historians, whose members had often been men of affairs and statesmen rather than professors.

Hart was an excellent and conscientious teacher who knew how to create a dramatic effect but who also knew how to stimulate his students to think and to make intelligent judgments; he did not want them to memorize. He took a narrow and uninspiring course and related it not only to the past but to the present. He expanded the course both in chronology and scope; to express his view that history was the whole life of the people, he taught more than politics though he felt America's political contributions to be the most important aspect of her history. He was extremely concerned about teaching methods; much of his interest extended beyond the college to the secondary school; in the field of method he made early and real contributions.[58]

The situation at Harvard when Hart arrived in 1883 was hardly encouraging despite the challenge it must have presented. Harvard, although it possessed a tradition of interest in American history reaching as far back as Jared Sparks,[59] possessed no developed course in the field. Henry Adams had taught it and taught it well, according to his students,[60] if not to him. He was convinced that students learned best through disagreements, a method akin to the medieval disputations (Hart would thoroughly have agreed with him), and it was in this manner that he attempted to teach. Had Adams remained at Harvard, American history might have become a stimulating and popular field of interest, but in 1877 he left Cambridge for Washington.[61]

Adams' successor, Henry Cabot Lodge, a thorough Federalist, taught Adams' course in colonial history and a course in the history of the United States to 1840. He did not seem to have great success, for it is reported that "Channing used to say that after Lodge's class at Harvard had dropped from fifty to three, that scholar decided to give up teaching for politics." [62] In any case, Lodge left in 1879, and colonial history was incorporated by his successor, Isaac T. Hoague, in a single course, the only one given in American history: "The Constitutional and Political History of the United States." It was in this course that Hart enrolled in his senior year, 1879–80. When Hoague became ill in 1880–81, the course was transferred to Freeman Snow, primarily interested in international law, and at the end of that year it was found expedient to consolidate the two half-courses into a single half-course covering the period to 1850. Thus the course stood when Hart took it over—a dry, factual half-year survey of two periods in American history. The first of these was the period of settlement as it led up to the Revolution; the second was the period after the formation of the Constitution, seen only as leading up to the Civil War.

To this rather barren state of affairs, Hart brought the stimulus of his own personality. He was a man of strong opinions and great enthusiasm, described by one of his students, Oswald G. Villard, as "a storehouse of information" with a "passionate devotion to our country." [63] His course reflected his distinctive personality. He had an impressive system for the collection of the information from his reading; different colors of paper meant original sources, secondary sources, original ideas, and so on. He would bring his formidable collection of notes with him to lectures though he did not always use it.

At exactly six and three-quarters minutes past the hour Professor Hart entered lower Massachusetts at the double-quick, bearing a huge green bag full of notes, and closely followed by a perspiring assistant, bearing an even greater bag stuffed with supplementary data. This tri-weekly procession, which Professor Hart headed with the air of a Roman general bringing home the spoils, was generally greeted by the class with a burst of applause.[64]

The course gained coherence from a basic philosophy stemming from the themes Hart saw in America's past. It was a philosophy reflecting the attitudes of his period: optimism, progress, democracy, morality. In the first place, there were what Hart termed fundamental principles, some of which were these:

(1) No nation has a history disconnected from that of the rest of the world: the United States is closely related, in point of time,

with previous ages; in point of space, with other civilized countries.

(2) Institutions are a growth, and not a creation . . .

(3) Our institutions are Teutonic in origin: they have come to us through English institutions.

(4) The growth of our institutions has been from local to central: the general government can, therefore, be understood only in the light of the early history of the country.

(5) Under a federal form of government, there must inevitably be a perpetual contest of authority between the States and the general government . . .

(6) When parties become distinctly sectional, a trial of strength between a part of the States and the general government must come sooner or later.[65]

These opinions were hardly original with Hart although the last was an extremely perceptive evaluation of the American political process. He shared with other historians of his time the belief in the analogy between history and biology, especially the belief that the evolutionary truths of the latter could reasonably be applied to the former. He believed in the "germ theory" of institutions, in the Teutonic origins of American democracy, and in progress. He summarized his beliefs neatly in his editor's introduction to the last book in the American Nation series, a book he himself wrote, called *National Ideals Historically Traced*. The early volumes of the series, he said,

have aimed to describe the development of the United States from the deep-lying roots in European civilization up through the mighty trunk to the topmost branches. Hence none of the writers have confined themselves to events: they have dealt with the great men who have been exponents of the thoughts and aims of their fellows; they have taken account of the customs, the moral standards, and the political conceptions which underlie both events and men . . . Each has consciously or unconsciously learned from Charles Darwin, who is the great historical master of our age in that he has taught us how, in the world of mind as in the material universe, there is steady progression from one condition to another; for human institutions also follow a law of natural selection, by the survival of those which are best adapted to their surroundings . . . The United States of today is not a miracle, but a steady and measurable growth, still enlarging, still to put forth new branches for the world's advantage.[66]

The essence of America's gift to the world was democracy. He once said that true Americanism "believes that this country has the greatest mission that was ever put into the hands of human beings . . . to demonstrate that a great Democracy can well and properly govern itself." [67] The roots of democracy lay in the Anglo-Saxon past. There was, he said, an Anglo-Saxon instinct for government; it lay in the character of the race. Nevertheless, the fullest possibilities of this democracy had been developed in America.[68] The most important fact about America was that she had made democracy and especially the federal plan of government actually work by combining new opportunities with the heritage of the Teutonic race, a heritage which combined the "greatest love for personal freedom" with the "greatest respect for law." [69] Therefore Hart devoted the early part of the course to a discussion of the roots of American institutions in England, where American freedom originated. His explanation for the Revolution, though actually more complex than that of a "single cause," could be expressed, he said succinctly in one lecture, simply as the fact that "the mother country tried to govern a lot of people who were perfectly well able to govern themselves."

Hart traced the important principles of democracy and federalism from the settlement of America to the present in an attempt to trace the meaning of America as it had been and as it had come to be. He devoted much attention to the West, especially to the question of territorial expansion which, ironically, had been both a cause of nationalism as internal improvements unified the country and a factor in the coming of the Civil War. The Civil War held a focal point in his view of American history because it tested the system of federalism and settled the question of union. Hart's views and his course did not remain static, however. Gradually, America emerged as a world power, and as imperialism played a more important role in current events, he emphasized it more in his lectures. For imperialism was also related to the main theme of the course, the growth and establishment of democracy; the question was one of the possibility of further expansion of democracy and democratic principles.

The course, as he taught it, reflected his belief that history was more than the collection of names and dates and political events which had been taught to him. Although he was interested in the evolution of institutions, he was not interested in their theory or their formal structure, but in how they functioned within their social context. History should examine the "causes, motives, and standards which have directed the practical policy of the country." [70] He believed that "the foundations of true historical knowledge of our past are the actual conditions of common life: of country, town, and city; of farmer, artisan, merchant, and slaveholder; of church, school, and convention." [71]

This view of history was reflected in *National Ideals Historically Traced*, in which he attempted to examine not ideals as we would use the word, but attitudes of Americans as revealed by events and changes over two hundred years of American history. The book was certainly his most original work, his own interpretation of American life; and as he said to Charles Eliot, it was

the result of twenty-five years' thinking. In the multifarious life of America, with its many points of approach, a man may write a book which, without being strikingly in error, nevertheless gives a partial and misleading view of the whole subject; and I hope I am sound in the main, for doubtless no treatment of social and political conditions can go far beyond one's own experience of life. The book is the writer.[72]

This book summarizes the attitudes evident in the lectures and outlines of the course although it is much more than a restatement of the lectures, and an evaluation of the book is in many ways an evaluation of the course.

This inadequately appreciated book presented as a key to our democratic development the struggles that resulted in the improved status of disadvantaged persons—slaves, freedmen, women, immigrants, and industrial workers. It emphasized the role of public education in democratic advance. It traced in a fashion quite acceptable to progressives the new devices to make democracy more effective and more articulate. And it gave much the same weight to the frontier and the Industrial Revolution in the development of democratic movements as an historian today might give.[73]

While this is perhaps too high an evaluation of the book itself, it does suggest that Hart can be fairly judged as moving toward a concept of history which included the economic and the social as well as the political. Although Hart devoted much of his time to political material, he attempted to introduce elements of economic and social history, as he understood them (though not as we understand them), into his course.

His attempts to introduce these elements were primarily descriptive; he did not have a sense, as one does today, of the ways in which political and economic and social phenomena may be causally interrelated; in this he is typical of his generation. Yet even without this sense of inter-relations, he managed to include much in his courses that was revolutionary for the time: whenever he moved into a new period, such as the formation of the Union or the presidency of Jackson, he included a section on the state of America, its books, its educational system, its newspapers, its religion.

His treatment of slavery partially reflects this newer approach to American history. Even though he still devoted a great deal of his course to the Civil War (since he felt that Union was the most important theme in our political history), he did not teach the Civil War as it had been taught him. The lectures he had attended on slavery were almost entirely constitutional and legal, with very little attention given to slavery itself. When Hart lectured on slavery he gave increasing attention to slavery as a system of labor and of society and to its effects on the South. He detailed the Southern arguments for slavery and the Northern arguments against it, and he gave one lecture on slavery as it was on the plantation, on how the slave was fed and clothed, on his education and religion. He tried to maintain a balanced attitude toward the system, but he did say, in the end, that by definition slavery as a system "*must* exist with blood, iron, and tears." Eventually his interest in the South, and in the Southern situation after the Civil War, resulted in two trips to the South, the Lowell Lectures given in the spring of 1908, and a book, *The Southern South*.

The title of his course remained "Constitutional and Political History of the United States," and certainly the largest proportion of the material was devoted to these themes. Beneath the political lay other material of a less usual sort, and more of it, in time, came to occupy his reading assignments, many of which were source books edited by him. These collections tended to exclude constitutional material and to include descriptions of other elements in the life of the people. In this way Hart foreshadows the widening interests of later historians.

Hart also expanded his course in terms of chronology. In 1883, when he began to teach, the course reached only to 1850. In June of 1884 he had reached the Kansas-Nebraska Bill, and in June of 1886 Buchanan and coercion. In 1887, and for several years thereafter, the course ended with Reconstruction. There were lectures scheduled on state and municipal governments in 1885, but none of the lecture notes available for the period includes such material (perhaps proving nothing more than that the students cut these lectures).

The outlines and notes available for the period of the nineties are inadequate and reveal almost nothing about any changes that did take place. But by 1900 the balance of the course must have shifted somewhat, for the lectures on the Monroe Doctrine had increased in number although the course still did not go beyond Reconstruction. However, by 1911, the last year for which any notes from the course are available, changes are evident. The notes are only partially complete, but when supplemented by examinations and a list of paper topics, they provide a clear picture. Hart devoted a large part of the first semester to the Revolution and the formation of the Constitution; continued with westward expansion, the Bonus Bill, the growth of parties, and the election of Jackson; and included much more material about social and economic life than had appeared in the earlier lectures. There was even a question on the mid-year examination asking for a description of improvements in the methods of travel to the West between 1817 and 1837. Paper topics for the second half of the year were much more closely related to contemporary events than they had been, and included such topics as "Needs of Civil Service Reform," "Dependencies," "The Protectorate of Cuba," and "Federal Control of Corporations."

Thus Hart tried to present American history not only as names and dates and constitutional cases, but also as people attempting to solve real problems. Evidently he succeeded, for among several warm letters from former students is one from a man then teaching at the University of Minnesota, thanking Hart "for the feeling you always convey that history is not a cold abstract science like that of the astronomer who discovers that Mars has two moons, but is human, vital, and of enormous value in enabling men to shape a worthy future for the Republic." [74]

Hart made great changes not only in content but also in the method of teaching history at Harvard. The question of method was widely debated during these years; it is to be remembered that history was rarely taught in 1880, and when it was taught, it was taught poorly, by the least interesting and most rigid methods. College teaching was only beginning to break away from learning by rote and recitation. It was by no means agreed that there was a method for teaching an undergraduate superior to that of memorization of a set body of material. Professor John W. Burgess of Columbia made in 1885 a clear distinction between the teaching of graduate and undergraduate students. Although it was a necessary and proper function to attempt to develop critical powers in graduate students, from whom original work should be expected, Burgess believed in a rather different approach in the case of the undergraduate.

> In the gymnasium,—the first three years of the School of Arts, —the method is, of course, the gymnastic method, and the purpose sought the gymnastic purpose: that is, the daily drill upon text-books and hand-books of history by recitation, question and answer, as required studies, for the purpose of fixing and classifying in the mind of the student the elements of historical geography, the chronology and outward frame of historic events, biographies of historic characters, and the definitions of historical terms and expressions.

If this basic foundation were not achieved, he felt that there would be nothing upon which graduate training might build. He was not interested in the new approaches:

And if, while so many of our Colleges, both great and small, are seeking to become Universities through the fallacious process of simply making their gymnastic studies elective and optional, some Apostle of the Gymnasium would arise and found Academies which would stand true to the gymnastic method and purpose, such an one would do for the development of the true University a far greater work than the College which ceases to be one thing without becoming the other.[75]

Hart disagreed strongly with this point of view. His ideas of teaching reflected newer attitudes toward the purpose of a university—that it was not a place in which to teach boys a series of agreed-upon facts, but a place to stimulate their own thinking. Hart wanted his students to draw their own conclusions rather than to accept his ready-made generalizations.[76] He felt, as he said to A. Lawrence Lowell, that "the object of Harvard College is to train up students who will disagree with their instructors," [77] and he was interested in developing a method of teaching that would not only allow but require them to do so.

He was not interested in disagreement for its own sake, purely as stimulus; he was interested in it only if it were well reasoned and could be supported by appropriate references and facts. It was the function of education, especially in history, to train resolute judgment. Language and science, he maintained, were means of teaching observation; mathematics taught logic; but history taught judgment, and thus the best statesmen were so often careful students of history.[78] He wanted first to teach his students the proper and scientific use of the sources and second to require them to use their own powers of judgment. Properly done, the first achievement should lead directly to the second.

Hart also thought visual learning often more effective than rote learning. For this reason he made extensive use of maps (on most of his examinations there was a map question), and he systematized certain kinds of data on charts. He said many years later to Morison, "There was a time in my academic career when I was known to a circle of irreverent youngsters as 'chart Hart!' " [79]

In the early years of his teaching Hart had to spend more time in giving students information than he really wanted, partly because secondary school teaching was entirely inadequate and students knew so little "coming in," and partly because there were few adequate written works. (Hart himself wrote several texts in an attempt to fill this gap.) Most available work was "superficial," and "if the instructor does not himself supply accurate and detailed information, his students will not have it." Often, Hart said, there was "positive misinformation" and there was no narrative covering the period after 1820 which could be used in colleges. [80] In fact, Hildreth and von Holst had written the only histories of the United States since the Revolution available at that time. [81] Since these volumes were extremely long and detailed, they presented problems of their own. Gradually, as more adequate secondary works became available, Hart could devote more time to theme assignments and later to one of his pet teaching techniques, weekly special topics, or what is currently called "the problem method."

Even from the beginning, however, Hart required outside papers and collateral independent reading on every topic. [82] Many of the readings were chosen because they presented a point of view different from that of the lecturer. Reading and a critical attitude toward what one reads were the basis of a proper historical method, according to Hart. He was fond of quoting the advice of a German professor on the first requisite of historical study: "1) Read; 2) Read widely; 3) Read very widely." [83]

As a teaching aid, Hart developed a complicated printed outline for the class, the early editions of which were printed on one side of the page and left blank on the other so that the student might interleave his own notes. These outlines were regarded as essential to the course and were printed at the expense of the student.[84] They were copyrighted by Hart, but he made no profit from them; any surplus funds were put into buying books related to the course for students' use in the library.[85] There were many revised editions of this guide, which gradually expanded beyond lecture outlines to include suggested references for readings and advice on note taking, all designed as aids for the student. The later editions, after 1901, were designed also as aids to teachers and included lists of possible lecture topics for a series of ten, twenty, fifty, or one hundred lectures in American history. Also included were lists of possible paper topics, not only for weekly reports, by then a developed system, but also for special research reports. Hart reported to Eliot that his systems had worked so well that he had extended them to his courses in government and diplomacy, and the final editions of the guide were therefore manuals of the history, government, and diplomacy of the United States, widely used and praised outside the University.[86]

The logical outcome of the outside reading system was an increase in written work, which from Hart's point of view could be used for two purposes, first to teach exactness and then to teach "independent judgment." The written work was required in a prescribed form, to be written in three columns per page, the middle column for text, the left hand column for "reference" (what we would call footnotes), and the right hand column for outline. Students were offered a wide variety of subjects since the main purpose of the work was for them to investigate something in which they were really interested. The exacting requirements, which from one point of view could certainly be regarded as rigid (themes were sometimes required on specified colors of paper),[87] were absolutely necessary, Hart thought; for prescribed form taught exactness in historical work, "where exactness is indispensable." [88]

In addition to the outside research papers, Hart required weekly papers exemplifying the problem method. Most of the constitutional history in the course was handled in this way. Hart felt that its questions were particularly suited to the problem approach and believed that it was worth taking time every week to allow (or to force) the student to reason for himself. He set up a general topic for the week, for example Jacksonian Democracy, and assigned readings. Students did the work and arrived in class to write for fifteen minutes on one of these three topics:

1) Did Jackson degrade the public service?

2) Was Jacksonian democracy the same as Jeffersonian democracy?

3) Did Jackson believe the judgment of the people better than his own?

Hart was proud of this system and wrote to President Eliot that the system of reading and outside library work was a

method which has been worked out in twenty-five years' teaching at Harvard, and rests upon the belief that the best way of dealing with such subjects is to furnish students with a body of selected readings to easily accessible books, and then to require them to penetrate more deeply into a series of topics which illustrate the more important questions which arise in the course. I think that the students believe the weekly written exercise to be the most helpful part of the course.[89]

He felt this to be one of his greatest contributions to teaching. He wrote to Lowell, toward the end of his teaching career, that if he were beginning again, he would use the problem method even more since the basic literature had increased in volume and improved in quality:

I hope it may be remembered for righteousness that next after Henry Adams and Henry Cabot Lodge, Channing and I have the honor of introducing on a considerable scale the study of special topics in American history.[90]

Hart's examinations allowed the student a chance to think for himself. Some of the questions were, of course, intended to test reading and factual knowledge acquired in the course of the year, and on every examination there was a bibliographical question. There were always spot quotations to identify, but there were also chances for the student to use what he knew, to exercise "trained judgment." On the midyear examination in his first year of teaching Hart asked: "Who made the Constitution? State the theories on both sides, and specify reasons for holding your own opinion." Often the student was given a quotation and asked to comment on it, to state whether or not he felt it agreed with the facts. For example, one examination gave a quotation suggesting that the Missouri Compromise had been impractical and had merely "postponed the inevitable."

Thus, in method and in content, Hart had revitalized the teaching of American history at Harvard and had made of it something far more stimulating than the program which he had been offered as an undergraduate. He had applied his ideas of history as a science to his teaching and had attempted to develop in his students the judgment that was the most important characteristic of the historian as scientist. For this purpose, he realized that the technique of learning by rote was completely outmoded, and he developed several techniques to replace it. From the very beginning of his career he had been in the vanguard of methodological thinking; his essay for G. Stanley Hall's book on methods of teaching American history was highly regarded by Herbert Baxter Adams of Johns Hopkins, who said that Hart's course outline, which embodied his methodological suggestions, may be said to represent the best attempts now making in our schools in the study of American institutions, and is substantially an outline of the courses and the work at Columbia, Cornell, and Johns Hopkins.[91]

It was with real satisfaction that Hart noted in 1901 that colleges now taught not by rote, but by papers, quizzes, and collateral reading.[92] Learning was now a matter of training the mind and not a matter of acquiring a set body of facts alone.

Hart's interest in improving the method of teaching history was not confined to the college level, for he realized that it was absolutely necessary to improve the standards of work in the secondary schools if there were to be any rapid improvement at higher levels. Consequently, he took an active part on the various committees of the nineties designed to investigate the teaching of history in the schools and was a member of the Cambridge School Committee for many years. He was much interested in the problem of framing entrance requirements for the colleges, and he served on the Faculty Committee on Admissions Requirements which considered this problem.[93] Obviously if more New England colleges, with their great influence, required history for entrance, more secondary schools would teach it to meet the new demands, and the colleges would have more to build upon.

It is important to note that Hart's interest in reforming the secondary-school curriculum was not primarily directed toward introducing new subjects, even history (though this was, of course, desirable), but toward changing the methods in these schools, much as those in his own classes had been changed. People were seeing the "absurdity" of the rote system, he felt,[94] and were beginning to direct their efforts toward the far more important goal of training the student to "use his powers resolutely and directly upon an unexpected question." [95] Thus reasoning and judgment were as important at the secondary-school level as they were in college; they were the means of learning.

At the other end of the scale was Hart's work with graduate students, carried on mainly in the seminar that he directed with Edward Channing from 1885 until it was divided in 1906.[96] In the early years the group was composed primarily of very bright undergraduates, but by 1900 it consisted entirely of graduate students, many of whom published their work. This is not the place to enter into a discussion of the proper definition of a seminar. Hart's seminar did not fit the narrow description of a seminar as students working as a group on a single body of material capable of contrary interpretation.[97] Each student followed his separate researches in a topic in American history quite unrelated to the other topics; Channing and Hart divided their students between them on roughly chronological grounds yet operated the same seminar. In this sense, they directed a group of thesis writers rather than a seminar. But in the wider definition of a seminar as a small group of students stimulating each other by criticism and suggestion and working in much closer relation to their professors than was possible in regular class work,[98] the Channing-Hart endeavor was a seminar.

In any case, Hart felt that he led a true seminar, in which the student carried on original research from the sources and made interpretations which added to the sum of historical knowledge.[99] As history could be a science, so these seminars, like the libraries, were laboratories in which research, scientifically pursued, produced useful results. Hart was proud that the early publications of the Harvard Historical Studies were primarily works which had originated in his seminar (many, in fact, were works for which he had been the advisor and the editor when they came to publication).

In this seminar were included all of the doctoral students who graduated from Harvard in American history in these years.[100] Most became teachers at other colleges across the country and some became distinguished members of the historical profession (Siebert of Ohio State and C. R. Fish at Wisconsin, for instance). More interesting than the students themselves was the long roll of institutions at which they taught: Brown, Smith, Dartmouth, Pennsylvania, Michigan, Chicago, California, Missouri, Illinois, Indiana, Stanford, Wisconsin, and Northwestern. Hart was proud of the fact that Harvard had sent men all over the country and that he had had a share in extending Harvard's influence in education.[101] He had somewhat the same attitude toward them that Herbert B. Adams had toward the Johns Hopkins students—that they were founding colonies across the face of the United States.[102]

Hart therefore studied and influenced the methods of teaching history at all levels, from the secondary schools through the college and university. He had trained a group of students who would teach, if not necessarily by his methods, at least hopefully according to his "scientific" standards. His students would thereby further improve judgment and increase knowledge in history. He followed the careers of his students with interest, therefore, and was eager to help any of them when he could, both from personal liking and for professional reasons.

Just as Hart followed the careers of his students within the profession, so he followed with interest the fortunes of the profession itself. It cannot be over-emphasized that when he arrived at Harvard, there was no profession of American history, and his concern with the growth of the profession, with which his own career coincided, is thus understandable. His interest was both general and specific; that is, he acted always from a strong sense of furthering the cause of the profession, and he did, in organization and professional work, whatever he thought to be useful and needed. He once wrote to President Eliot that

I have never believed that the American public will be induced to respect the professor and his calling more by merely giving him a larger salary; that is not the prize for which highly eminent men look, they find it in reputation as men of learning and of force, in what may be called accidental honors and rewards.[103]

Feeling this way, he was eager to search out honors for other members of the profession. He wrote, again to Eliot, about two former students, one president of the University of Arizona and the other at Montana, to ask if they could not be given some recognition by Harvard, perhaps an honorary degree, to increase the respect in which they were held in their communities and therefore their influence. In 1898 he suggested to Eliot that Harvard offer the use of its buildings to the American Historical Association, which was to meet that year in Cambridge, in order to lend Harvard's prestige to the Association.[104]

Hart, despite the fact that he was a man of strong opinions, was not dominated by professional jealousy, and thus he was able to have concern for the profession as a whole. An interesting example of the way in which his attitude toward contemporaries was expressed can be seen in his opinions of Charles Beard. Hart disagreed entirely with Beard's interpretations of the Constitution; indeed, Harvey Wish has said that Hart looked on Beard's book "as something almost indecent." [105] Nevertheless, just after Beard resigned from Columbia to protest what he considered an infringement of academic freedom, Hart wrote to President Lowell that he disagreed with Beard on the economic influence on the Federal Constitution but that "his work both in history and government is first class . . . If there is the slightest possibility in the suggestion of bringing Beard here,

Munro and I can furnish the good academic reason there-
for." [106] Furthermore, he also wrote to Beard:

I most deeply and conscientiously express the belief that nothing would induce you to resign . . . except the conviction that
you were in fetters. I am acquainted with your writings as are most
of your brethren in history and political science and can bear testimony to their originality, forcefulness and patriotic feeling. We
disagree in the most friendly manner on some questions of historical interpretation and political organization. We agree completely
in loyalty to our country.[107]

Perhaps such attitudes help explain Hart's ability to devote
so much effort to cooperative endeavors such as the compiling of sources expressly for the use of others and his devotion
of time to the professional necessities of the organization
itself.

Hart was not a member of the American Historical Association when it was founded at the Saratoga meeting in September of 1884, but he joined the group almost immediately. He was in wholehearted support of its purposes—that
it should gather together people from various universities,
the "amateur" historians together with the "professionals,"
for the promotion of scientific research, exchange of ideas,
coordination of projects, and furtherance of common interests. When the organization had trouble in its early years, he
was active in suggesting solutions to its problems, and it was
his efforts among others that brought about the turning
point in the life of the association.[108] The Modern Language
Association was organized a year before the American
Historical Association; and the American Economic Association, a year after the American Historical Association. Thus
the historians were operating under compulsions similar to
those in all the academic groups, the need to define a professional status and to solve common problems.

Hart was closely connected with the establishment of the

American Historical Review. The idea of founding such a "scientific journal" seems to have occurred to several men at different institutions at about the same time, further indicating the widespread and parallel growth of professional needs and interests at several leading academic institutions. One early letter came from John T. Short at Ohio State to Herbert B. Adams in 1881.

> I am considering the feasibility of starting a Journal of History and Political Science, to serve as a medium of publication for the most advanced thought and thorough investigation in our field . . . [It would] find recognition and have a mission . . . in furthering historical studies throughout the whole country.[109]

Nothing came of this idea, and in 1890 Adams wrote to Andrew D. White at Cornell with regard to his own plans:

> I find the Modern Language Association publish their papers in quarterly parts, forming a volume each year. The example strikes me as excellent. We are now in a position to begin the development of an *American Historical Review*, as *The Nation*, after the appearance of our last annual report, recommended us to do. What do you think of the idea? [110]

Harvard's ideas on the subject may be traced back to November 16, 1892, when the History Department appointed a committee of two, Charles Gross and Hart, to draw up a scheme for establishing a historical journal. Harvard's plan, it seems, was always intended to be a cooperative project with other colleges. In any case, at a meeting of the American Historical Association in December 1894 historians from Cornell and Harvard learned of each other's plans, and upon the urging of various people, notably George B. Adams of Yale, it was decided that a meeting would be held in New York in the spring to draw up some sort of program. Hart was a member of this committee [111] and was a member of the original editorial board. He was elected secretary-treasurer, and obviously he must have put much work and time into the establishment of the new journal. Unfortunately, none of the correspondence from this period survives, but those indications of some of his efforts at persuasion that do remain in the journals of the time stress the concept of the maturing of a science: "one of the measures of the interest in a science is . . . [its] journals." [112] Hart was a strong supporter of, if not an instrument in, the transfer of ownership of the *Review* to the American Historical Association.[113]

Hart's work for the profession was more than merely organizational. One senses that whatever he felt needed to be done, he set himself to do. An examination of a few of his editorial undertakings reveals the nature of the tasks required by the profession at that time. He often discussed the need for adequate bibliographical guides to the materials of American history; in part his own course guides had been designed to fill such a gap, and the Channing and Hart bibliography in fact originated in the organization and teaching of Hart's course. According to Lester Cappon, who possesses the only correspondence known to be extant on the matter, it was Hart who proposed to Channing the collaboration on a guide already begun by Hart.[114] Much of its material was, in fact, drawn from Hart's *Course Outlines,* and after the *Guide* was published, the format of the *Outlines* changed— they thereafter included much less bibliographical material.

One of the chief advantages of the *Guide's* bibliography was that it extended to the Civil War, whereas Justin Winsor's earlier *Narrative and Critical History* had gone only as far as the period of the Constitution. The *Guide* included more than lists of books; it contained sections on method and suggestions for teaching, lists of possible libraries varying with the amount of money one wanted to spend, and suggestions for paper topics. The bibliography itself included textbooks; works in geography; travel books; periodicals; newspapers; United States records; works of statesmen; autobiographies; and even lists of historical novels, poems, and ballads.[115] Hart had intended to continue the *Guide* to 1885, but neither space, money, nor time was sufficient. The book received an excellent review from the *American Historical Review* and, according to Cappon, "became the handbook of every advanced student of the subject." It sold 9,000 copies in seventeen years, an excellent, even amazing, record for the time. It was certainly a much needed tool for the profession and filled one of the gaps of which Hart had long complained.[116]

Another lack, of which he had often complained, was the absence of published source materials for the use of students. There were a few books of sources, but none was adequate and none reached the present time. What Hart wanted was not constitutional documents or political and legislative enactments. He had in fact helped to edit just such a series of documents in the American History Leaflets, which he and Channing edited from 1892 to 1913,[117] and he felt that there were enough constitutional and political documents available to serve the teacher's purpose. In his *American History Told by Contemporaries* he therefore bypassed constitutional materials in favor of diaries, travels, autobiographies, letters, and speeches which were preferred "as being more real and more human." [118] In these books sources were treated not as materials for research, but as illustrations giving "particularity and *local color*" [119] to the important events of history and making them vivid and memorable to the student. He tried to choose material to illustrate social, political, and occasionally economic conditions, to show how ordinary people lived, and when possible to give both sides of an issue. Such a collection of documents was an excellent teaching technique and was directly in line with Hart's view that history should teach more than the political events and activities surrounding great leaders. By occasionally presenting conflicting materials, it also illustrated the problem approach and the desire to teach a student to think for himself.

Hart edited many other books and collections of articles; none of them reveals new concepts or great contributions to the study of history except the American Nation series. It is in connection with the editing of this truly monumental work that Hart is usually remembered. The work is monumental in several ways: in sheer size (there were twenty-seven volumes, an outstanding collection at the time), in the speed with which it was completed (four years elapsed between the publication of the first volume and the publication of the final volume), and as a symbol of the shift from the old history to the new history. It was a monument to the first generation of American professional historians.

Since 1898 at the latest Hart had urged the writing of a general history of America by the "cooperative method." [120] The American Historical Association had considered the possibility of preparing the work under its auspices but had decided that it did not come under the functions of the Association as such; therefore Hart had arranged with Harper and Brothers for the publication of the work under his editorship. Again, there is almost no correspondence remaining to illuminate the progress of the work; we have only the history itself.

The editor's introduction sets forth the goal of the series, which was to give an "intelligent summarizing of the present knowledge of American history by trained specialists." [121] The books were intended to look beyond the high political events and the activities of great leaders and thus to follow Hart's own ideas about the proper study of American history.

The point of view of *The American Nation* is that the purpose of the historian is to tell what has been done, and quite as much, what has been purposed, by the thinking, working, and producing people who make public opinion . . . For this is not intended to be simply a political or constitutional history: it must include the social life of the people, their religion, their literature, and their schools. It must include their economic life, occupations, labor systems, and organizations of capital.[122]

As in any series in which different writers take part, the results were uneven, and variously received, although in general all volumes were praised by the reviewers. In an article concerning the whole series, in the *American Historical Review*, a writer who had followed all the reviews and had collected personal opinion stated that "The specialist generally has been disappointed in the treatment of his particular field, either because it was inadequate and sometimes inaccurate or because he found in it nothing that was new." [123] This writer continued with the observation that most men regarded those volumes outside their field very highly and that in general the work was both readable and accurate. The point of interest here is less the opinion of specific volumes in the series than it is the fact that there now could be "fields of study" in American history. Twenty-five years earlier the field of American history itself had been suspect. The volumes of the American Nation series were written by twenty-four men, only two of whom were not professional historians, that is, who had not received graduate training and were not then employed by a university. In this sense the work was a monument to the achievements of the first generation of scholars, as well as to the untiring energy of its editor.

Hart himself wrote two volumes for the series, the concluding volume, *National Ideals*, and the sixteenth volume, *Slavery and Abolition*, *1831–1841*,[124] a balanced account of the growing divergence of North and South, of the conflict over civil rights, and of the gradual growth of sectional rather than national political parties. It is an excellent book that has dated surprisingly little in fifty years.

The American Nation series represents Hart's last really important contribution in the field of American history, appropriately embodying his ideas as scholar, teacher, and professional man. Afterwards his interests turned more and more toward studies of American government, and he became chairman of this department in 1910. He continued to teach his course in American history, and he continued to write and publish a great deal along the lines laid out in the early part of his career. He remained a figure on the American historical scene for many more years, writing, speaking, and attending meetings, but the "New History" grew without really involving him in any way. It is indicative of his place in the field as a representative of the first generation of scholarship that he was known, even in 1914, as the "Grand Old Man" of American history.[125]

The field's growth in organization and self-awareness had been one of Hart's primary interests, equal to his interest in teaching and scholarship. He had been a part of almost all the important aspects of its development and had taken part in all its necessary activities. At the end of his career he summed up the work of the first generation in a review of the work of his own life:

Looking back over fifty years since I began a systematic graduate course in history, I see how it was inevitable that I should spend my lifetime chiefly in building up the fields of history and its allied subject of government, by assembling and publishing materials, by writing textbooks, by forming groups of allied scholars in coöperative historical enterprises, and by stating historical conclusions in books dealing with limited fields . . . The developments of the subject in which I take most pride and pleasure are the opening up of source material, the combination of groups of scholars on historical tasks too great for any one mind, and a share in introducing stimulating methods for undergraduate lecture courses and for the historical training of advanced students. For all the weary hours spent over bibliographies and source books and textbooks, at the end of fifty years I have the satisfaction of believing that I was one of a group of young men who made history and government vital subjects for college and graduate school.[126]

Indeed, Hart is an excellent example of that first generation which attempted to create an American school of American history. His philosophy of history embodies the ideas of progress, optimism, morality, evolution, and the Anglo-Saxon influence upon American history in which his generation believed, as well as the concept of history as a science. As a science, history would be accurate and objective, and its method would achieve all the benefits gained by the physical sciences. The methods by which it was taught would advance it as a science, for students would learn the proper treatment of historical sources and, by exercising judgment, would learn to draw generalizations from them. Bolstered by such a discipline, historians could help the public to understand their society; the study of history would thus have a utility of which Hart himself was especially aware as a result of his special interest in public affairs.

The need for a revolution in the teaching of history, with which so many of these men were concerned, did not come primarily from the hope that it would allow accurate historical generalization, even on a limited scale. It derived primarily from the fact that the new methods taught the student to think for himself, to exercise the faculty of judgment upon new materials and new questions. It thus reflected a new sense of skepticism toward truth in general. No longer was the student to be given a body of material, accepted and labeled as "truth," the memorization of which would be equated with education. "Truth" was now considered as not necessarily final or, at least, as not easily available. "Truth" in a specific field, such as history, required its own techniques of discovery, and it required trained individuals to employ and teach these techniques; hence the union of the writers and teachers of history which so many noticed as the hallmark of the new profession.

It is this philosophy which Hart so well exemplifies. He took part in all of the important aspects of the growth of a new profession; he was interested in scholarship and teaching and in the profession itself, and his concerns reflect the concerns and attitudes of many of his contemporaries. Although he made no brilliant syntheses or original contributions, his ideas were extremely sound and provocative, and they were widely expressed in terms that the public could understand and in which they could take an interest. For history in this period was still written for the public although, as the monograph grew in importance, there grew also the tendency, so much more prevalent today, for the historian to be read only by other members of the profession. In this development Hart is a transitional figure, and it is ironic that the profession whose foundations he helped to lay in the expectation that its growth and development would bring it much closer to the public, has, in fact, become increasingly separated from it.

Hart felt it his duty to bring learning to the public because he viewed history as a science with lessons to teach. His career advanced the growth of a profession which believed that the lessons of history could be learned only by acknowledging that they did not consist of revealed truth and that meaning must be searched for scientifically. His work thus embodies the most general implication of the changes in the teaching of history at Harvard, the shift in men's ideas about learning and its proper techniques.

WILLIAM JAMES

AND THE NEW

PSYCHOLOGY

SHELDON M. STERN

THE DEVELOPMENT of physiological psychology within the course of nineteenth-century European intellectual history would itself require detailed examination on both historical and philosophical grounds. It must suffice for the scope of this essay, however, to recognize that the new emphasis upon the relations of body and mind was a product of the late-eighteenth- and early-nineteenth-century emphasis on man's historicity. Although the affirmation of man's evolutionary nature had its roots in the works of Jean Jacques Rousseau, George Friedrich Hegel, and Karl Marx, not until Herbert Spencer and Charles Darwin was it synthesized into a coherent scientific doctrine. After the publication of *The Origin of Species* European consciousness recognized the need to appraise man as a part of the developmental process of the natural world. Darwin gave new sanctity to the physical dimension of existence, and the mind itself did not escape the implications of this new insight into the relation of natural man to the natural world.

The work of Alexander Bain and Spencer in England, of Hippolyte Taine and Charles Renouvier in France, and of Carl Stumpf and Wilhelm Wundt in Germany all had in common a basically new approach to the study of man's mind. Physiology was related to psychology, and the centuries-old bond between philosophy and psychology faced a serious challenge. During the decade of the sixties, physiological psychology in Europe began its steady course toward recognition. America did not get its first significant taste of the new psychology until the middle seventies.

In the last half of the sixties a young Harvard medical student, William James, spent a year in Germany studying the latest strides in physiology. During his visit James became interested in the possibility of approaching psychology in a scientific rather than in a speculative manner. Writing to his father in late 1867, James concluded that "As a central point of study I imagine that the border ground of physiology and psychology, overlapping both, would be as fruitful as any, and I am now working on it." [1] Another letter of the same period indicated that physiological psychology had made a deep impression upon the mind of the young James: "It seems to me that perhaps the time has come for psychology to begin to be a science—some measurements have already been made in the region lying between the physical changes in the nerves and the appearance of consciousness . . . (in the shape of sense perceptions), and more may come of it." [2] By May of 1868 the idea of bringing the new psychology to America had become uppermost in the thoughts of William James: "I have a (perhaps erroneous) suspicion that psychology is not à l'ordre du jour until some as yet unforeseen steps are made in the physiology of the nervous system; and if I were able by assiduous pottering to define a few physiological facts, however humble, I should feel that I had not lived entirely in vain." [3] The extent to which the soul-searchings of a sickly young man were eventually to transform the development of American thought could hardly have been discerned in the winter of 1868.

James's assertion that psychology must become a science indicates that up to this point in its history it was something else. In actuality, there was no such discipline as psychology before 1870; the study of the mind remained subordinate within the larger framework of metaphysics. It was no more than a colony within the empire of theology. Mind, often with a capital *M*, was regarded as an a-physical entity, with any relation to the body in general, and even to the brain, largely ignored. René Descartes had concluded that man's essence, mind, "has no need of space nor of any material thing (or body). Thus it follows that this ego, (this mind,) (this soul,) by which I am what I am, is entirely distinct from the body . . ." [4] With this assertion he had fixed the role of psychology for the next two centuries.

Psychology at Harvard during the period from 1860 to 1875 reflected the status of this area of study in American higher education. [5] Between 1860 and the inauguration of President Eliot in 1869, psychology was treated as a minor aspect of the study of logic and metaphysics. Professor Francis Bowen [6] offered a series of readings in the philosophy of mind, while in no way recognizing the conception of the mind espoused abroad. In 1869, in the Divinity School, Professor Charles Everett [7] began a course known as the "Science of Thought"; his use of the term *science*, however, was highly subjective. Not until the period from 1870 to 1872 did Bowen introduce into the Department of Philosophy Harvard's first well-structured course in the philosophy of mind. The readings, which included John Locke's *Essay on Human Understanding*, Noah Porter's *On Human Intel-*

lect, and Victor Cousin's *Philosophy of the XVIIIth Century,* evaluated mental activity in a strictly subjective and speculative fashion. The terminology of such a course would have been familiar to Descartes or Spinoza.

Bowen advanced ideas wholly contrary to the insights of the new psychology. He asked his students, for example, to differentiate between the philosophy (or psychology) which they had studied, on the one hand, and the realm of science, on the other. Bowen built the course around the Cartesian dualism that had characterized all philosophy of mind up to this point. Like Descartes, he divided the world into realms of mind and matter; science dealt strictly with the latter. Bowen thus identified philosophy as pure science, removed from physical links and differentiated between the "matter" and the "form" of thought. Harvard's first course in psychology dealt more often with questions of moral responsibility than with an empirical approach to the physical nature of the human mind. That the study of mind was, and must remain, outside the area of scientific inquiry was the real theme of Bowen's course.

During the same years Professor Everett continued "The Science of Thought." Everett's method was strictly theological and logical; he bypassed any scientific consideration of the phenomenon of thought. Terminology such as "analogy," "syllogism," and "integration" characterized Everett's lectures. Basically, the course dealt with the steps by which theological doctrines were to be related to the logical functionings of the mind.

A Board of Overseers' Visiting Committee, in an 1871 report on the progress of elective study, complained of the slighting of psychological courses at Harvard. "Psychological studies cannot be said to rank very high among us. They are neither taught by as many teachers, nor studied by as many students as they might be." [8]

In the following academic year, perhaps in response to the complaint voiced by the Overseers, Professor Bowen changed the name of his course to "psychology." Bowen substituted Cousin's text for Porter's but made no significant change in content. He reviewed the old Platonic concept of the unreliability of our knowledge of the material world and advanced the argument, that in matters of matter, man's ability to "know" is hampered by a lack of certainty. Rejecting J. S. Mill's concepts of experience, extension, and association of ideas, Bowen maintained, in Cartesian terms, that only our knowledge of the nonmaterial or ideal world can be exercised with certainty. Bowen's emphasis on the unreliability of material knowledge is *the* point at which he and William James parted ways, for the latter's concept of psychological knowing depended upon a thorough knowledge of the physical constitution of both mind and body.

Another problem which Bowen treated in his "Psychology" course was that of "the possibility of our conceiving and knowing God as he really is—in his essential attributes." One of James's many tasks would be to remove theological and metaphysical terminology from psychology at Harvard and to channel the study of the mind in the direction of empirical verification as opposed to that of introspective speculation.

Professor Bowen's course change, which amounted merely to a change of title, did not please the watchful eye of James Elliot Cabot of the Board of Overseers. The 1873 report concluded wryly: "In psychology there has been no change, so far as we are aware. We have no wish to reflect, or to seem to reflect, upon the Plummer or Alford professors, by whom philosophical studies have long been ably and faithfully taught. They will agree with us we are confident, that neither the number nor the spirit of those who take electives in philosophy is what it ought to be." [9]

Although James had begun teaching at Harvard as an instructor in anatomy and physiology as early as 1872, he did not initiate the new psychology until the academic year 1875–76. A brief review of the content of James's course in "Comparative Anatomy and Physiology of Vertebrates" is nevertheless worthwhile since similar subject matter formed the core of his psychology courses for the next two decades. James dealt with such questions as the structure and function of nerves, the development of the ovum, the constitution and circulation of the blood, and the effects of alcohol, both physiological and psychological, upon the human mind. James emphasized two points which were of significance to his subsequent work in psychology. First, he insisted that problems be handled with specific reference to experimental proof. Second, although the course technically dealt with the anatomy and physiology of vertebrates in general, James dealt primarily with the human animal. This emphasis on the experimental and the human was crucial for the new psychology.

Before beginning a technical analysis of the range and content of James's psychology, a brief summary of the dominant ideas which formed the heart of James's psychological thought is in order. Physiological psychology came upon Harvard suddenly, but it did not spring full-grown from the forehead of its innovator. William James's concept of psychology was a processive entity, and its evolution continued throughout his career on the Harvard faculty. When James received his medical degree from Harvard in 1869, he gave little hint of becoming one of the most renowned American thinkers of the nineteenth century. But it was just this medical background which provided James with a kind of "therapeutic concern" for his fellows. He became a "physician of the soul." [10]

Drawing upon the insights of Bain and Wundt, James believed deeply in the physiological relation of the mind, hence thought and knowledge, to natural functions. "He refused to isolate the natural world and its processes on one side, and mind on the other, and then to look upon mind as the witness of events in which it does not share." He insisted that mind participates in the course of nature. Perceiving, knowing, believing, and thinking are all bound up in man's physical relation to the physical world about him. These are natural processes with deep roots. James's approach to man was biological rather than metaphysical, theological, or logical. His epistemology was natural experience. James shifted the view of human psychology from subjective introspection to controlled experimentation; he was not reluctant to identify man with the material world. These insights may seem rather superficial in the contemporary world, but without them there could have been no modern psychology.

James, however, was fully aware of the danger that lay in the alliance between mind and body. As a result, his most famous psychological concept, the stream of consciousness, ran counter to Spencer's physical-psychological determinism as well as to Cartesian cerebralism. James's notion of the stream of consciousness held that "consciousness is not primarily a matter of cognition or intellectual acts" (that is, not merely a knowing affair). "Our mental life," James wrote, "like a bird's life, seems to be made of an alternation of flights and perchings . . . The resting places are usually occupied by sensorial images of some sort, whose peculiarity is that they can be held before the mind for an indefinite time, and contemplated without changing; *the places of flight are filled with thoughts of relations . . .* contemplated in the periods of comparative rest . . . Resting places are the *substantive* parts of the stream of thought— the places of flight the transitive parts." [11] The folly of introspective psychology was that it ignored these relations between mental events, and treated the process of thought as a series of separated, a-physical entities.

Consciousness, then, for James "was impulsive, passional and volitional throughout its course, and intellectual only at intervals"; but consciousness was *more* than an automatic function of the brain and nervous system. The brain as the instrument of consciousness did have the power of selectivity, and man was more than a physical automaton.

Finally, there is James's concept of the role of the will in belief, opinion, and knowledge. He insisted that human volition must and does substitute for our lack of adequate knowledge. Often we cannot know the full truth about a situation before we act on it. We are forced to act without the knowledge we would like to have, the will becoming a substitute for these facts, and helping to create the actions which full knowledge would demand. "We are entitled to exercise a will to believe."

With these ideas William James transformed the face of the Harvard Department of Philosophy and, eventually, the foundations of American psychology. James first attempted to introduce physiological psychology at Harvard in the small group of graduate courses offered by the Faculty of Arts for 1875–76. With his commitment to specialization and physiological study as the primary requisites for an independent psychological science, James embarked in this course upon the difficult task of breaking down many hallowed traditions. He recognized the pluralistic implications involved in bringing independence to psychology, and he was intent upon demonstrating the futility and sterility of the arguments and categories of introspective psychology. After examining the "psychology" of both Professors Bowen and Everett, we find in James's graduate course a thorough shift in direction and approach. The material more closely resembles that of James's course in anatomy and physiology than it does that of the courses of Bowen or Everett. But it was precisely this kind of distinction which James tried to break down, for he refused to accept any rigid differentiation between the problems of physiology, psychology, and philosophy. His emphasis was upon the naturalness of mental activity. Stated briefly, the course covered two principal areas: physiology, *per se*, and physiology as it applied to the broader range of psychological and philosophical problems. James paid a considerable amount of attention to such questions as the distinction between efferent and afferent nerve processes, the role of the ganglia of the brain, and the tracing of the various processes involved in muscular effort.[12] But James's primary task concerned the relating of the already familiar body processes to the functioning of the mind. He offered a serious challenge to introspective psychology when he asked, "Can actions accompanied by intelligence be conceived under the form of reflex action?" This question represents one of James's most significant themes—that intelligence is not some separate or extra-physical force which deals solely with mental phenomena. Indeed, intelligence might, he implied upon finer analysis, be proven to be another variety of physical reflex. Although James never agreed with Spencer in conceiving of man as a mere conscious automaton, he nevertheless used the concept of intelligence as reflex in order to establish more firmly the physical nature of mental activity.

A second task explored by James in relation to the concept of natural mind was that of the elimination of the absolute in dealing with mental phenomena. Not only did he refuse to grant visions of the "spiritual" to a detached and antiphysical mind; he also, although binding the mind to physical roots, refused to fix or dogmatize these physical roots. James rejected absolutes in the physical realm as well as in the speculative realm. Even when considering views concerning the function of the cortex, he refused to accept any single possible explanation as final. The categories that Bowen had used to differentiate mental and physical phenomena, James used to substantiate their relations: he related space perception to the functioning of the senses; he broke down the supposed dichotomy between the inner and outer world and demonstrated that the inner world was subject to the identical physical forces and processes as the outer world; and he treated the metaphysical problem of free will in the revolutionary context of Spencer's theory of the conscious automaton. James, in dealing with physiology, was able to reflect upon such philosophical concepts as cognition of the real world and freedom of the will. Such subject matter demonstrated his hope of breaking down the artificial divisions of human experience which were basic to introspective psychology.

The Overseers' Committee which had complained in previous years about the lack of psychology at Harvard finally acknowledged in its report for 1875–76 that something of value had been added to the Harvard curriculum. "We are glad to learn that a course upon the relations of Physiology to Psychology has been established, and we hope that it is to be incorporated into the department of Philosophy. The ignoring by philosophers of the physical side of mental phenomena has had the natural effect of exaggerating the importance of materialistic views . . . It is not the immediate business of Philosophy to edify, but to help us to understand the facts of life . . . we must take care not to turn our backs upon any, because they do not suit our preconceived opinions." [13]

Although it is outside of the range of this essay to describe in detail the founding of the Harvard psychological laboratory, it is nevertheless valuable to deal with the laboratory as it reflected the opportunity for the students of the new psychology to engage in firsthand empirical research. James's principal tenet, the need for specialized and controlled experimentation as opposed to uncontrolled speculation, had inspired the founding of the psychological laboratory; despite the later protestations of G. Stanley Hall,[14] James did found the laboratory as early as 1876 when the treasurer reported a $300 allowance for such research.[15] Hall's claim that the laboratory was not used for psychological purposes merely because it was identified as a "physiology" laboratory during its first seven years is irrelevant. James never accepted such a rigid distinction between physiology and psychology, and there is ample proof that the laboratory was used for psychological research long before its name was actually altered in 1883.[16] The laboratory was a natural concomitant of James's graduate course 18, for advanced courses were incomplete, in James's opinion, unless they provided materials for original research.

By the fall of 1875 James realized that experimentation; removal of religious, metaphysical, and logical terminology; and the need for specialists as instructors were the primary requisites for the success of psychology as an independent science. Writing to President Eliot in December 1875, James expressed his desire to establish psychology as a specialized field, taught by men with a firm background in physiology. Psychology could no longer be taught, he insisted, by men "whose education has been exclusively literary or philosophical," for they "are too apt to show a real inaptitude for estimating the force and bearing of physiological arguments when used to help to define the nature of man . . . Shall students be left to what languid attention professors educated in the exclusively literary way can pay to the subject?" [17] When James asked for the union in one instructor of the physical and philosophical approach, he was describing the very design that he was introducing at Harvard.

Remaining an instructor in anatomy and physiology,

James, partially as a result of the Overseers' praise for the 1875 graduate course, began undergraduate psychology in the fall of 1876. The catalogue description of the course as Natural History 2, "Physiological Psychology" (using Herbert Spencer's *Principles of Psychology*), did not give the curious student body a clear definition of its content. The promise that the course would deal with Herbert Spencer created a distinct wave of interest. In a letter to the *Harvard Crimson* in November, 1876, a student expressed pleasure that evolution would be offered at Harvard.[18] (Some students had simply associated Spencer's name with his fame as an evolutionist.) James responded to the desire for a course in evolutionary philosophy in 1879, but that was not his intention in 1876. Regardless of the temporary confusion, the lectures apparently received widespread acclaim in a short period of time; by November students were appealing to the Natural History Society to request that Professor James repeat certain of his lectures for the benefit of those interested students not enrolled in the course.[19]

Natural History 2 represents a concise summary of James's concept of psychology as a science independent of, and yet intimately related to, other fields of learning. The basic theme of the course was the manner in which the various parts of the body may affect each other and may influence the process by which men think and feel. James lectured on the existence of untraced physical impulses in the mind and then asked, "Why does he [Spencer] call a certain kind of sensation the mother tongue of thought?" This question reflects James's emphasis upon the theme that thought, like the movement of an eye, is a natural phenomenon affected by and affecting the identical physical processes which characterize the rest of the organism.

James presented a subtle mixture of problems that typified his idea of the overlap between physiological psychology and philosophy. In treating the age-old problem of the existence of an external reality, he conducted an experiment dealing with relative reactions to the temperature of water depending upon the state of the body temperature; similarly, he considered such philosophical questions as the meaning of materialism, the perception of time, the reasoning of metaphysicians, and the relative validity of various arguments. He continued to argue for a many-sided, pluralistic universe in which all aspects of existence blend into each other and become indistinguishable from the context of all life. James thus combined his physiological and psychological data to test the ability of his students to reconcile the facts of experimental psychology with an honored metaphysical principle. "Psychical changes either conform to law or they do not. If they do not this work is sheer nonsense; no science of psychology is possible. If they do conform to law there cannot be any such thing as free will." James answered the former affirmatively but, employing his concept of the role of the will, kept from relegating man to the Spencerian status of a smooth-functioning physical automaton. By maintaining the existence of psychological laws and yet supporting a concept of free will, James not only revealed his own originality and distinction from the Spencerian school but also demonstrated that the concepts of physiological psychology could be meaningfully applied to the most pressing questions of man's existence. (The only evidence of the use of the laboratory in this course comes from the memory of one of James's students, who, writing years later, declared that Natural History 2 "proved to be almost a purely psychological course. The text book being the 1200 page synthetic philosophy of Herbert Spencer. Four or five times a week were mostly taken up by lectures of the professor . . . The laboratory in Lawrence Scientific School was often referred to in those lectures.") [20]

The success of this first attempt at introducing physiological psychology to the students of Harvard College was applauded by James Elliot Cabot of the Overseers: "The new course in Psychology seems . . . to be an important addition to the department, as affording an introduction, with a firm footing upon the physiological facts, to the study of the connection of body and mind, and of the physical conditions of knowledge. The treatment has been of necessity somewhat tentative . . . But the course has already abundantly justified itself by the interest and the mental activity which it has called forth in the attempt to deal at first hand with psychological facts. If it suffers from the lack of well-assured and accredited doctrine, it is thereby to the same extent saved from the dangers of dogmatism, on the one hand, and the mere historical retailing of opinions on the other." [21] Psychology had come to stay at Harvard.

Now an assistant professor of physiology, James succeeded in 1877 in shifting his psychology course into the Philosophy Department. James did encounter difficulty as the change was opposed by the stalwart of rationalistic psychology, Professor Francis Bowen.[22] Despite objections, the 1877–78 catalogue listed a strange bedfellow among the Department of Philosophy offerings in Cartesianism, ethics, German philosophy, and political economy—James's course, entitled Philosophy 4, "Psychology." Since James was not content to allow his lectures to remain static, Spencer's text was temporarily shelved in favor of Taine's *On Intelligence*, a work which particularly interested James because of its original approach to the phenomenon of insanity and to the uses of applied psychology.

In emphasizing Taine's highly empirical approach, James again demonstrated the direction toward which he was guiding the study of psychology. Most of the lectures dealt with technical points covered by Taine, but there is ample evidence that James continued the exclusively physiological lectures begun in the Natural History Department. James expected, for example, a detailed understanding of the anatomy of the spinal cord and an analysis of the process by which the optic nerve excites the sensation of light. James recognized no real division between knowledge of physiology, psychology, and philosophy, and the course illustrated his conviction that the study of man's mental life cannot be complete without an adequate consideration of the constitution of the human body. He reviewed Taine's outlook on such problems as the nature of the ego, the concept of word power, and the significance of hallucination, especially as they related to physiology. In asking for a physiological-psychological analysis of the concept of "real being," James treated a hallowed philosophical doctrine in a vitally new context. The lectures touched upon anatomy, upon psychology, and finally upon metaphysical problems; James could not have summed up his own attitude more concisely.

James was aware that in introducing thinkers whose works had never before been assigned to Harvard students, he was faced with the need of preventing their ideas from being taken as *the* truth. Realizing that the aura of science or Darwin could sanctify Taine in the student's mind, James concluded his course by requiring a list of any inconsistencies or errors to be found in *On Intelligence*. An identical question concerning Spencer had been asked during the previous year.

The Report to the Overseers summed up the new course enthusiastically: "The course in Psychology offers a great deal of interest and stimulus to thought, which cannot fail to be of great advantage to those of the students who are sufficiently grounded in the matter to be able to test for themselves the methods of investigation and the fundamental assumptions which prevail in the 'scientific' school of philosophy at the present day." The Overseers went on to request increased course work in elementary psychology as a means of preparing more students for advanced work. Warning against the possibility that the physiological approach to thought would merely substitute one set of meaningless facts for another, they expressed confidence in the "eminently liberal and inspiring method" of instruction.[23]

A final glance at James's maiden year in the Philosophy Department reveals that Professor George H. Palmer offered introspective psychology in the required Junior philosophy course. Palmer, however, did refer to the new psychology at a number of points during the semester. He provided his class with a list of books in scientific psychology, along with comments as to their worth. Included in this list were selected works of Spencer, Bain, and Taine. Palmer described Spencer as "superficial and easy," Bain as the "drybones of Mill," and Taine as a mere "restatement of Spencer." Palmer apparently held the new psychology in slight regard, but it is to his credit that he acknowledged its existence. Despite his personal views, he was instrumental in bringing James into the Department of Philosophy.[24]

Relative to the magnitude of the changes in psychology at Harvard from 1875 to 1877, the academic year which began in the fall of 1878 was one of consolidation rather than one of innovation. James continued "Comparative Anatomy and Physiology," Philosophy 4, and Graduate Course 17. The catalogue reports that James again changed his required reading, substituting Bain for Taine; but the Dean's Report, as well as James's examinations, indicates that he finally decided to omit Bain and return to an analysis of the thought of Herbert Spencer. As a result, Philosophy 4 generally repeated the material which James had given in his first physiological psychology course in the Natural History Department. James seems to have felt the need to emphasize Spencer again, and he was disappointed in the drop in enrollment in comparison with that of the course on Taine (from 23 to 18 students).

The fact that in 1878 James was in the Philosophy Department did not hamper his emphasis on physiology. He considered such questions as nerve processes as a possible explanation of consciousness, covered the delicate (but to James primary) question of the "interaction of the sciences and the arts," treated "the significance of touch in the advance of intelligence," and dwelled upon Spencer's theory of the effect of the environment on the organism. James continued to employ both anatomical and psychological insights as a means of providing a fresh approach to the greatest of all philosophical problems, man's relation to the physical universe.

The organization of James's early courses is fairly clear. He apparently spent most of the first semester in reviewing the physiological data and used the second semester in applying them to philosophical problems hitherto treated as independent of anything as mundane as man's physical experience. This division was flexible, but it generally represents the procedure by which James tackled his material. By the end of the year James had lectured on such physiological subject matter as the universal law of nervous action, the origins of cognition, and the conduction between sensory and motor neurons, but James repeatedly directed this knowledge toward a critical analysis of philosophical problems. Trying as always to demonstrate the artificial nature of any division between physiological psychology and philosophy, James questioned his class on Spencer's concept of the substance of mind and asked for a full account of "your instructor's statement on the problem of free will."

At the same time that James was steadily undermining the artificial categories of introspective psychology, Professor

Francis Bowen, in his examination in Contemporary German Philosophy, continued to uphold an absolute distinction between mental volition and physical action. His refusal to recognize the growing proof of their intimate connection reflects a tenacious attempt to keep the mind separate from the supposed crudities of anatomical investigation. The spirit of Descartes was not easily shaken.

One further significant step in the advancement of American psychology occurred in 1878 when Granville Stanley Hall earned the first Harvard Ph.D. in philosophy and psychology with a thesis on a subject which broached both areas, "The Muscular Perception of Space." [25] Not for another decade and a half was this degree to be awarded with any regularity.

Once again the Overseers were impressed by the progress of Dr. James. "The examination-books of the class in Psychology showed in some instances remarkable originality and acuteness of thinking. The instruction has included, besides occasional theses, a good deal of discussion in the class-room, which was carried on with much spirit." [26] Tempering their enthusiasm, the Overseers again warned of the need for more introductory psychology in order to strengthen the caliber of the more advanced offerings.

James made a significant change in 1879 when he dropped undergraduate psychology and substituted Philosophy 3—"The Philosophy of Evolution," with Spencer as the primary source—and Philosophy 5—"Contemporary Philosophy," based primarily on the work of his friend Charles Renouvier. The change represented, to a degree, James's attempt to provide a more diversified set of courses; more significantly, it reflected his desire to demonstrate the validity of the insights of physiological psychology in fields other than psychology proper. In a sense 1879 was the most important year in the history of psychology at Harvard, for it marked James's initial thrust into the adjoining areas of philosophy. By 1892 he had established the value of psychological data for almost every area of philosophical inquiry.

An examination of "The Philosophy of Evolution" indicates that James did incorporate psychological material into his lectures. Since this was not technically a course in psychology, however, physiological considerations were cut down. James dealt with Spencer's concept of our "thinking faculty," his use of the "idea of self," and his emphasis on the need for philosophy to accept the objective world as part of its fundamental data. In a physiological and psychological framework, James considered the "knowability of reality and the validity of Atheism, Theism, and Pantheism." Students considered these problems in a genuinely revolutionary context.

In the same vein James used "Contemporary Philosophy" as a vehicle to bridge the gap between physiological psychology and philosophy. He devoted his lectures to Renouvier's consideration of such problems as Being, the idea of Infinity, the notion of freedom of the will, and the definition of philosophic certainty. But it is not coincidental that James emphasized a modern philosopher with much to say about physiological psychology; for he included references to Renouvier's stand on problems such as the effect of the "passional and volitional" on thinking, his position "with respect to the connection of mind and body," and his attitude on the relations between muscular movement and the will. James was apparently motivated in 1879 to drop physiological psychology *per se* in order to demonstrate the plausibility of applying psychological methods in a more widely recognized philosophical context. He showed in 1879 as never before that the problems of man in the world are the common property of physiological psychology and philosophy. He brought these disciplines as close as they had ever been.

Equally significant is the gradual spread of the material of physiological psychology in courses not taught by James. Francis Bowen, who in 1880 asked his students in Philosophy 1 to "distinguish Thought strictly so called from those separate sensations and perceptions of individual things which form the mere data, or crude material, of knowledge," referred to the work of Bain in the same course. Furthermore, in his course on logic George Herbert Palmer employed Carpenter's *Physiology*, a work used by James during his brief stay in the Department of Natural History and assigned once again in his psychology course for 1880. The new psychology was gradually beginning to attain respectability.

The modest advances made at Harvard seem more striking in both their boldness and uniqueness when one considers the lack of any comparable innovation in psychology over the rest of the nation by 1879. Writing indignantly in the British journal, *Mind*, G. Stanley Hall complained that in more than three hundred secular colleges in the United States few fields of study were ignored as consistently as psychology. "The great open questions of psychology and metaphysics are made to dwindle in number and importance as compared with matters of faith," Hall declared, and "philosophical instruction seeks to inoculate the mind with insidious atrocities which too often close it forever . . . all branches of mental science have come to be widely regarded as the special appanage of a theological curriculum." Hall pleaded for psychology as an independent science, concluding with the hope that psychology would be initiated at the universities at Berkeley and Baltimore. Hall reserved his praise solely for James's efforts at Harvard.[27] James's effect on American psychology was thus barely perceptible by 1879.

At the start of the academic year 1880–81 James's transfer

into the Department of Philosophy was solidified by his appointment as an assistant professor of philosophy. (He became professor of philosophy in 1885.) Continuing the "Philosophy of Evolution" and advanced psychology, James abandoned "Contemporary Philosophy" in order to reinstate "Physiological Psychology" as Philosophy 5.[28]

James began his psychology course in September 1880 with a minimum number of remarks concerning the purpose of the course, intending to develop the purpose as the lectures proceeded. His first task was to provide a reading list, which was considerably larger than that stated in either the catalogue or the Dean's Report. In addition to Bain's *Body and Mind* (which J. S. Mill had called a natural history of the mind) James assigned more technically anatomical works such as Henry Maudsley's *Physiology of the Mind*, Bastian's *The Brain as an Organ of the Mind*, Henry Calderwood's *Brain and Mind*, and Carpenter's *Mental Physiology*.

James began his lectures with an analysis of reflex action, defining it as unconscious nerve processes uncontrolled by the will; in addition he discussed the constitution and function of the brain; and using a series of drawings, he began the experiments which continued throughout the two semesters of study. One experiment (on frogs) aimed at determining whether intelligence was present in a given action and whether intelligence was itself a purposeful action. In similar experiments, on guinea pigs and dogs as well, James attempted to trace the physiological foundation of phenomena usually regarded as extra-physical (that is, thinking, and so on). After discussing at length various problems connected with thinking as a mechanical process, James concluded that "the height of animal intelligence depends on the development of his hemispheres, for these permit him to escape from servitude to present sensation. They permit the past and future to enter into his motives of action . . . That man has the highest intelligence who is actuated to widest consideration of time and space." James thus suggested that man's capacity to attain the highest forms of mental prowess was directly related to the development and maturity of the hemispheres of the brain. The very ability to engage in philosophical speculation could not be fully appreciated without a realization of the physiological roots of all mental achievements.

James also lectured on the case for Spencer's theory of the conscious automaton and then proceeded to undercut Spencer's position with his own concept of freedom of the will. "All these preliminary lectures," James concluded, "show that there is a strong tendency to connect the highest forms of mental life with the lowest nervous action." Having considered Spencer's concept of thinking, in which man's most exclusive possession is treated as merely a highly complicated reflex action, James demonstrated that the mind did and indeed must possess the power of discrimination. He thus reconciled physiological data with freedom of the will, for James never intended to detach man from responsibility for his own actions under the guise of an inescapable physiological determinism. Once again he had combined the data of physiological psychology with the most sensitive of philosophical problems.

In a similar fashion James continued to explore the Spencerian doctrine which, challenging centuries of theology, asserted that the organism grew out of the environment instead of being created with it. James used the data of physiological experimentation to bear out the Spencerian theory and, in typical Jamesian understatement, declared, "The whole study of psychology has accordingly changed."

In short, James considered problems both physiologically and psychologically, and then in relation to any philosophical implications. In this context, he dealt with the reliability of material knowledge in terms of experiments on the nature of eyesight, treated the age-old problem of the cognition of space and time in terms of skin and muscle receptivity to sensation, presented a detailed analysis of the significance of psychosomatic diseases, and on the basis of concrete empirical investigation rejected the use of the *a priori* in scientific analysis.

The most striking example of James's binding together of anatomical, psychological, and philosophical data occurred in his treatment of the imagination. After conducting a number of experiments on the nature of mental images and imagination, James applied his findings to the conflict of nominalism and conceptualism, which began with Plato and Aristotle and emerged as one of the primary philosophical tensions of the Middle Ages. Focusing on a more modern period, James contrasted George Berkeley's conviction as to the necessity of particular images (nominalism) with John Locke's belief in general images (conceptualism). James concluded that the difference between their views may have been one of physical make-up. "May not Berkeley have a keen visualizing faculty, and Locke be utterly devoid of one?" Although James never reduced an individual's philosophy solely to a function of mental chemistry, he nevertheless was convinced of the need to open the eyes of the philosopher to the *possibility* that at least some part of his thought was the function of his physiological make-up. James explicitly demanded that the anatomical foundations of human thought be understood as a vital factor in even the most abstract of mental acrobatics.

In 1907 James wryly described the assumptions of introspective psychology:

Rationalism is comfortable only in the presence of abstractions. This pragmatist talk about truths in the plural, about their utility and satisfactoriness, about the success with which "work," etc., suggests to the typical intellectualist mind a sort of coarse lame second-rate makeshift article of truth. Such truths are not real truth. Such tests are merely subjective. As against this, objective truth must be something non-utilitarian, haughty, refined, remote, august, exalted. It must be an absolute correspondence of our thoughts with an equally absolute reality. It must be what we *ought* to think unconditionally. The conditioned ways in which we *do* think are so much irrelevance and matter for psychology. Down with psychology, up with logic, in all this question! [29]

Philosophy 5 was an attempt to wreck forever the contrived unrealities of this world of Rationalism.

James continued advanced psychology in 1880–81, but for the first time the course was listed among the offerings of the Philosophy Department rather than among the small number of courses in the graduate division. Undergraduate psychology, meanwhile, remained largely unchanged with the exception of the reinstatement of Taine as the primary text. James asked his students to prove that physical sensations were at the root of hallucinations, questioned his class on Taine's theory of space perception, dealt again with nominalism as opposed to conceptualism, and in a typically Jamesian fashion, requested that his students "make Idealism as plausible as you can in two or three pages." James's request for a defense of Idealism, a position for which he had little sympathy, again reveals that Jamesian psychology shared the pluralistic world of Jamesian pragmatism.

The academic year 1882–83 was filled with developments of major significance for the future of psychology at Harvard. James, having earned a year of rest, prevailed upon President Eliot to appoint as his temporary substitute a young Californian for whom he nurtured growing affection and respect. In September 1882 both graduate and undergraduate psychology were turned over to twenty-seven-year-old Josiah Royce. Royce, who received his A.B. degree from the University of

California in 1875, had spent more than a year in Germany studying all aspects of German thought. Naturally attracted to physiological psychology, Royce was fortunate enough to have studied with both Hermann Lotze and Wundt. On returning to the United States, Royce took his Ph.D. degree at Johns Hopkins and after a few uncertain years found himself, at least temporarily, an instructor in psychology at Harvard University. The years revealed differences between the thought of James and Royce, but their friendship was strengthened. Royce was to remark many years later that his closeness to James was a living example of unity in difference.

Royce reduced undergraduate psychology to one semester and retained Taine as the major text. The young instructor was apparently feeling his way cautiously in 1882. Royce was thus basically Jamesian in considering the areas at which psychological and philosophical problems intermingle. Physiological considerations appeared in lectures on sensations, images, and external perception; Royce's query concerning "the general nature of the evidence that connects higher mental life with cerebral hemispheres" can be traced to earlier James examinations. The only trace of Royce's individual interests occurred in his consideration of experiments in attention and mental activity, concepts from which G. Stanley Hall was beginning to work out a coherent psychology of education.

The academic year 1882–83 was also marked by the appointment of G. Stanley Hall to teach psychology (including experimental psychology) at Johns Hopkins University. By 1884 Hall achieved the rank of professor, although technically in philosophy. Hall's transfer to Clark in 1889, where he founded a psychology laboratory, was to lead to further advances in American psychology.

Royce was retained by Harvard, and 1883–84 marks the

first year in which psychology was taught by more than one instructor. Royce's continuation of his one-semester course in psychology, the resumption of James's Philosophy 2 (formerly Philosophy 5), and the maintenance of advanced psychology gave the department three psychology courses for the first time. Of equal significance is the fact that James reintroduced the "Philosophy of Evolution"; in addition, Royce began a course in ethics which included Spencer's psychology among the required readings. Five courses dealt to some degree with the new psychology.

In his half-year course, Philosophy 1, "Lectures on Special Philosophical and Psychological Problems," Royce began in earnest to develop his own distinctive approach to psychology. Besides the course title itself, which suggests a critical and problem-centered content, evidence indicates that Royce began to differentiate the purpose and scope of psychology on the one hand from its tangible results on the other. Royce questioned the complete joining of philosophical and psychological problems; he distrusted the assumption that they did not reflect distinct elements in human experience. Although he did acknowledge the intimate connection of philosophy and psychology, he insisted that philosophy must stand apart from psychology as the critic of its assumptions, values, and scope. Royce asked his students to *contrast* the spheres of philosophy and psychology by selecting a problem with both a philosophical and psychological aspect and then differentiating them.[30] Royce feared the submergence of what was in his view philosophy's primary task, evaluating the methods and assumptions of human thinking. If philosophy became too closely identified with psychology, he sensed the loss of its individual identity; in addition, he feared the consequences of psychology's proceeding upon its assumptions free of criticism and without a realization of its own limitations. Royce hoped to keep open the possibility of receiving psychological insights from disciplines outside of anatomy or science in general. Royce emerged as the philosophical psychologist while redefining James's role as that of the physiological psychologist.

James meanwhile gave the "Philosophy of Evolution"—that curious mixture of physiological, psychological, and philosophical material. He asked his class to relate mechanically a candle flame and an animal body as examples of moving equilibria, to discuss the idea of the mind process as adjustment to and correspondence with the environment, to question the validity of various religious attitudes, and to consider the problems of "Reality and the Unknowable." "In ethics," James asked, "what are physical, biological, psychological and sociological views of conduct respectively?" James continued to undermine what he considered artificial categorizations of human experience.

While James attempted in the "Philosophy of Evolution" to demonstrate the relation of psychology to ethics, Royce, in his ethics course, pursued an identical goal. What, Royce asked, are the "respective general bearings of biology, psychology, and sociology upon the problems of ethics?" Royce, as well as James, feared rigid distinctions; nevertheless, he upheld the need to avoid a complete blurring of lines. While James denounced the folly of introspective psychology in not facing up to the unity of mental life,[31] Royce insisted that the areas of mental consciousness must remain distinct and separate.

A description of the content and character of advanced psychology (Philosophy 8, 1883-84) emerges from the recollections of one of James's students. Writing to Ralph Barton Perry during the early thirties, R. W. Black described James's graduate course and the laboratory as

a laboratory in Lawrence Scientific School where there were some human brains in alcohol, which I did not consider myself physiologist enough to cut up, also there was some electrical apparatus for measuring time reactions. We would press a key the instant we saw a spark. I noticed my reactions seemed to take less time than the others and asked how we know whether we were in reality responding to the spark or to the metallic sound of the contact. He stopped experimenting and I never knew whether I had raised a doubt in his mind or exposed the procedure, that is whether he was testing to see which we would respond to. He had some staples with a pin and a screw in each the width of the staple apart and we all stripped to the waist or rolled up one pant leg and he would try them on the skin to see if we felt the contact as one or two. He said I had the most insensible calves he ever saw and I thought perhaps they needed washing. If I were there now I should improvise apparatus and try experiments on my own account, but none of us seemed to realize the opportunity we had to build up a laboratory . . . There was a sort of barber's chair at the laboratory and we would sit in it and look at a bright object on the wall preparatory to being hypnotized . . . When it was my turn I grimaced when he approached me after I had stared awhile at the object and he said "You can't be hypnotized." But with the doubts that creep into our minds with age, I now recall that it occurred to me one evening that I would "loaf over" to the laboratory and see what was going on. I was an unbidden guest and James said "Couldn't you keep away?" So now I wonder if he "Suggested" my coming.[32]

The work on hypnosis is particularly informative as it reflects James's interest in the aberrations of the human psyche. By mid-1884 James's interest in psychical research led him, along with some associates, to form the Society for Psychical Research. Despite Royce's skepticism and Hugo Münsterberg's eventual doubts, James never lost faith in the relevance of this dimension of the human mind.[33] The laboratory described by Black was renamed in 1883–84, becoming officially known as the Psychological Laboratory.

Royce temporarily ceased to teach psychology in 1884–85 while James continued both his undergraduate and graduate courses in addition to the "Philosophy of Evolution." The evolution course remained a vehicle for relating psychological ideas to previously introspective subject matter. In what ways, James asked, for example, "is it possible for scientific discoveries to influence ethics?"

In "Modern French Philosophy," given that same year, Professor Bowen asked his class to differentiate physical from psychical phenomena. One student explained physical phenomena as being observed and involving the use of the senses. On the other hand, he defined psychical phenomena as immediately known and not involving the senses. "They are undulutable [sic]." James had realized that challenging centuries of cherished philosophical assumptions was not an easy task.

The following year James again carried on all lectures in psychology. Undergraduate psychology was reduced to a single semester as part of a full course known as "Logic and Psychology." James lectured on the four classes of reflex acts and proceeded from such physiological considerations to questions on the relation of speech and thought and to psychological definitions of distance and empty space.

By the end of the year, James's impact was at last measurable. In a letter to the Board of Overseers, Andrew P. Peabody, chairman of its visiting committee, after praising the philosophical faculty, indicated the committee's feeling that it might be expedient if "rudiments of mental and medical science should be among the required studies." [34]

The next four years of psychology at Harvard, 1886–87 through 1889–90, represent the most exciting years of the James era. Illustrating the Philosophy Department's insistence on presenting varied points of view on the same subject matter, James and Royce began teaching courses with identical titles and reading materials. Both Philosophy 2 and Philosophy 3 were called "Logic and Psychology" in 1886–87, and both employed Bain as the major text. (Although audit-ing was possible, a student could elect only one of the two courses.) James dealt primarily with the philosophical implications of physiological data; curiously enough, he barely touched physiological questions, *per se.* He lectured on "all the facts involved in the free will controversy" and on "moral sense, sympathy, and tender emotion" as the result of natural stimuli. James also challenged one of the cherished assumptions of introspective psychology in asking for an explanation of "the Lockian or analytic doctrine, that our consciousness at any moment is a sum or cluster of simple ideas." In short, James asked for a discussion of his own concept of the stream of consciousness. Never before had a James course involved so much of the psychological-philosophical, and so little of the purely anatomical.

Royce's lectures are equally confusing in the light of his previous psychology courses; he largely ignored philosophical considerations. He did consider "a way out of the Idealist-Realist controversy." On the other hand, Royce weighted his course with purely physiological questions: the influence of sensory experiences on our perception of the external world; evidence on the relation of the brain to mental life; distinctions between the sense of seeing and the sense of hearing. It appears that James and Royce deliberately reversed themselves for a year, each temporarily adopting the other's approach to psychology. Such an assumption cannot be positively substantiated, but an extraordinary closeness existed between these two men despite the distinctions in their thought and it was fully in character for each to attempt to understand the other by temporarily adopting the other's methods.[35]

Royce introduced *Physiological Psychology* by the American psychologist G. Trumbull Ladd as his primary reading assignment for 1887–88 while James continued to use Bain.[36] James, however, seemed to be looking for some way to revivify his course; he asked his class "If the course were given another year, how should you wish it improved?" By the next year James had given up Bain and followed Royce in adopting the work of Professor Ladd.

Meanwhile, G. Stanley Hall, chafing under the low regard for psychology in American philosophical journals, founded the *American Journal of Psychology* with the aid of the Johns Hopkins faculty. James was delighted with this development. Another historic step in the advance of American psychology was taken in Philadelphia in late 1887 when the University of Pennsylvania announced the appointment of Dr. James M. Cattell to the first professorship of psychology in the United States. Cattell, along with Hall, had studied under Wundt in the late seventies. The university further stated that a laboratory for psychological experimentation would be in operation upon Cattell's assumption of the new professorship. In 1888 the University of Wisconsin established the second American professorship of psychology.

In 1888-89 the reversal of approach which characterized the teaching of psychology at Harvard during the previous year was no longer evident. Making use of Ladd for the first time, James's course was more physiological than at any time since its first appearance in the Department of Natural History. A typical examination read as follows:

Explain by diagram either a, b, or c.
a) a cross section of the spinal cord and nerve roots, marking the anterior and posterior aspects;
b) the internal ear;
c) the embryological development of the brain.

Similar questions asked for descriptions of the corpora striata of the brain, an evaluation of the phenomena of color contrast, and an account of the function of the hemispheres of the brain.

One further aspect of this course is enlightening in regard

to James as a teacher. Indicative of his deep personal regard for his students, James concluded the year by asking: "State what psychological problems you personally need to have cleared up," "How would you organize a treatise on psychology if you were writing one?" "Suggest any improvements in the course." Such questions provided an atmosphere of "give and take" in which students knew that thoughtful comments would be well received.

On completing the first semester of his course in "Logic and Psychology" Royce broke under the physical and mental strain and was forced to leave the University for the remainder of the year in order to regain his health. During the first semester, however, Royce did complete a course on the "Philosophy of Nature," in which he evaluated historically philosophies of man's relation to nature, culminating in the environmental psychology of Herbert Spencer. Royce dealt with the psychological evaluation of man as the cumulative result of centuries of development, from Bruno, through Hegel, to Spencer. Toward the end of the course Royce brought the problem of man and nature up to the midnineteenth century, stating that "the thought of man corresponds to the unity of the body . . . If the whole body is affected there will be a corresponding change in the mind . . . The body is the dynamic unit." In treating psychology as a part of the evolution of natural philosophy and in recognizing the processive character of man's quest for psychological knowledge, Royce gave the new psychology the distinction of having a history. James meanwhile continued advanced psychology, with seven graduates of other universities taking the course during 1888–89.[37]

When Professor Francis Bowen, stalwart defender of speculative psychology, retired in 1889, President Eliot offered the Alford Professorship to William James. James's reply of October 20, after expressing his humility at being offered such a renowned professorship, stated his case for the creation of a professorship of psychology at Harvard. Undoubtedly referring to the creation of such professorships at Pennsylvania and Wisconsin, James reasoned that a similar innovation was necessary to keep Harvard "in the foremost files of time." [38] Psychology, he insisted, was growing steadily away from philosophy and necessitated special training and individual recognition. Declaring that such a professorship would attract new students, James insisted that the institutionalization of psychology was a necessity since he would not live forever. Before the end of the year President Eliot replied by naming William James professor of psychology.

With Royce's recovery and return in the fall of 1889, James and Royce resumed simultaneous courses in psychology. James continued to use Ladd's *Physiological Psychology*, devoting the course to anatomical problems with scant reference to philosophical considerations. The catalogue identified the course as "Logic and Psychology," but the title recorded by a student, "Logic, Physiology and Psychology," is closer to James's design. The following brief outline reflects the scope of James's psychology lectures.[39]

Part I—detailed study of the nervous system
a) division of nerve fibers
b) definition and function of ganglia
c) function of medullated nerve fibers
d) structure of the outer membrane of medullated nerve fibers
e) excitability and conductivity of nerves
f) afferent and efferent nerves

Part II—detailed study of the spinal cord
a) constitution of the white matter
b) constitution of the grey matter
c) anterior and posterior portions of the spinal cord
d) its relation to the brain

Part III—detailed study of the brain
a) continuity of the medulla and the spinal cord
b) the cerebellum—grey external—white internal
c) cerebrum and corpus striatum
d) bridge of the brain

Part IV—electronic nature of the nerves
a) test with galvanometer on interrupted nerve currents
b) explanation for increase of heat
c) brain as the center of automatic bodily activity
d) continuous interaction of the skin

Part V—the nervous system
a) the nervous system in general
b) sympathetic nervous system
c) cerebro-spinal nervous system

Part VI—the eye
a) three coats—sclerotis, cornea, and choroid
b) the physiological process of vision—image, index of refraction, etc.
c) iris, retina

Part VII—the ear
a) internal ear, concha, and auditory bones
b) external meatus, tympanum
c) Eustachian tubes
d) semi-circular canals
e) cochlea and auditory nerves

Part VIII—machinelike nature of the body
a) chemical constitution
b) arrangement of nervous elements
c) the interaction of different parts of the body

Philosophy 2 embodied the conviction which James had voiced to President Eliot almost fifteen years earlier: that psychology can be adequately taught only by those who have a "first hand acquaintance with the facts of nervous physiology." [40] But a mystery remains as to why James had largely abandoned the philosophical considerations which he had nursed for more than a decade. Although he concluded his course by briefly stating the relation of the data covered to pathology and psychiatry, his closest brush with philosophy amounted to a few remarks upon the similarity of internal and external experience.

The solution to the enigma of James's shift in emphasis was Josiah Royce. In 1880 James had been the only instructor in psychology at Harvard; he had little choice but to consider the philosophical dimensions of physiological psychology within the compass of his single course.[41] By 1889, however, James could bequeath the philosophical problem inherent in psychology to Royce and focus his own course upon a rigorous foundation in nervous physiology. James always felt that anatomical facts must precede all attempts at philosophical generalization; Royce, on the other hand, was primarily interested in the method, assumptions, and values upon which psychology based its findings. The student could therefore sample two widely divergent concepts of the role of psychology. James, however, had much sympathy for Royce's critical approach and within a few years abandoned scientific psychology for philosophy. But holding fast to the concept of unity in difference, James and Royce in 1889 embarked upon two different roads, allowing the student to choose his own way according to his own will and initiative.

Royce's Philosophy 3, in contrast to James's Philosophy 2, reveals a striking lack of the use of diagrams and drawings, despite use of the same text in both courses. Royce opened his course by stating its ultimate aim—to deal with science and to criticize its foundations. "Philosophy must analyze the significant processes of life . . . and the ideas applied to the basis of science." Philosophy must evaluate "the significance of the pre-suppositions of science." Having once defined the scope of the course, Royce attempted to define the scope of psychology. "The purpose of psychology is to study the laws of mental life—to discover the regularity of mental life

. . . A perfect psychologist . . . considers why I now remember some old forgotten fact, why the thought item rose in my mind. Why do I love this or hate that, or why do I forget this? Psychology is natural history of mental life . . . Psychology helps us to observe our natural life *which it is the purpose of philosophy to evaluate* [my italics]. Psychology examines causes and philosophy estimates values." Royce spent almost two weeks of lectures defining the scope of philosophy and psychology and, most significantly, the relations and distinctions between philosophy and psychology. The Roycian aversion to a total blurring of lines between these two facets of experience, evident as early as 1883, became the theme of Philosophy 3.

Royce's lectures on the technical subject matter of psychology began in mid-October with a consideration of the connection of mind and body and a definition of consciousness. James discussed the problem of consciousness in terms of the physical processes upon which it is constructed. Royce was more interested in criticizing the assumptions which prompted Ladd to treat mental life as merely equivalent to consciousness. Royce concluded that Ladd had ignored unconscious life and that its mere existence proved that mental life was more than consciousness. James, as an experimental psychologist, had amplified the problem of consciousness with his concept of the stream of consciousness. Royce approached the problem not as a scientist but rather as a philosophic critic.

Extending the historical approach to psychology which he had begun during the previous year, Royce explained the significance of the new psychology as based upon its relating of mental and bodily phenomena (as distinguished from the study of the psyche, in the Greek sense). Royce illustrated this distinction with a long series of historical examples of "prejudices against believing that higher parts of mind-thinking, enjoying beauty, are affected by the body." He concluded that "without certain nervous conditions in higher mind, it would not take place." Royce's use of psychology within the context of history gave his arguments a convincing validity. Even when in agreement with James, Royce, as his methods attest, thought through the problems of psychology on his own.

An example of Royce's ability to refine the scope of psychology is his position concerning the vicarious nature of psychological experimentation. "Mind thinks easily of external things, but it is difficult to analyze our own experiences." Royce insisted that psychology, essentially the vicarious viewing of others, was subject to the will. Such insight on the part of Royce revealed a shading of the doctrine of the will which James himself apparently failed to emphasize. Royce's techniques amounted to amplifying psychological doctrines, not only by relating them to philosophical problems but also by subjecting them to critical philosophical evaluation. James analyzed the character of mental phenomena with the aid of experimentation; Royce lectured on the same topic by treating lyric poetry as an expression of the bond between ideas and emotional feelings.

Despite his original defense of the relation of mind and body, Royce did not accept this idea without warning that psychology must remain open to disciplines other than physiology. "The facts of psychology are to be found wherever we can find them," Royce observed. "No one department is to be more especially used than another." Royce demanded that once physiological psychology had broken down artificial divisions of human experience, it was further obligated to prevent the establishment of new dogmatic categorizations.

Royce lectured on physiological subjects such as reflex action, the function of the brain, and medullated nerve fibers in terms of method and problems with only scant attention to physiological conclusions. At one point Royce advised his class, "Details may be read but are not important." He devoted his time to pointing out the "conjectural nature" of much anatomical evidence: "The matter of method is most important," he stated. "Look out for sound methods of reasoning." In the midst of a lecture on the function of the ganglia, for example, Royce attacked Ladd's conclusions as "dogmatic and unwarranted."

In short, Royce refused to accept the conclusions or presuppositions of science at face value. James, too, had avoided this pitfall, but Royce made it the point of his course. When dealing with the scope of man's intelligence, he criticized physiological psychologists for ignoring the study of the mental capacity of women, observing that such necessary work "is buried beneath a mass of social matters." Royce criticized physiologists for emphasizing the comparison of man to animals to the exclusion of the comparison of man to man. Royce made numerous assignments in Ladd which the students used for detail not covered in class; he spent his lectures keeping Ladd under the thumb of critical philosophy.

Royce temporarily abandoned Ladd in early January when he treated his class to a series of lectures entitled "Excursions into philosophic problems of the relationship of the human mind and body." With obvious enthusiasm, Royce attempted to relate the new emphasis upon mind and body as a dual-faced unity to the following philosophic hypotheses:

1) The Materialistic hypothesis: "Is mind an incident to the turmoil of certain ganglia?"

2) The Spiritualistic hypothesis: "Does mind exist above physical roots giving them a meaning and an end? Does the soul inhabit the body or organize it?"

3) The Monistic hypothesis: "Does mind run parallel to nerve processes, being inseparable yet independent?"

Although in his next lecture he performed experiments upon the brain of a frog to determine its effect on other parts of the body, by the end of the week he lectured on "The Idealistic Form of the Monistic Hypothesis."

Roycian psychology actually complemented rather than contradicted James in most respects. There was nevertheless a strain of thought throughout the Royce lectures which indicated a basic distrust of the physiological elements upon which James placed his faith. When Royce concluded that the "world must exist for higher interests than can be satisfied by it," he insisted on a meaning for the natural world which lay somewhere beyond material experience. At this point James and Royce could not be reconciled.

James and Royce presented two distinct and yet related views of experience and each maintained an individual manner of presentation reflecting his own temperament.[42] One former student made a comparison in a letter to James's son when the latter was editing his father's letters.

I have a vivid recollection of James's lectures . . . and the side that students saw of him generally . . . he seldom followed for long an orderly system of argument or unfolding of a theory, but was apt to puncture such systematic pretensions . . . with some entirely unaffected doubt or question that put the matter upon a basis of common sense at once.

. . . Professor Royce's style of exposition was continuous, even, unfailing, composed. Professor James was more conversational, varied, broken, at times struggling for expression—in spite of what has been mentioned of his mastery of words. This was natural, for the one was deeply and comfortably installed in a theory (to be sure a great theory), and the other was peering out in quest of something greater which he did not distinctly see. James's method gave us in the classroom more of his own exploration and aperçu. We felt his mind at work.

Royce in lecturing sat immovable. James would rise with a

peculiar suddenness and make bold and rapid strokes for a diagram on the blackboard—I can remember his abstracted air as he wrestled with some idea, standing by his chair with one foot upon it, elbow on knee, hand to chin . . . Once in the effort to illustrate he brought out a blackboard. He stood it on a chair and in various other positions, but could not at once write upon it, hold it steady, and keep it in the class's vision. Entirely bent on what he was doing, his efforts resulted at last in his standing it on the floor while he lay down at full length, holding it with one hand, drawing with the other, and continuing his flow of commentary . . . If this suggests lack of dignity, it misleads, for dignity never forsook him, such was the inherent strength of tone and bearing.[43]

After his appointment as professor of psychology James attempted to raise money for the expansion and improvement of the psychology laboratory. James's letters to various friends written during this period contain references to "clipping" them for contributions. By August 1891 James had obtained more than $4,000 and thus assured Harvard of a first-rate psychological laboratory.[44] When James's activities in behalf of the expansion of experimental psychology are coupled with the almost exclusively physiological emphasis in his courses in 1889–90, it is difficult to understand the fact that he was actually losing his interest in the scientific aspects of psychology. Nevertheless, James's correspondence at this time indicated a growing aversion to "brass-instrument" psychology, and by 1890 he was thinking of a successor to take over the new laboratory after its opening in the fall of 1891. James was sympathetic toward the psychology taught by Royce in 1889, and the nature of their courses might well have reflected an agreement between the professors to present two distinct views as a kind of pedagogical experiment.

In the fall of 1890 the University formally created a new system of course division—undergraduate, middle group, and graduate instruction—which has survived to the present day. The Philosophy Department offered psychology in all three areas, and, in terms of the expansion of instruction and facilities, 1890–91 marked the high point in the maturation of Harvard's psychology during the James era. An introductory course for freshmen and sophomores was divided equally among logic, psychology, and metaphysics. James, gradually turning away from psychology, taught the metaphysics portion; introductory psychology was assigned to George Santayana, who had begun teaching in the Philosophy Department in 1889.[45]

Philosophy 2 (middle group) was distinguished in the fall of 1890 by the use of a new text, the *Principles of Psychology* by William James. Published days before the beginning of the semester, the *Principles* established James's international reputation.[46] With the adoption of James's text, the scope of the course was conspicuously expanded.[47] In that year the departmental announcement stated that

Professor James's *Principles of Psychology*, used as a text book with either an oral or a written recitation occupying the first ten minutes of the hour . . . For the philosophy of the senses Bernstein's *Five Senses of Man*, or its equivalent, will be required of the student. The lectures will amplify and extend the books in the experimental, historical, and philosophical directions. The brain will be studied practically by models, and by the dissection of the sheep's brain by each of the students. The newly equipped laboratory will permit adequate demonstration to be made of the phenomena of the various senses, and of the experimental methods recently used in the exact measurements of mental facts.[48]

A student in Philosophy 2 later described the course as abounding in "sustained intellectual analysis"; James impressed his class with frequent invitations to criticize both the presentation and the method and conclusions of his text.[49] He was pleased with the expanding laboratory, the increasing enrollment in psychology, and the broadening of the psychological curriculum. But he was preparing to relinquish all association with the teaching of experimental psychology.

James temporarily continued his seminar in advanced psychology which he described as a comprehensive two-year course characterized by individual research into specialized experimental projects.[50] The goal of the course was a finished essay upon the subject of one's experimental research.[51] According to the *Announcement of the Department of Philosophy*

the instructor and the students together will make as exhaustive a study as possible of the psychology of the feelings, including the subjects of pleasure and pain, and what is known as Aesthetics. The basis of the work will consist of reports on the literature of this subject, made steadily throughout the year by all members of the class. To this will be added essays and lectures in which all will in turn bear a part. In addition to this seminary work, laboratory exercises . . . will be specially arranged for each man according to his interests and needs. Several psychological investigations are under way; and the apparatus in the Laboratory affords a means for acquiring familiarity with . . . important experimental problems. The opportunities for human brain anatomy are good.

Psychology was adequately represented on both the elementary and middle-group levels. Santayana's brief undergraduate course included considerations of the formation of positive and negative after-images and the distinctions between the origins of illusions and those of hallucinations, dreams, and hypnotic trances. That both of these topics had been part of the course material of Philosophy 2 indicates that the new introductory course maintained a considerable degree of sophistication. Santayana's treatment of the extent to which "all our emotions and actions are selfish in the last analysis" was a further reflection of many problems dealt with on a more advanced level during the previous decade.

James's Philosophy 2 revealed a shift in emphasis. While using Ladd, James had concentrated upon physiological topics; using his own text, James paid more attention to the social and philosophical aspects of psychology. He contrasted modern psychology with phrenology, defined his concept of the "fringe," and paid particular attention to the philosophical significance of psychological freewill. James's personal predilections became far clearer in 1890 than they had been the year before; his teaching of metaphysics, as well as the new orientation of Philosophy 2, suggests again that the 1889–90 course reflected a deliberate attempt to present a point of view which differed from that of Josiah Royce.

The new apparatus first mentioned in 1890 was finally moved into the remodeled Dane Hall laboratory shortly before September 1891. There, the upper floor, consisting of one large lecture room and two large laboratory rooms, was assigned to Professor James. James was, however, already determined to give up supervision of the new laboratory. To him something impersonal and sterile seemed to characterize the very laboratory which his efforts had made possible. By 1891 he was searching for someone to replace him, someone who could combine a precise knowledge of experimental psychology with the vision necessary to preserve experimental psychology's humanity.[52]

James felt that Harvard demanded a man of the highest quality, a man of genius rather than a "safe" man.[53] Impressed by the astute writings of a twenty-eight-year-old German psychologist, Hugo Münsterberg, James was soon convinced that he had found the right individual.[54] The appointment of Münsterberg, James felt, would be his "greatest stroke" for Harvard.[55] Communication with the young psychologist produced positive results, and on April 25, 1892, Hugo Münsterberg was appointed professor of experimental psychology and director of the psychological laboratory. In order to assist Münsterberg in his initial year, during which time James was to be on leave, Herbert Nichols was appointed instructor in psychology for 1892–93.[56]

Undoubtedly looking forward to a year of rest in Europe, James devoted himself to an enormous program in psychology for 1891–92. Aided by neither Royce nor Santayana, James took over all three levels of psychology courses in addition to a series of voluntary lectures to teachers on topics in psychology.

James's assumption of the psychology portion of Philosophy 1 was partially a result of the publication in 1891 of a briefer version of his *Psychology*. The complete edition would have been far too complex for a course which ran for only one-third of a semester. Before long the students began to refer to the original edition as "James" and to the shorter volume as "Jimmy." [57] Slightly irritated at the need to prepare a condensation only a year after the publication of the original edition, James could not hold back a bit of sarcasm when describing "Jimmy" to his friend and publisher, Henry Holt. "By adding some twaddle about the senses, by leaving out all polemics and history, all bibliography and experimental details, all metaphysical subtleties and digressions, all quotations, all humor and pathos, all *interest* in short, and by blackening the tops of all the paragraphs, I think I have produced a tome of pedagogic classic which will enrich both you and me, if not the student's mind." [58] Despite James's half-serious complaints, "Jimmy" was ideally suited for ten weeks of lectures.

James continued to alter the almost exclusively physiological approach of his earlier courses. He briefly considered the properties of the nerves, the eyes, ears, and skin, as well as the relation of the brain and the mind, but the presence of exhaustive anatomical studies underwent a marked decline. What was more striking, however, was the appearance of subjects barely treated by James when he had used Bain, Spencer, or Ladd: the historical development of psychology through Hobbes, Spinoza, Kant, and Spencer; the pedagogic importance of the study of instincts and attention; and the critical value of the study of abnormal psychology. James had crossed onto the road traveled by Royce, convinced that experimentation which lost sight of the human dimension was both misdirected and meaningless.

James's seminar on mental pathology was to be the last time he would teach advanced experimental psychology. (During Münsterberg's absence, 1895–97, James assisted instructors who had been selected to substitute for Münsterberg. Upon the latter's return, James relinquished all association with experimental psychology.) A student in mental pathology described James as "ready to do sympathetic justice to the most unaccredited, audacious, or despised hypotheses. His thought was that there is no sharp line to be drawn between 'healthy' and 'unhealthy' minds, that all have something of both. Once when we were returning from two insane asylums . . . I remember his saying, 'President Eliot might not like to admit that there is no sharp line between himself and the men we have just seen, but it is true.' " [59]

The growing division between experimental and problem-centered psychology, which had begun to make itself felt toward the end of the eighties, was finally institutionalized in 1892 with the arrival of Münsterberg. Neither James, Royce, nor Münsterberg admitted that tension existed among their views, but friction did eventually develop. Münsterberg, vigorously pursuing experimental psychology, gradually gave the impression of being irritated with both

James and Royce. As the nineties wore on, Münsterberg became for James an example of cold "scientism" in psychology.[60] Actually, Münsterberg gained a wide reputation in the United States, not for his experimental work, but rather as a popularizer and promoter of science and its methods. James, who had thought of Münsterberg as a humanistic experimenter, was hardly satisfied with his actual performance.[61]

The psychology courses given during Münsterberg's first years at Harvard indicate that the division between problematics and experimentation widened. The idea of unity in difference, that varied points of view were good for the student's intellectual development, was to some extent obscured by the seeds of antagonism. Philosophy 1, which under Royce in 1892 took the expected Roycian pose of criticism of method and values, was in 1893 divided into two half courses. Santayana took over Philosophy 1a, which was more physiological than critical, while Royce taught Philosophy 1b with a more philosophic tint. Philosophy 2, which Nichols taught in 1892 using the texts of both James and Ladd, was in 1893 divided into two half courses. Münsterberg took the semester of experiments while James handled the lectures and critical theses. The advanced psychology seminar reflected the same developments, for when it was divided into Philosophy 20a and 20b, the former was conducted largely in the laboratory by Münsterberg,[62] and the latter was conducted by James as a seminar dealing with psychological problems.

During the same period the Department of Philosophy incorporated two new courses of psychological interest into its program. Professor Charles C. Everett, who twenty years before had taught "The Science of Thought," introduced a course on "The Psychological Basis of Religious Faith." [63] Everett's former course had been concerned solely with logic and speculative theology, but the new offering revealed an awareness of the implications of the new psychology. Professor Everett continued to emphasize traditional theological topics; but his reference to the role of the feelings in religious belief, as well as a question on Spencer's views on science and theology, reveals the penetration of psychological data into theological philosophy.

James had applied psychological conclusions to evolution and contemporary thought in general; Royce had used psychological thought in ethics and cosmology; Everett had recognized the relevance of the new field in theological questions; but George Santayana was the first to devote an entire course to the history and problems of aesthetics in terms of psychological data. Initiating "The Psychology of Taste and the History of Aesthetics" in 1892, Santayana breathed new life into an aspect of philosophy which had remained largely unchanged since the Renaissance. Santayana treated aesthetics in the context of psychological insights: "What materials besides sensations of sight and hearing can we find in aesthetic consciousness?" "In what way may instincts and vital processes affect our sense of beauty?" "What is meant by forms and habits of apperception?" "Write on the presence of a sensuous value in the higher works of art." This union of aesthetics and psychology reflected the success of James's intention to destroy unnatural bifurcations in knowledge and experience.

Professor Münsterberg returned to Germany in 1895 to spend the following two years deciding whether to make a permanent shift to Harvard. By the middle of 1897 he had reached a decision; Münsterberg returned to Cambridge to remain at Harvard until his death in 1916. Under his vigorous leadership the work begun by James was advanced with remarkable efficiency.[64] As early as 1892 Münsterberg left no doubt that he would assert the full authority of his role as professor of experimental psychology. Although he was technically expected to cooperate with Münsterberg, James had no desire to retain any authority in the experimental field.[65] In 1897, symbolizing the change in his thought, James relinquished his professorship of psychology and was renamed professor of philosophy. From this point on Harvard psychology became largely the story of Hugo Münsterberg. The friction between James and Münsterberg rarely came to the surface, and to a considerable degree, the latter carried on the attempt at unifying human experience which the former had begun:

But who, then, [Münsterberg wrote] are the students for whom such psychological work comes in question? Are they only future professors of Psychology? Whom else does all this concern? I might perhaps more simply ask: Who is there whom all this does not concern? Certainly those who wish to devote themselves especially to Psychology and Philosophy will always select for themselves this most engrossing work; but the conviction is growing with surprising rapidity that other departments ought not to hold back, unless they wish to forfeit the greatest practical advantages . . . and there is no danger that the highest dignity of our mental life will suffer injury from this study, or that our moral strength and our aesthetic treasures will be destroyed . . . when we learn to understand even the most subtle processes of our soul-life . . . Experimental Psychology stands thus midway between the sciences of mind and of nature. It is thus rightly the unifying central science; or rather, I would say, it ought to become this central science. Yes, it ought to become that, it can become that, and it will become that, when the universities rightly understand its true advantages and their highest duty.[66]

Under the leadership of Hugo Münsterberg psychology at Harvard entered its second era.

THE EDUCATION

OF EDUCATORS

AT HARVARD

1891-1912

ARTHUR G. POWELL

THE FORMAL study of the educational process in America commenced during the third decade of the nineteenth century. If this study at first was limited to the reminiscences of schoolmasters like Samuel Hall, it quickly became an explicit, theoretical endeavor whereby rules of school practice were deduced from an impressive "science of the mind." This development occurred largely within the walls of normal schools, specialized academies which offered a review of elementary subjects for prospective common-school teachers and a course in educational theory to round out the curriculum, much as the senior moral philosophy course rounded out the curriculum of the classical college.

The colleges themselves were generally uninterested in the new subject. The Amherst faculty, it is true, wrote in 1827 that the science of education "lies at the very foundation of all improvement." [1] But the trustees did not support the faculty's recommendations for a course of study and the idea died. By ignoring education as a subject for study, the colleges rejected the notion that teachers needed special training beyond the usual prerequisites of good character and knowledge of their field. Indeed, teaching in common schools was scarcely recognized as a "career" at all.

A series of events in the last third of the century conspired to involve colleges and universities for the first time with the study of education. The normal schools, especially in the middle west, pressed state legislatures to accept, and then require, normal training in place of the traditional local examination for licensing in the common branches. The rapid increase in public high schools created a demand for secondary teachers that could not be met by the older sources of supply. Most normal schools tried to widen their function and enhance their prestige by preparing secondary as well as elementary teachers. The greater number of high-school graduates became a source of students as many normal schools, again primarily in the midwest, began to offer one, then two years of collegiate training. As burgeoning state and local educational bureaucracies became staffed by graduates of normal schools rather than of classical colleges, sympathy for formal training in education increased within the educational establishment. Almost without exception, observers concluded that elementary teachers with normal training were invariably superior to the vast majority without it. Why not the same good results if all prospective high school teachers received this training? These arguments, and the danger of normal schools' gaining valued public funds, moved presidents of several state universities to offer courses in education as early as the seventies. Iowa acted in 1873 and Michigan followed six years later.

Massachusetts had been the cradle of the normal-school movement. But her normals, surrounded by older and wealthier colleges whose graduates dominated the Commonwealth, were much weaker than their midwestern counterparts. In the eighties they were still state-run academies preparing common-school teachers. Yet demands among teachers and principals for "trained" secondary teachers and administrators grew as fast as the number of high schools in Massachusetts. The Report of the Board of Education for 1889–90 recognized that

the demand for teachers with normal training is no longer confined to the primary and grammar schools. The increasing importance of superintendence renders it almost imperative that those who engage in this department of educational work should have both theoretical and practical instruction in pedagogy . . . The teachers in the secondary schools are coming rapidly to perceive that something more than learning and scholarly abilities is requisite to the successful discharge of the duties of their office.[2]

In fact no such training was offered anywhere in Massachusetts. But by 1887 several educational associations had begun agitation to supply it. Their requests caused the Board of Education to appoint in 1889 a special committee to study the matter.

J. B. Sewall, headmaster of Thayer Academy, told the 1889 meeting of the New England Association of Colleges and Preparatory Schools that Harvard was the proper institution to provide the training. Teaching was unquestionably a profession, he asserted, but had not been regarded as such by the prestigious New England colleges. Only their action could enhance the repute of teaching. In the lively discussion that ensued, President Charles W. Eliot rose to repudiate Sewall's suggestion. The best way colleges and universities could advance teaching, he believed, was to "teach the subjects which are to be taught in the colleges and high schools and academies in the best manner we can." In any case, most teachers did not regard their calling as a profession. Therefore colleges had good reason for not attempting to teach the philosophy of education. Higher educational history, moreover, was "the most terrible history in the world . . . because there is no good history of teaching and no history of good teaching." Eliot, however, said that he would welcome "very heartily" the conversion of a Massachusetts normal school into a "high" normal school to train high-school teachers.[3]

Eliot's opposition to the proposal that Harvard take the initiative caused many supporters of secondary teacher education to petition the Board of Education to seek the establishment of a "higher normal school" in Boston. They wished not to expand the course of study at existing normal schools but to found a new school to offer a one-year course in professional education for "college graduates or those of equivalent education." The institution would be financed by a $15,000 annual appropriation from the legislature. Despite the support of many distinguished educators—Presidents Elmer H. Capen of Tufts and William F. Warren of Boston University among them—opposition to the plan quickly arose.

John W. Dickinson, Secretary of the Board of Education, was known to believe that one more normal school was unnecessary and undesirable.[4] He wrote Eliot and renewed Sewall's suggestion of the previous summer: "What do you say to establishing a pedagogical department in Harvard College?"[5] And Eliot himself refused to support the proposed legislation when hearings were held in March 1890.[6] The bill failed to pass.

Eliot's shifting positions were critical to the fortunes of

the "higher normal school" bill. His apparent reversal from "very heartily" supporting a higher normal school to lobbying vigorously against it did not alone kill the proposal. Just as crucial was his decision to establish such a "normal course" at Harvard, despite his prior public opposition to Sewall. Indeed, it was understood by all interested parties that if the "higher normal school" bill was defeated, Eliot would act at Harvard.[7] In early October 1890 Eliot introduced at a faculty meeting "the subject of a possible Normal Course of one year designed to meet the demands of those who sought legislation from the General Court in 1889/90 in favor of such a project." [8]

Eliot's opposition to an additional state normal school, even a "higher" one, is not difficult to explain. He had never respected the work of the existing normal schools. In the late eighties his contempt increased as he investigated in detail the effectiveness of Massachusetts public schools. Such articles as "An Average Massachusetts Grammar School" and "The Gap between Common Schools and Colleges" were critical accounts of how and what children learned; Eliot could not help questioning the quality of institutions whose graduates staffed ineffective schools. He said late in 1890: "There are several high schools in the cities in which the instruction is now better than it is in the state normal schools. What ground is there for supposing that by the establishment of another state normal school the instruction given in the high schools would be improved?" [9]

But why did Eliot take the radical step of establishing a program in pedagogy at Harvard when he so clearly doubted its value? The incessant pressure on Harvard by the proponents of pedagogy should not be completely discounted. Men like Sewall and Boston Superintendent of Schools Edwin P. Seaver were Eliot's friends and their judgment carried weight with him. They argued that pedagogical training for high-school teachers was inevitable in Massachusetts. How much better to have Harvard's matchless traditions and resources support this training than a weak, new state school! Would not the cause of education suffer if Harvard stepped aside? Seaver, for one, cautioned Massachusetts teachers in July 1890 that Eliot's rejection of Sewall's proposal might not be final: "The inference cannot be fairly drawn that a great university has pronounced itself against the plan of a normal college within the university. This discussion is not yet a year old. There are ways of convincing a practical-minded president." [10] Thus the debate was framed in terms of "either-or." Either Harvard would act or another weak normal school would be created.

There is no evidence that these arguments alone convinced Eliot to establish the "normal course" at Harvard as the lesser of two evils. His decision was more positive than that, and did not involve a change in his opinion of pedagogy. On the contrary, Eliot's suspicions of education as a field of study were as strong in 1891 as they had been in 1890. His action becomes understandable only when we realize that he had no intention of establishing the study of education at all. Harvard would offer "training" for those intending careers in high-school teaching, but the role that education courses would play in this training was thought by Eliot, from the first, to be minimal. In addition, Eliot was more concerned with particular problems at Harvard College than with the wishes of Massachusetts schoolmen. The administrator of the program would, in Eliot's view, be more concerned with improving Harvard's relations with secondary schools than with training teachers.

This initial incomplete commitment to the study of education impeded that study's development at Harvard for more than half a century. Paradoxically it also insured the program's survival, for the apathy of the Harvard faculty eventually allowed the education professors to develop their own curriculum.

Once Eliot had chosen to establish a "normal course," the vexing question remained of what that course should be. Especially concerned was Josiah Royce, who, as Chairman of the Faculty Committee on the Normal Course, was charged with the responsibility for defining it. In 1890 no obvious model appeared.

Pedagogy had always been the least important, if most pretentious, subject offered by normal schools. Their principal business consisted of offering intensive review courses of the common branches and, sometimes, of those subjects on the secondary level. Yet a variety of authors had produced by the Civil War a large literature on the "science of education." They saw pedagogy as more complex and profound a subject than their predecessors who had taught helpful hints on classroom management.

These educators called themselves "scientists" before Darwin lent prestige and currency to that word. By "science" they usually meant a body of fixed principles or laws. "Science" was a synonym for these laws, rather than for the method by which they were obtained. Obtaining laws seemed less a problem than applying them to school practice. Gabriel Compayré, a French scholar, wrote in 1887 that science was "the experience of the ancients and of all those who have preceded us." [11] The most relevant set of laws comprised faculty psychology, or the view that the mind was divided into various compartments such as will, reason, and imagination which could be developed and improved through practice.[12] To most educators, the existence of faculties was "common sense."

In the last four decades of the nineteenth century educational scientists appeared in large numbers on both sides of the Atlantic. Perhaps the most widely read was Herbert Spencer, whose influential *Education: Intellectual, Moral, and Physical* appeared in 1860. Spencer, unlike those "common sense" theorists who had written about education, appealed directly to natural science for the clues necessary to understand man and society. His heavily factual works gave the appearance of a method based on induction. But he was interested less in finding a method for educational science than in promoting his conception of the nature of reality. Spencer believed social science should emulate the natural sciences and be grounded on facts. But he was not an exponent of this kind of science in his own educational work. Instead, he merely repeated and dressed with new phrases like "evolution" traditional notions of faculty psychology. Thus "education must conform to the natural process of mental evolution—that there is a certain sequence in which the faculties spontaneously develop, and a certain kind of knowledge which each requires during its development; and that it is for us to ascertain this sequence, and supply this knowledge." His emphasis on evolution was stronger than that of other writers but was by no means original. And nowhere did Spencer offer evidence for either the existence of faculties or the sequential nature of their development. Similarly, his call for educational method based on known laws resulted in assertions offered without evidence: teaching should go from the simple to the complex, from the concrete to the abstract, from the empirical to the rational; the education of the child should recapitulate the evolution of the race; if the child showed interest in his work, the teacher would know he had been successful. The goal of education was complete living, and a curriculum based on science would best achieve it.[13]

Thus Spencer's importance in the development of the field of education was not in the originality of his conclusions but in the backing he seemed to give to empirical conceptions of science. More respected in university circles than the earlier American theorists, he offered hope to those who would expand the domain of the study of education. (An 1859 normal-school convention had felt constrained to pass a formal resolution that education was "truly and eminently a science.") [14] Many accepted his categories confident that they were somehow more genuine than the speculations of the earlier theorists. The results were generally ambiguous. Spencer and his followers [15] offered little more than deductive speculation and a vague respect for facts.

Philosophical idealists competed with Spencerians for the allegiance of normal-school instructors. They too claimed to be "scientists." The American William H. Payne admired Spencer's brilliance but disliked his "narrow utilitarianism." Instead Payne would "replace sensation by idea" that a child might better approach the Ideal. Like Spencer, however, he perceived the "laws" of the mind as encompassing the various mental faculties. Payne even worked out in tabular form the disciplinary value of each faculty—high, medium, and low. [16]

For materialists like Spencer and idealists like Payne educational "science" was an honored if vague synonym for lawfulness, system, regularity. None offered an empirical method; all shared a deductive tradition of obtaining truth, though Spencer was less aware of this than the idealists. The materialists and the idealists shared, thereby, the same method that characterized all the popular movements of American educational reform in the nineteenth century: the Pestalozzian influence at Oswego Normal School in the sixties and seventies; the Froebelian kindergarten movement thereafter; and the Herbartian movement of the nineties. All these popular movements provided closed systems of theory and they were all appropriately named for individual philosophers. All were popular precisely because they were prescriptive. More than Spencer or the idealists they offered easily understood directions buttressed by complex and mystical rhetoric. Yet few of those who flocked to them, or to the Spencerians and idealists, perceived that anything was amiss. They saw, at long last, a content for education: learned books, difficult theories, complex terms.

Josiah Royce recognized these traditions as he pondered the proposed normal course at Harvard. His reflections, directed at the question "Is there a science of education?" were published in the first two issues of Nicholas Murray Butler's *Educational Review*. President Eliot had refused an offer to present the negative side of the same question.[17]

Royce rejected the notion that education was a science. He criticized those who built rigid systems of method from universal laws of educational ends. Human nature was the product of evolution and would vary according to time and place. Universal laws were therefore nonexistent, and the dream of them a relic of seventeenth-century mechanistic philosophy. Royce supported the intuitive method of teaching of the German idealist, Wilhelm Dilthey. Admitting that the growth of children was not wholly arbitrary, he nevertheless emphasized that the end of this process could not be foreseen. Unlike William H. Payne, Royce did not build a rigid educational theory from his idealist assumptions.

Having defined his position, Royce suggested several general conclusions for the training of teachers. If there were no science of education, a teacher should still know all he could of the subject he was to teach. Yet certain branches of science, especially psychology, might prove useful. Although these might have to be forgotten at any moment in teaching, Royce contended that to know what to forget could make a great difference. Finally, the teacher must be a man of ideals since the end of education was an ethical one. In short,

Royce advocated a limited training of teachers but rejected the scientific pretentiousness of the "pedagogical system" of his day.[18]

On November 11, 1890, Royce presented to the Faculty the completed report of his committee. Internal strife on the committee had been such that Royce eventually wrote most of the report himself. The organization of the suggested curriculum closely resembled that proposed for the unborn state normal college. It was to be a program of one year's length open to both men and women, to prepare teachers for Massachusetts high schools. Admission requirements would be similar to those of the Harvard Graduate School. Controlled by a special committee and offering special courses, it was to have little connection with Harvard College.

The program of study was to be based on eight courses in the methods of teaching particular academic subjects, given by regular members of the Faculty of Arts and Sciences. Each course was to emphasize content and effective ways to present it, rather than "methods" per se. Prospective history teachers, for example, were to study textbooks, chronology, and biography and would be expected to audit regular Harvard history courses. No mention was made of "laws" of method. Their absence testified to Harvard's rejection of the "methods" approach of normal-school "scientists." [19] Harvard education courses were not to be divorced from the academic subjects themselves and were to be taught by the appropriate academic departments.[20]

If these "subject-method" courses were the core of the committee's proposal, Royce's view that other materials might have some value was also accepted. A series of lectures on psychology was to be offered. Finally, an instructor in the "art of teaching" was to be appointed.[21]

During two meetings the Faculty struck down coeducation, increased the number of subject-method courses, and jettisoned the hated word "normal" wherever it appeared. On December 16 the revised plan was adopted by a 29-14 vote.[22] The Division of Philosophy agreed to provide shelter for the new program, and Royce and the committee began the task of persuading Harvard professors to teach subject-method courses. William James reluctantly agreed to lecture on the psychology of teaching.[23] The only matter that remained was to choose an instructor in the "art of teaching" and define his functions.

For reasons still not wholly clear, Eliot selected Paul Henry Hanus of the Colorado State Normal School for the position.[24] Eliot scarcely knew Hanus. They had met briefly in 1883 and again in Denver during the spring of 1891. Hanus was friendly with Eliot's son, the Reverend Samuel A. Eliot of Denver, and after dinner one evening in the latter's home President Eliot suddenly offered Hanus the position. Although Hanus had been teaching pedagogy for less than a year, his conception of it must have impressed Eliot. Largely absent was that pretentious scientism that Eliot knew Harvard must avoid.

Hanus had come to America as a boy of four in 1859. His stepfather was an industrial promoter, and the small family moved about the country as new enterprises opened up. A boyhood spent in rural Wisconsin, New York's Hudson River Valley, and Denver made Hanus's schooling fragmented and incomplete. Upon three occasions he set out to become a druggist. But a chance attendance at a City College of New York commencement "served to fix [his] determination to get a college education, somehow, sometime." By 1878 he had obtained a B.S. from Michigan. Drifting to Denver after college, he taught high-school science and mathematics, taught mathematics at the University of Colorado, wrote a book on geometry, became an amateur geologist, became principal of a high school, and in 1890 was made professor of pedagogy in the newly opened Colorado State Normal School at Greeley.

Hanus's interest in pedagogy did not derive from any scholarly acquaintance with the subject but from Colorado's pressing need for more competent educators. In 1884 and thereafter he was called on to lead teachers' institutes throughout the state. His addresses, derived from his own experience, helped crystallize his thinking and heighten his interest. Many of the influential books on pedagogy were unavailable in Colorado at this time, and Hanus was forced to visit schools and familiarize himself with "conditions as they actually were."

With this background he taught courses in educational psychology, principles of pedagogy, and pedagogical history in his one year at Greeley. He later told Eliot he had known little about these subjects and had relied heavily on his own experience. Yet knowledge was not in great demand at Greeley;[25] and Hanus, for all his lack of training, was the only faculty member who held a college degree. Undoubtedly some of the Greeley atmosphere's fanatical devotion to idealistic system-building [26] influenced Hanus. But he was dissatisfied with his new job, and contemplated returning to his Denver high school the following year. He told Eliot his battle was for education "on what might be called its practical side."[27]

Untrained in systematic pedagogy and never having studied in Europe, Hanus had been well-insulated from the extremes of educational thought. His whole education, and most of his teaching, had on the contrary been devoted to science and mathematics. His "practical" attitude toward the study of education, indeed his suspicion toward pedagogy as it then existed, probably recommended him to Eliot.

Eliot found it difficult to specify Hanus's functions with any exactness. Generally, he was to deliver lectures (rather

than teach courses) on the art and history of teaching, visit
those schools which sent many students to Harvard College,
conduct a summer school for teachers, take part in teachers'
institutes and associations, and serve as general agent for the
new program. Eliot added that "the function is really one
which you are gradually to create." [28]

However tentative these functions were, they did not suggest a large teaching load for Hanus. Presumably he would
be frequently absent from Cambridge. The teaching for
which he was responsible encompassed the "history and art"
of education. "History" meant, in the lexicon of 1890, comparative educational philosophy. "Art" referred to the rou-
tines of managing school and classroom. Both were periph-
eral to the subject-method courses, and both steered clear of
educational "science." Thus the Hanus appointment and his
expected function were thoroughly consistent with Royce's
general plan.

Almost immediately after these aims and procedures were
espoused they proved impossible to achieve. During the early
years of the study of education at Harvard they were abandoned and new and unexpected aims emerged. Three kinds
of changes illustrate this process: shifts in the formal relations between the program and the University; the decline
of subject-method courses; and the different function the
program came to serve.

During 1891–92 Hanus's lectures were not offered for
credit to Harvard undergraduates, but the next year "The
History of Educational Theories and Practices" and "The
Theory of Teaching" counted toward the A.B. degree. By
the following year all courses were open to candidates for the
A.B. or A.M. degree. After 1894 courses were gradually
opened to Radcliffe students. In 1891 four students attended the pedagogical lectures; by 1904, 194 Harvard and

64 Radcliffe students were enrolled in the courses.[29] An un-foreseen new constituency for the new offerings had developed.

Education also became more autonomous within the Division of Philosophy. In 1899 the program became a department in the Division of Philosophy and Psychology; in 1901 Hanus was given tenure; in 1906 the education courses won independence from philosophy and were formed into a separate division. Education thus gained crucial control over scholarship allotment as well as welcome liberation from Hugo Münsterberg, an ardent opponent of pedagogy and Chairman of the Division of Philosophy. A year later the Division of Education was authorized to grant the Ph.D.

Although all of these remarkable changes eventually gave education a relatively secure position in the Harvard curriculum, they were not accompanied by any significant growth in faculty admiration for education. "Considerable opposition" accompanied the faculty decision to give undergraduate credit for taking education courses.[30] Respected men such as Barrett Wendell joined Münsterberg in decrying the validity of pedagogy. Wendell observed that the trouble with teachers was "old-fashioned ignorance, not neglect of 'pedagogy.'" [31] Others, such as Byron S. Hurlbut, an assistant professor of English soon to be Dean of the College, informed Eliot that Hanus's students were weak and his courses easy.[32] Wendell believed that if pedagogy had to be taught at Harvard at all, it should be separated from the College as were the Observatory and the Bussey Institution.[33]

This latent opposition never coalesced. Instead a majority of the Faculty saw fit to give Hanus more, not less, authority in the 1891–1906 period. Indeed, Hanus said in 1894 that objections to education as a proper subject for university study had "well-nigh passed away." [34] How did this come about?

Hanus was no pedagogical extremist and shared Royce's suspicions of a "science" of education. From the beginning he received important support from men like Royce and James who agreed that some technical training of teachers was desirable.[35] Royce admitted to Eliot that opening education courses to undergraduates would end the power of the faculty committee which controlled them, but he supported Hanus anyway.[36]

Hanus was popular throughout the state and had, as Albert Bushnell Hart suggested, broadened the constituency of Harvard.[37] The *Journal of Education*, a Boston periodical not friendly to Hanus in 1891, said in 1900: "There is no young man in the country who has done more that is desirable for the cause of education without doing anything specially undesirable in the past ten years than has Mr. Hanus." [38] He promoted his educational wares on all occasions especially through lengthy reports to the Committee on Instruction; through the aegis of the Harvard Teachers Association, founded in 1892; and through debate at faculty meetings.[39] Hanus recalled with pleasure how a hostile but fair-minded Faculty had responded in 1892 to his argument that it was unfair and illogical for Harvard to offer courses and not give credit for them.[40] Yet this promoter often had moments of tactlessness, as when he suggested that Harvard only appoint professors who possessed training in pedagogy.[41]

Circumstances apart from Hanus himself played their part in the growing authority of the education program. As more states required high-school teachers to have professional training, Hanus's tenure became more secure.[42] Moreover, the Harvard faculty, aside from a few zealots, became disinterested in the fate of education.[43] Their apathy only helped the program to become more solidified. The growing autonomy of education, indeed, owed as much to this apathy as to the conscious efforts of Hanus. The most significant evidence of that apathy was the rapid decline of the subject-method courses. Abdicating the central role in the curriculum it originally held, Harvard's faculty left a curricular vacuum which Paul Hanus and his associates quickly filled with courses on pedagogy itself.

The subject-method courses lasted but two years. In 1894 a new kind of methods course, basically different in purpose from the original, was introduced. "Methods of Teaching Science in Elementary and Secondary Schools" dealt with physics, chemistry, physical geography, botany, zoology, physiology, and mathematics. The instruction, significantly enough, was given "mainly by persons engaged in teaching science in elementary and secondary schools" [44] rather than by a Harvard professor of science. Two years later a similar course in language methods was offered. By the next year the Department of Education alone was responsible for those courses. Between 1899 and 1906 an effort was made to revive three of the old subject-method courses taught by regular Harvard professors of the particular subjects, but none of the courses took hold.

Hanus did not oppose the subject-method courses in this latter period; indeed he welcomed them and despaired over their demise. But their death was made inevitable by the faculty itself, which neither accepted nor supported them. Royce had experienced difficulty in recruiting teachers even in 1891.[45] Many professors did not know what was expected of them, or did not believe that "methods" courses of whatever stripe could be useful or dignified.[46] In addition, the job was time-consuming. Dean LeBaron R. Briggs wrote Eliot: "I doubt whether the college teachers can thoroughly master high-school teaching without drawing off too much energy from work that, *as college teachers*, they are bound to do." [47] For similar reasons the lectures on psychology were abandoned after two years. James delivered them the first year, Royce the second. James's lectures, later published as *Talks to Teachers on Psychology* in 1899, were probably the most memorable contribution of the education program in its formative years. With subject-methods and psychology abandoned, the curricular field was left to Hanus. His conception of its purpose marked a third departure from the expectations of Royce and his committee.

In his first address in New England, Hanus revealed his own hopes for the new program. Teachers, he thought, should be trained first in scholarship. Psychology was important—"not textbook psychology, but . . . a knowledge, obtained through observation and reflection, of the mind's development and processes . . ." The history of teaching should be studied to furnish "ideals" for comparison and judgment in the light of today. Educational theories in general should not be evolved by speculation but "obtained from educational facts,—from the data obtained through the study of psychology, of educational systems past and present, and by observing the work of skilled teachers." Such sentiments, of course, would not have disturbed Royce. Yet Hanus went beyond Royce when he asserted that teacher-training programs should not merely train teachers narrowly, but expose them to the great educational questions that baffled mankind. The curriculum, the proper time for specialization, the educational uses of science, and reform were all matters of importance and should be part of the teacher's training, perhaps the most important parts.[48] Thus courses about education itself rather than subject-method courses taught by academic scholars, stood at the center of Hanus's conception of the proper curriculum.[49] As the years passed, Hanus articulated more clearly the central importance of training in education for everyone's liberal education:

> College and university courses on education and teaching are still quite generally regarded as purely professional courses, de-

signed only for those who intend to teach. The idea that education in its historical, theoretical, and practical phases deserves to be studied, and to some extent should be studied by all college students, irrespective of their future profession, is still quite as novel as was the demand which was made repeatedly and ultimately heeded some years ago that the mother tongue deserves to be carefully studied by all persons seeking a liberal education.[50]

Liberal training in education would aid everyone because every citizen had dealings with educational institutions. As for educators themselves, such training would make them leaders and not mere technicians. By "educational leaders" Hanus meant not only an alert and creative teaching force, but a corps of trained principals and superintendents as well. Indeed, before 1900 most of the graduate students of education at Harvard were teachers and principals attempting to become principals and superintendents.

Hanus believed, in sum, that professional training should stress the traditional disciplines applied to education—history, philosophy, psychology—rather than subject-methods. The aim was not simply to staff Massachusetts high schools, but to train leaders—administrators, teachers, and a knowledgeable citizenry. All these developments were summarized in the description of "general aim" first published in 1898 in the Department of Education's bulletin:

I. To discuss Education as an important function of society as well as of the individual, and hence of interest to all university students whether they intend to become teachers or not.
II. To offer to university students who look forward to teaching in secondary schools the necessary professional training for their vocation; and to teachers already in service professional inspiration and guidance.
III. To offer to university students who have already had experience as teachers and to all teachers of suitable age and attainments appropriate professional training for future activity as principals and superintendents of schools.

Doubtless the role of training superintendents made more sense to certain faculty members than that of training teachers.[51] Even Eliot later confided to Hanus, "We ought to aim distinctly at training superintendents." [52]

In the years from 1891 to 1906 an autonomous division had replaced a "normal course" run by a faculty committee. The courses were no longer associated with the traditional academic subjects, but they now were concerned with "education" and were taught by specialists in that field. Harvard and Radcliffe undergraduates could elect most courses, and those courses offered a "liberal culture" as their rationale for existence. Not without genuine pride could Hanus say in 1906: "During the fifteen years since courses in Education were first offered at Harvard the aims and scope of Education as a university study have broadened and deepened. Without abating its just emphasis on the adequate technical preparation of the classroom teacher, the university study of Education now emphasizes other important areas of that study formerly overlooked, or, at least, not generally recognized." [53]

These changes in aim and organization provided intellectual opportunities for Hanus as his courses gradually moved to the center of the curricular stage. What he did with those opportunities can be perceived only by examining the curriculum itself.

Aside from the methods courses already mentioned and the lectures on psychology, the Division of Philosophy offered lectures by Hanus on three basic subjects in 1891. These were soon after translated into formal courses: "History of Teaching and Educational Theories," "Theory of Teaching," and "Art of Teaching." By 1906 the "Theory" course had become the basic introduction to education while the "Art of Teaching" comprised a graduate-level treatment of the organization and management of schools and school systems. Every new course in this fifteen-year period derived from one of Hanus's three original courses: a short-lived comparative treatment of European school systems, a version of educational organization and management for undergraduates not planning careers in the schools, an additional course in educational philosophy, and graduate "seminaries" on education and the history of education.

The "History of Teaching and Educational Theories" became in its second year the "History of Educational Theories and Practices," a revealing title which was retained throughout the period. As taught by Hanus the course was admittedly concerned with comparative philosophy. Hanus was little interested in history and was happy to turn the course over to George H. Locke in 1897 and then to Arthur O. Norton in 1899. Norton, who taught it until 1912, emphasized history rather than philosophy. He announced in 1901 that "the purpose of the course is to trace the historical development of modern schools and universities, with especial reference to their ideals, studies, modes of teaching, and organization . . . Attention is given to the effect of political, social, and religious ideals . . ." Here was an effort to see education "in its relation to the history of civilization." Hanus supported the new approach: "It means understanding what the educational ideals of a time are; how they are the outgrowth of contemporary social, political, economic, and religious conditions . . ." [54] And Norton added, "The new view is, in brief, that the history of education is genuinely and primarily history. As one branch of general history, it is intimately related to other branches, such as social and political history." [55]

History was no longer conceived of as comparative theory, but neither did it assume a narrow institutional approach. The aim was to demonstrate that educational developments were inextricably linked with all other developments in society. The student would study not only Plato but also Athenian society, not only Vittorino da Feltre but also Renaissance Italy. In this broadened sense the history of education could serve a more useful purpose in the liberal curriculum's effort to train leaders. History could create one aspect of the "professional attitude." Norton revealed this motive in 1904:

It [history of education] should impart a sense of solidarity with the academic past; that the teacher may regard himself as the dignified maintainer and perpetuator, within his sphere, of whatever is honorable and enduring in educational tradition . . . The steadying and ennobling effect of worthy traditions, worthily upheld, in any human endeavor, is too obvious to need discussion . . . But most of our [educational] institutions lack such influential traditions. This is particularly true of our public elementary and secondary schools, where to my mind they are most needed . . . The first professional aim of the history of education, therefore, is to supply in some degree this lack of immediately present examples by giving to students the sense of kinship with a great past, to which they owe at least the duty of maintaining its best traditions so long as these do not stand in the way of progress.[56]

Norton was not alone in this effort to turn history to professional use. Thomas Davidson's A History of Education had sounded the call in 1900, and Norton used Davidson's text in his course.[57] Norton was less successful, for his particular aim—to relate educational history to other forms of history —was more an aspiration than an accomplishment.

Despite his published articles and the changes in course descriptions Norton's course continued to be dominated by philosophers and the curricula of particular schools. In 1901 the only material that covered years after 1700 dealt with Rousseau, Pestalozzi, and Froebel. In 1904 Herbart was added, together with a few remarks on English and German schools of the nineteenth century. American education was not mentioned at all. Only rarely, and typically in isolated sentences, did Norton discuss the social sources of educational change. He noted, for example, that seventeenth-century developments in agriculture and trade helped bring about special schools in those areas and that conceptions of social "laws" were reflected in educational institutions.

His failure to carry out the professed objectives of the course should not surprise us. There were few precedents for cultural history; the mainstream of academic historiography concerned itself with institutions at the turn of the century. What is surprising is that Norton, and Hanus, should profess this approach at all. Without it, prospective teachers could still be given a sense of "kinship with a great past," as Paul Monroe and Ellwood Cubberley would soon prove. Cubberley, for example, found that kinship in the development of free, secular, and compulsory public education in America.[58] Yet Norton and Hanus wished to find it in the ways educational institutions reflected broader social changes. While their dream led to no scholarly achievement, it was not insignificant. But that significance will become clear only when we examine the course that became central in the curriculum, the "Theory of Teaching."

The title of this course was changed to "Introduction to Educational Theory—Discussion of Educational Principles" in 1895 and "Introduction to the Study of Education—Discussion of Educational Principles" in 1902. The change from "theory" to "principles" marks Hanus's growing confidence in the existence of "principles" rather than opinions. In 1891 his course comprised two distinct parts. In the first students would be led to see that "psychological principles underlie all right methods. An application of the laws of acquisition to the development of methods naturally follows." The second part of the course would examine an educational classic, such as Rousseau's *Émile* or Spencer's *Education*.

The course quickly revealed a pronounced Spencerian bias. Bain's *Education as a Science* and Compayré's *Lectures on Teaching* were the texts during the first year. Examination questions, surviving only for the years after 1891, are preoccupied with lawfulness and system. In 1892 students were asked to discuss the "psychological sequence" of the "unfolding of the leading components of mental life" and the logical "sequence of subjects" in the transition from "the concrete to the abstract." Hanus wrote in 1895 that education was "an organic process with an unbroken sequence corresponding to the child's advancing mental, moral, and physical development from one end of his school life to the other. This conception naturally leads to a consideration of aims, means, and methods appropriate to different stages of the work . . ." Such a view almost paraphrased Spencer. It was no surprise that Hanus felt the purpose of education to be "preparation for complete living." Such preparation meant "the acquisition of knowledge drawn from the two fields of all human activity—*man and his experience and achievements, and external nature*; and training to intelligent and productive activity in the use of this knowledge, and to proper enjoyment of it." [59]

Decrying those teachers who lacked particular aims, Hanus began his course with an extended discussion of educational goals. They became more numerous and explicit as the years passed. He early distinguished between the aimlessness of the "fortuitous" education that the environment provided and the purposefulness of formal school education. By 1895 he spoke of the "special aims" of elementary and secondary education. Elementary education would "nourish the mind of the child through the course of study which should comprise an orderly presentation of the whole field of knowledge in its elements, and to provide for the exercise of all his powers." [60] It should, in short, open up the mind of the child and let the world in.[61] The special aims of secondary education

consist in the discovery and the special development of each pupil's dominant interests, in so far as these interests represent possibilities of development in harmony with the general aim of education, and in the constant use of the course of study as a means of intelligent experimentation until the pupil's self-revelation is complete.[62]

Hanus presented a theory of learning based essentially on faculty psychology which was to make clear to future teachers how these aims of "opening up," "discovering," and "revealing" could be accomplished. The "interests" of the pupil originated in distinct "instincts" and were the outward manifestations of them. Hanus identified several "interests" —the intellectual, the artistic, the constructive, and the ethical. By 1901 he had added the physical and the religious. The interests of the child were not to be treated casually by the teacher, for the kinds of behavior, what Hanus termed incentives, that arose from these interests were necessary prerequisites to the development of skill or "power" in any subject. Indeed, "during the school period aversion and evasion are more frequently cultivated than power and skill through the forced pursuit of permanently uninteresting subjects—subjects for which the learner has no capacity." If interest preceded the incentive which could yield power, and this was Hanus's point, the crucial question became how to develop particular interests. Here lay the relevance of academic subjects, for a given subject could only yield certain incentives, though different subjects might yield similar incentives. In this vague and intuitive way Hanus had anticipated Edward L. Thorndike's demolition of the extreme doctrine of "transfer of training." [63]

In fact, the "educational value" of a subject—its efficacy in promoting the aims of education—could be determined by observing the *kinds* of incentives and powers it would yield. The "best" subjects, those which any curriculum should emphasize, were those which developed the "highest" incentives and powers. Hanus believed the highest incentives were those derived from man's ethical instinct. Literature, social studies, and art portrayed beauty, honor, duty, and love. "When they dominate the actions of men, they usually insure the best and most complete usefulness and happiness. The incentives growing out of those ideals are therefore higher than all others." He added that these subjects have "some educational value for all pupils, and all pupils should be required to give sufficient attention to them." Other subjects (he meant science) were, "in general, inferior in educational value to those of the group first considered." [64] All of these ideas had entered the curriculum no later than 1895 and were still to be found in varying degrees of intensity in 1906.

By his faculty psychology, his espousal of an evolutionary view of education, and the tone of his rhetoric (education was "preparation for complete living") Hanus proclaimed the deep influence of Herbert Spencer upon him. Others recognized that influence at the time: George H. Locke, a former colleague, observed in 1899 that Hanus's first book about education was fundamentally Spencerian in organization and tone.[65] His easy acceptance of "instincts," "incentives," and "powers" as legitimate categories of educational analysis placed Hanus squarely in the deductive tradition. Of course a Spencerian like Hanus would not admit to a deductive, speculative approach. He saw himself, and in part was, an empirical fact-gatherer.

Hanus's students in the "Theory" and "Art" courses were not exposed solely to the deductive theorists, for they were forced to study contemporary educational problems. School reports and statistics, as well as philosophical treatises were documents for class analysis. Students visited schools, were given opportunities to teach in them, and often wrote lengthy term papers to describe their observations. One student recalled "the feeling of working in a laboratory," [66] after experiencing a Hanus course.

More directly, Hanus taught a "seminary" devoted to investigating contemporary issues. Research papers were demanded from the students; in 1902, for example, they studied the results of the elective system in school and college. Questionnaires were sent to secondary-school students and to Harvard graduates, to the latter because of their mature ability to "estimate justly and impartially" the influence of electives on themselves.[67] Hanus lamented the small number of replies but concluded that the elective system was worthwhile. No analysis of the data was attempted; the numbers "pro" and "con" were tallied and a judgment was rendered. Although Hanus himself questioned the questionnaire method a year later, such concern for "research," primitive as it was, revealed an inductive, empirical temper. Hanus knew that mere speculation was ineffectual; it had to be opposed by "observation," "experiment," and "actual facts." Yet this laudable effort to be empirical did not suggest any precise procedures. Hanus knew the general direction in which to travel but not which road to take. Thus he first espoused but later criticized the questionnaire method. Similarly, he supported with vigor President Eliot's Schools Examination Board.

The latter was a body of Harvard professors organized in 1892 to examine confidentially those secondary schools willing to pay the fee involved. The professors would visit and study a school for two days, and "since the object of an examination is to subject the aims, the organization, the equipment, and the efficiency of a school to thorough scrutiny and frank discussion," Hanus wrote, "the examination can not be exclusively nor especially directed to ascertaining the attainments of the pupils." The Schools Examination Board was more interested in catching "the spirit of the place" by "personal inspection." "Accuracy and completeness" would prevail, for the inspectors were impartial "specialists." [68] Here was "observation" of actual practices but the results would largely be the opinions of men whose judgments were informed solely by "experience."

Hanus, who served as the Board's secretary, had little choice but to pay lip service to its findings regardless of his real feelings. His national reputation confirmed his interest in "practice" over "theory." He was known for "a thorough examination and careful interpretation of tendencies in actual school work." And James E. Russell of Teachers College, Columbia University, told him in 1903 that in "practical work" he had advanced farther than had most heads of university departments of education.[69]

Hanus's interest in using the empirical method to solve educational problems became more conscious and explicit as the twentieth century approached. Like many other citizens he was awakened in the nineties to the massive defects in American education and to how little was actually known about schooling. A plethora of problems suddenly existed; they were apparent enough, but their solutions were not. Solutions were offered, however, and choice became necessary. What choices to make became immediate and troublesome questions to departments of education.

Other professions striving for reform faced the same dilemma. In medicine, for example, a great variety of techniques and cures competed with each other for professional approval. The careers of certain doctors, located in strategic centers such as universities and foundations, consisted largely of pronouncing on what was scientifically true and untrue. Their power was great, and often they erred. Yet some kind of systematic authentication was necessary.[70]

In education the problem was even more acute; the very future of the young subject was at stake. Men like Hanus comprised the first generation of university specialists. They had to show results of some kind. And their task was made more difficult by the growing public criticism of American education. One of the most influential critics was Joseph Mayer Rice of the *Forum*. Rice had been a gadfly critic of American education since the early nineties, but in 1896 he published a particularly biting article entitled "Obstacles to Rational Educational Reform." The obstacles were the educators themselves, who could not agree to what changes, if any, were desirable or feasible. "Everything is speculative," wrote Rice. "Nothing is positive. 'I think' and 'I believe' are the stereotyped expressions of the educational world: 'I know' has not yet been admitted." He called for precise goals and a standard to specify what "satisfactory results" in education meant. And he exposed the inadequacies of educational "scientists":

> In a word, they have made the fatal mistake of exactly reversing the true order of things. Instead of proving the accuracy of their hypotheses by a study of the results of a given process, they have endeavored to prove, in advance, what the results of methods based on these hypotheses must be.[71]

In 1902 Rice still felt that the subject of education consisted of "opinions, of reviews of opinions, and of opinions based on opinions." [72]

In the nineties three kinds of authority claimed to provide education with reliable methods and conclusions. Herbartianism offered a closed philosophical system from which distinct methods could easily be deduced. The child-study movement offered a series of generalizations based on observable behavior. The numerous prestigious committees established by the National Education Association represented an effort to achieve agreement in educational policy by publicizing pronouncements of highly influential educators. How Hanus dealt with each of these movements illustrates his growing interest in an inductive, empirical method.

Johann Friedrich Herbart (1776–1841) provided the theory that lay behind the most publicized educational fad of the nineties. Like Spencer, Herbart stressed the importance of interest. Unlike him, he believed that history and literature were of most worth. But his intellectual resurrection was principally due to the formal method he offered the teacher. In the hands of his disciples the method usually involved five vigorously deductive steps: preparation of the pupil's mind, presentation of new material, association of it with the old, generalization, and application. The method was based on the concept of "apperception," which held that learning took place through the absorption of new experiences into an "apperceptive mass" of old learning.

Herbartianism entered Hanus's "Principles" course in 1894. Students were asked to discuss method under the headings of "preparation of the pupil's mind," "presentation of subject matter," and "applications." By 1897 Hanus subjected Herbartianism to harsh criticism and by 1903 treated it as a "fad" although he continued to employ some of its terminology. Recalling William James's discussion of the subject, Hanus commented that apperception meant nothing more than the commonplace notion that we take things into our minds on the basis of what was there already. Hanus found Herbartianism too rigid, too plodding, and, in the last analysis, too reliant on mere opinion.[73]

The child-study movement similarly demanded attention. Organized principally by G. Stanley Hall in the eighties, child study derived from the evolutionary doctrine that human beings pass inevitably through distinct stages of development. Moreover those stages recapitulated the development of the race, a secondary theme in Herbartianism but central to child study. Hall felt that the solution to educational problems would come only after the study of these stages. A chaos of "research" then commenced, ranging from the adoration of children by "scientific" schoolmarms to sophisticated studies of what children actually did.

Hanus was generally unsympathetic toward child study although it was incorporated in his course by 1892. He said in 1896 that child study's emphasis on individual differences had produced some good results but that "the bad results are hasty generalization, investigations to discover commonplaces, tendency to regard child study as furnishing answers to all the problems of education." [74] In 1898 Eliot told Hanus that he agreed with him on the questionable value of child study and expressed gratitude that enthusiasm for it had cooled.[75]

What disturbed Hanus most was that so much of child study was "non-scientific" or "pseudo-scientific." In the former category he placed the mystical "ladies of Worcester" and added that a good many teachers should be chloroformed at the age of forty. In 1903 he saw the questionnaire method as an example of the "pseudo-scientific" approach by which experiments were carried on by mail. Hanus believed cross-examination of the witness was necessary, but even that method should be accepted with caution. "Scientific" child study could only mean the study of individual children and the establishment of standards. Hanus praised the Chicago school system for finding useful norms of height and weight for children and for establishing a correlation between "physical physique" and school progress. Child study, then, only received Hanus's blessing when it was "scientific." By 1903, at the latest, Hanus used the word "scientific" to connote empirical investigation.

No movement of the nineties was more influential than the effort of distinguished educational committees to arrive at uniform and rational curricular procedures. President Eliot's Committee of Ten on Secondary School Studies was the best known, but many others sought a similar influence. At a time when relevant printed materials on contemporary education were rare, the committee reports served as texts in college courses. Indeed, the first education seminary at Harvard was convened primarily to discuss the Report of the Committee of Ten. Unlike the Herbartian movment or the child-study movement, the committee movement did not seek to convince by a special methodology. Dealing more with questions of broad policy, the various committees sought by force of their own prestige to impress some order on the American educational scene. Hanus heartily agreed with the desirability of this latter function but lamented that the committees did not go far enough. He generally praised the Committee of Ten, for example, but he did criticize it for failing to "define what a good modern secondary education is . . . The report was lacking in an illuminating, well-defended educational doctrine." [76]

Educational confusion inevitably resulted from such procedures. If Herbartianism and child study were unreliable, "guidance" had to be obtained from some other source. Hanus emphasized in 1902, "*We have not yet organized our educational doctrine, we have only formulated it piecemeal; and we have not organized our educational experience—we have not gathered the fruits of experience as we went along.*" [77] The deeper problem, Hanus recognized, was the reliability and respectability of educational knowledge itself.

How can we expect the great body of teachers to accept the programme changes which we recommend in the only spirit that will render them valuable—the spirit of interested, or at least intelligent, coöperation—as long as we have no such definite guidance? How can we expect the community to be impressed with the wisdom of changes that run counter to all tradition? . . . and to display the patience that must be exercised before such changes can commend themselves alike to all concerned? And how can we expect the schools to be free from persistent, usually well-meant, but pernicious meddling . . . ? [78]

Only by more "rational experimentation" and by results "actually achieved and collectively presented" could education find respect, influence, and truth.

When Roentgen announced his discovery, other physicists confirmed *his* discovery . . . The principles of science once established in this way, no one can doubt or belittle them . . . So must it be in education, if we are ever to escape from the quagmire of random and isolated experimenting in which each worker seeks to find the way out for himself, disregarding the landmarks and sign-posts that have already been set up by his predecessors.[79]

In all of this discussion, Hanus made two basic points: a more "rational experimentation" was necessary to determine the "principles" of education, and a closer network of educational leaders was needed in order to publicize those principles and guide the lay public. Hence his proposal that each large school system should be an "educational experiment station." [80] Hence also his lament that the educational committees had failed to provide "guidance."

Neither Herbartianism, child study, nor the committees yielded principles that could be universally acknowledged as true. Hanus had perceived this fact and the resulting methodological chaos it had brought to education. His criticism of all the movements had rested on their denial of empiricism, although he often appeared to call more for agreement between educators than for rigorous examination of what they had agreed upon. Still, Joseph Mayer Rice singled out Hanus in 1902 as one educator who supported his own criticisms. And Hanus later recalled his intellectual indebtedness to Rice.

Hanus saw the problem of obtaining an empirical method for education. Yet he was untrained and unable to formulate strategies to find it. His own interests were increasingly directed toward problems of administration, where school reports could be studied and generalizations induced, rather than toward the more complex problems of human learning. At the same time that he praised the Chicago school-board experiments, he justified his treatment of arithmetic by reference to his own experiences and reflections. This attitude, wherein introspective and empirical explanations could exist side-by-side, would plague Hanus and the coming Progressive generation as they sought from modern science what deduction had been unable to provide.

The increasing concern for empirical methods was in part a response to the weighty problems that education was called upon to solve. As the nineties progressed Hanus's courses reflected not only the move toward empiricism but also the increasingly "social" nature of education. The school aimed for the fulfillment of the individual, but to be fulfilled, the individual must "work with his fellow men for the continued improvement and happiness of the race." [81] Hanus made the implications of that remark explicit in 1897:

Together with this improved adaptation of the school to the needs of each individual, there is also a growing recognition of the important social function which the school has to fulfil. This is as it should be. The life of any institution of modern society depends on its efficacy in promoting public as well as private ends . . . Now, the material and the spiritual interests of men change with advancing civilization; hence, the primary social function of all education, and, in particular, of secondary education, is to adapt every individual to the civilization of his time.[82]

In 1898 his course in "Principles" dealt formally with that theme for the first time.

The aims of education were rephrased as social, cultural, and vocational. Besides developing the individual for his own sake, education should teach him to aid the community. And though "general culture" was still the "most precious" of aims, it should not be over-intellectualized because most boys were not interested. Instead, cultural education should "connect school interests with life interests." In fact, "general culture means, primarily, the capacity to understand, appreciate, and react on the resources and problems of modern civilization." [83]

Both culture and vocation were seen in social terms. Hanus feared what might occur if boys left school without vocational training to fit them to society. They might become "the prey of the demagogue and the social agitator" if the proper vocations were not found. He quoted with approval Andrew D. White's belief that education should extend the area "not of the license urged on by anarchists and the utopias pictured by socialists, but of liberty as developed healthily and steadily in obedience to the lessons of history and constructive thought." The school should foster a "wise conservatism." [84]

That these words were published in the emotional wake of the election of 1896 is not happenstance. Social, cultural, and vocational aims merged in a common effort to preserve a community that seemed on the verge of exploding. It is unnecessary to belabor the fact that deep social tension ran through the nineties, or that unprecedented immigration had unsettling effects on the Boston community. As wise conservator, the school could be a stabilizing institution, an agency of social control. "In my opinion," Hanus said in 1898, "one of the safeguards of the stability and progress of a democratic society is the diffusion of common aims and common interests among all classes. The most valuable, and potentially the most efficient, instrument for diffusing these common aims and common interests . . . is the secondary school." [85]

Hanus did not conceive of the school as primarily a restrictive agency, dispensing a common culture to fend off the revolution. Its response to industrialism should be more positive. Hanus contended that schools had always responded to the problems and demands of society. That, after all, was the meaning of the history of education. But Hanus felt contemporary schools were not fulfilling their traditional function; they were "divorced from life" [86] when they should be preparing for life. The argument, which appeared in his course no later than 1901, eventually ran as follows:

The public-school system of the past, with its "literary" training, was the best education for young people in an age in which they could not escape acquaintance with community activities; an age in which life was simpler; in which each person, whether child or adult, had a part to play; an age in which the children participated in the occupations of their parents, had their own duties to perform about the household, on the farm, in the store, the shop, the factory; an age in which the children, therefore, knew precisely what the occupations are with which society keeps itself going, by actual participation in them . . . Modern social conditions have changed all that.[87]

In earlier times the book-oriented education offered by the school was useful since it was unavailable elswhere and served, for example, to train the clergy. But books were now available outside the school. Other experiences, however, were not. Thus the school must

assume a responsibility for developing in children a consciousness of the part which they will ultimately play in the world's work, and a desire to equip themselves for it. The education which the community life no longer affords must be provided in the school.

That is to say, it is the duty of the public school to provide the children with a general acquaintance with our means of production, distribution, and transportation, with our institutions, our social organizations and activities . . .[88]

The school must not only adjust students to industrialism. It must balance out the evils of industrialism as well. As such it could become an engine for social reform.[89] John Dewey, of course, had sketched these same themes in his influential *The School and Society*, published in 1899. Hanus used the book extensively in his course, though it is difficult to judge how much his thinking was shaped by it. Both men were responding to the same kinds of urban developments. Both men accepted industrialism, feared its consequences, but were confident that education could ameliorate these consequences. As such they embodied the values of the Progressive generation.

If Dewey viewed these new educational responsibilities as a philosopher, Hanus viewed them as an administrator. To the latter, the *organization* of education was always the principal subject of interest. He quickly realized that if schools were to be responsible to society, the curriculum must be made more flexible. He early championed modifying the elective system for high schools,[90] and more particularly expanding the number and range of subjects taught. Realizing that all subjects, in order to thrive, must be made respectable, he abandoned the practice of pointing out the "high" and "low" educational values of various subjects. He even came to speak of science as having substantial educational value.

Until 1905 Hanus hoped that education for all could take place in one "comprehensive" school. Yet the increasing importance of vocational education rendered that desire unrealistic.[91] As late as 1904 Hanus told his students that the best solutions to the problem of vocational education were tactful management of pupils, manual training, and commercial work. But in the winter of 1904–05, while on sabbatical leave in Munich, Hanus discovered the German plan of separate vocational continuation schools. Elementary-school graduates could learn the broad aspects of a particular trade while simultaneously holding a job in it.[92] On his return to America, Hanus took a leading role in the growing nationwide campaign for industrial schools. As chairman of the Massachusetts Commission on Industrial Education, he traveled across the state propagandizing the cause.

Hanus felt the central problem of American education was the vast body of adolescents who left school in approximately their fourteenth year. The high schools as then constituted were oriented toward those who would later attend college. Hence the curriculum had little meaning to the majority. But outside the school, these students could not enter the job market with any hope of success. Employers wanted skilled labor, but the adolescents had no skills. What was needed was "an education that teaches them the significance of a skilled vocation, and that helps them to explore their capacities and their tastes for the vocations in which skilled labor is needed." [93] Hanus proposed the creation of an industrial school system outside the public-school organization. It would offer a four-year technical education on the secondary-school level. "General culture" would not sufficiently promote social mobility.[94]

All these ideas were incorporated in Hanus's courses. Not only did "vocational education" become one more topic to teach, but the concern for social reform increased. Even by the turn of the century, for example, attention was given to such topics as play and school hygiene. And although the vocational-education movement did not reach its full flowering until after 1910, it was evident that different types of educators with different skills would be needed for the future.

Most important, however, was the modification of the social implications of Spencerianism. Education would not only "adapt" students to a society that already existed; it would, within the limits of "wise conservatism," help eliminate certain evils of that society. Hanus was no George Counts, daring the schools to build a new social order, but as the twentieth century commenced he was able to give his students a sense of education's critical relevance to the industrial age.

Two major developments had occurred in Hanus's thinking in the 1891–1906 period. First, educational aims came to include the social and the school came to be seen as an agency for reform. Second, Hanus undertook to search for an empirical method to solve educational problems. Both developments modified Hanus's teaching but neither came to dominate it. No new courses devoted to the new concerns were introduced. There was no major enlargement of function, either to explore the curricular responsibilities of the vocational-education movement or to establish conditions in which more rigorous educational experimentation might have taken place. This was perhaps natural, for few perceived such new demands before 1900. Yet even after 1906, indeed until Hanus's retirement as Chairman of the Division of Education in 1912, the Harvard curriculum changed but little.

It was true that a course called "The Education of the Individual—Study and Treatment of Both Unusual and Normal Types" was offered in 1907. It tried to cultivate a "physician's attitude" toward pupil defects and diseases, toward the blind, the dumb, the feeble-minded, and the incorrigible. In preceding years "individual differences" had been discussed, if at all, in terms of "truant schools and reformatory schools." [95] Yet the course lasted but five years and was taught by an historian with no special training in psychology.

Aside from this course, what curricular differentiation there was proceeded along traditional lines. Two courses in educational philosophy appeared, and the graduate course in "Organization and Administration" split into three courses designed to train superintendents and secondary principals, secondary teachers, and elementary principals.

If Harvard's curriculum did not emphasize the twin functions of reform and research in the 1906–1912 period, those of several other institutions did. Not by accident, moreover, did these institutions assume national leadership in professional education while Harvard fell behind. Most notably, they created separate courses in developmental and educational psychology which were often committed to "laboratory" experimentation. The progenitor of Teachers College offered two separate courses in educational psychology by 1891. Admittedly speculative in the first year, one course used as a text in 1892 William James's *Briefer Course*.[96] Judging from examination questions, no Harvard education course used any works of James until 1902, when Hanus asked students in his "Principles" course to "Explain James's conception of the child as a 'behaving organism.'" Probably the book used then was *Talks to Teachers* (1899). But the dramatic changes in educational psychology at Teachers College began with the coming of Thorndike in 1899. That year he taught child study and school hygiene, but by 1902 he taught a research seminar on "Genetic and Comparative Psychology." Four other courses in educational psychology were soon offered, and Columbia became the center for research in that field.[97]

The University of Michigan was perhaps more typical than the expanding colossus on Morningside Heights. There a course in "Genetic Psychology" for education students was taught in 1901. But the transition there came in 1906 when courses in "Educational Psychology," using Thorndike's

Principles of Teaching as a text, and "Psychology of Childhood and Adolescence" were introduced.[98] A course which dealt with occupations, the church, and the home, among other topics, appeared in 1898.[99]

In both institutions empirical psychology was introduced soon after the turn of the century. Special courses in hygiene and social phases of education attested to the growing importance of the reform impulse. At both Michigan and Teachers College changes were typically introduced by newcomers to education departments. Men who had begun teaching education in the eighties, like Michigan's B. A. Hinsdale, were often content to uphold the "liberalizing" studies of history and philosophy.[100]

Harvard also lagged behind fiscally. In 1912 its appropriations for education were $10,250 as compared with Columbia's $156,750, Chicago's $30,516, Missouri's $20,800, and California's $16,000.[101] Hanus realized Harvard's financial deficiencies and sought to remedy them, but he could not accomplish this alone. Large sums of money were needed to expand the curriculum. Until 1907 the division contained only two regular instructors; until 1913 only three. How could these few men carry out the multitudinous functions the education curriculum of the twentieth century was expected to perform? But Eliot, his successor, A. Lawrence Lowell, and the Corporation proved unresponsive to Hanus's many requests for funds.

Believing that latent faculty opposition hindered expansion, Hanus suggested to Eliot in 1903 that a separate graduate school of education be established. Eliot replied that the Corporation's wish was to "reduce the number of separate schools rather than to increase it." [102] Through the annual reports to the Board of Overseers Hanus and his supporters continually spoke of Harvard's declining educational influence. She lacked the constructive imagination necessary to realize the great opportunities and responsibilities in the field. In 1905 Hanus noted that Harvard could offer but nine courses in education while Teachers College listed seventy-nine and Chicago forty-three.[103]

The most pressing need was for additional faculty members since "the essential minimum of technical training for prospective teachers is not covered." In 1907 Hanus believed, significantly enough, the greatest needs to be an instructor in educational psychology and an instructor in school hygiene and physical training. Long-range necessities included an instructor in elementary education, a model school, scholarships, and a library. The University, however, made no effort to increase the size of the teaching staff. Its only concession was to pay the salaries of instructors who, in their early years, had been supported by outside sources. The apathy which had originally aided education was now an obstacle.

Teachers College had grown in its early years with little help from Columbia, and an analysis of the sources of its support throws much light on Harvard's difficulties. The key to Teachers College's growth lies in its origin: "the purpose of the early leaders was not . . . to promote or to found an academic institution but rather 'to promote a cause.' " The cause was the uplift of struggling urban workers, and the original supporters were New York philanthropists like Grace Dodge who had little interest in teacher-training *per se*, but great interest in the regenerative potentialities of manual training and industrial arts. These New Yorkers made Teachers College possible and continued to support it, however reluctantly, as the institution expanded its functions to embrace academic concerns. When the philanthropy tapered off in the late nineties, Teachers College possessed a building and a staff large enough to handle an enrollment which could take up, through tuition fees, the financial slack. But always the earlier reform spirit continued.[104]

The Harvard program was oriented toward academic teacher education from its inception in 1891. And since the program never existed apart from the University, no Boston group could look upon it as its own. There is, moreover, no evidence that Hanus sought the support of Boston philanthropists in the nineties. In those years professional education at Harvard and urban social reform had little in common. The reformers themselves saw no connection between "schooling" and their concerns.[105] In addition, the program was rather invisible until education became a separate division after 1906. Thereafter it acquired its own Overseers' Visiting Committee and thus a forum for Hanus's promotions. Many of the visitors were philanthropists who later gave crucial aid to the division.

Lacking the reform base which enabled Teachers College to prosper in the eighties and nineties, Harvard's program foundered. It came to prosper only when bonds of common purpose united it and Boston reform movements. But when that development finally took place, Teachers College, along with Chicago, Stanford, and other universities, were already the leading centers for the study of education in America.

Until 1897 Hanus labored alone. Although he continually asked Eliot for assistance, the first additional instructor was supported by a group of Boston ladies led by Miss Marion C. Jackson. Their object was not to expand the course offerings but to repeat them for the benefit of Radcliffe students,[106] but the move effectively freed Hanus from part of his teaching load. More important, it enabled practice teaching to be established on a firm footing. It had been necessary to promise local teachers free admission to Harvard education courses in order to obtain visiting rights in their classrooms for Hanus's students. But since most of the teachers were women and hence ineligible to sit in Harvard classrooms, offering courses at Radcliffe was a strategic move as well as an expression of concern for the training of women teachers.[107] George H. Locke received Miss Jackson's benefactions but after two years left for the University of Chicago. Arthur O. Norton, a student of Hanus's, who had received his B.S., A.B., and A.M. from Harvard, replaced Locke and remained until 1912.

But the most significant appointment, and the only other until 1912, was that of Henry Wyman Holmes in 1907, for Holmes's position was made possible by Boston social reformers who saw him as a prophet for their cause. Hanus first met Mr. and Mrs. Joseph Lee in 1900 when, at Royce's suggestion, he appealed to them for funds to begin an educational library.[108] They responded favorably and the acquaintanceship ripened. A Harvard alumnus, Lee was also a leading reformer and philanthropist. One account of him concluded that "in the late nineteenth and early twentieth centuries Lee had represented the quintessence of the creative social conscience of New England." [109] At once a Brahmin, a Unitarian, a Democrat, a supporter of birth control, and an immigrant restrictor, Lee saved most of his energies for helping underprivileged youth to help themselves. He became best known as the "father of American playgrounds." Lee and Hanus shared few common interests during the nineties but, in 1907, one year after Hanus's appointment as Chairman of the Massachusetts Commission on Industrial Education, the Lees offered to support a new instructor in education for five years.[110]

Their object, especially that of Mrs. Lee, was to locate strategically a disciple of Friedrich Froebel, German mystic and the father of the kindergarten.[111] Consequently they stipulated that the instructor offer a course on Froebel's philosophy. Although Hanus realized that much of Froebel's philosophy was then in disrepute, he saw the offer as an opportunity to develop a program for future elementary-school principals. A Harvard graduate (A.B. 1903, A.M. 1904) and former student of Hanus's, Holmes was interested primarily in elementary-school administration. Neither Holmes nor Norton specialized in "research" or "reform." Their own interests, together with the circumstances of their coming, did not portend new departures for the curriculum.

Yet between 1907 and 1912 the ties deepened between Boston social reform and noncurricular aspects of the Harvard education program. The Lees established in 1907 the South End House Fellowship to provide $600 for research in out-of-school educational opportunities for wage earners. The fellowship was jointly administered by the Division of Education, the Social Education Club, and the South End House.[112] A year later the Vocation Bureau of Boston was founded, the first of its kind, and Hanus soon became its director. Lee became a member of the Overseers' Committee to Visit the Division of Education, and other wealthy reformers, like James J. Storrow, began to show interest. The origins of Storrow's interests were typical. A prominent banker, he had been associated with the Public School Association of Boston, a reform group, since its establishment in 1894. In 1901 he was elected to the Boston School Committee and, in an unfamiliar role, consulted Hanus for advice. He thereafter served for many years as sympathetic leader of the Overseers' Committee for Education.

Between 1912 and 1920 the benefactions of the philanthropists poured in and the curriculum exploded. The twin impulses of research and reform were embodied unmistakably in special courses with newly hired experts to teach them. We cannot examine these courses in detail, but it is necessary to sketch the magnitude of their impact on the curriculum.

A total of twelve education courses was offered in 1912. By 1916–17, the last school year before America's entry into the First World War, twenty-six courses were given and five more listed in the catalogue. New courses in educational psychology, educational experimentation, and educational measurement were introduced, and old courses, like Hanus's seminary in administration, were relabeled as "quantitative." Holmes, who had become the division's chairman in 1912, told the Overseers in 1914:

Questions of individual learning must be studied in the laboratory; questions of class-room procedure must be studied experimentally in the school itself; questions of organization and administration must be studied statistically from school records. In the effort to meet these requirements the Division of Education maintains a laboratory of educational psychology in Emerson Hall, and under the Joseph Lee Foundation for Research in Education it cooperates with the City of Newton in using the school system of that city as a laboratory in which experiments and statistical studies are carried on . . .

The three formal "aims" of the education curriculum, as printed in the official register, had not changed since 1898. But a fourth aim was added in 1913: "To afford opportunity for original investigation and experiment in Education and for constructive contributions to educational theory and practice." Though Hanus and Holmes tried their hand at some elementary statistical studies and though creative scholarship was produced by such newcomers as Alexander Inglis, the major responsibility for this emphasis on empirical research fell to Walter F. Dearborn. Dearborn was brought to Harvard in 1912 from the University of Chicago after a concerted effort to obtain Thorndike failed at the last moment.[113] Dearborn, the scientist, replaced Norton, the historian, whom President Lowell declined to reappoint. Dearborn's educational background was strikingly dissimilar to that of Hanus, Holmes, or Norton. He had not attended Harvard but had studied extensively in Germany and possessed both the Ph.D. and the M.D. degrees. Trained as an experimental scientist, he was well prepared to direct research in educational psychology.

Reform followed research into the curriculum under the benevolent guidance of men like Lee. Speaking of the new pedagogical developments, the Boston *Evening Transcript* noted fittingly in 1916: "In Harvard's choice of new courses for 1916–17, the impressive point is the close relation they bear to society's own choice of new courses." [114] New departures in industrial education had created a demand for educators with appropriate skills, and Harvard devised new courses to supply them: school hygiene, the administration and conduct of play and recreation, the philosophy of play, and vocational guidance. Lee himself taught a course in play. In 1917 the Vocation Bureau of Boston became an agency of the Division of Education and was renamed the Bureau of Vocational Guidance. Under the leadership of John M. Brewer, another new appointee, the Bureau offered courses on vocational subjects in the Boston area, carried on research, and counseled labor and business. [115]

Hanus himself was not essential to these changes. Increasingly in the years after relinquishing the division chairmanship, he took on the role of elder statesman. In his special field of administration, he tried to adapt his thinking to the empirical and quantitative concerns of the day. He had said in 1910, "Individual opinion and 'authority' still tend to be inculcated when the emphasis should be on methods of securing facts and on experimentally proving or disproving alleged principles of procedure." This seemed a categorical rejection of the speculative tradition; but, as earlier, it was one thing for Hanus to espouse such thoughts, another for him to devise techniques to carry them out. This continual dilemma was illustrated by his notable survey of New York City's schools in 1911–12.

The New York Board of Estimate had appointed a Committee on School Inquiry in 1911. The latter engaged many scholars to conduct the investigation and appointed Hanus to direct it. Following a year of study, preliminary reports began to appear. Several of these, including that of Hanus himself, were quickly subjected to intensive and bitter criticism. Much of this criticism was politically motivated as Hanus repeatedly emphasized in later years, for his largely negative judgment on New York's schools naturally offended the men who ran them. But the opposition went deeper than that and challenged the methodology of the survey itself.

Was the report, asked one critic, an example of expert *investigation* or merely of expert *opinion?* Did the New York Committee on School Inquiry hire Hanus to discover and analyze the salient facts about the schools or to judge them according to his own personal ideas of what a good system should look like? "There are many men in the United States who are able to give expert opinion upon phases of education, but an opinion proves nothing. You can never convict a man on expert opinion . . . It is never either proof or demonstration." Thus, critics alleged, the results of the survey told more about those who conducted it than about the schools themselves. Had either G. Stanley Hall, Hugo Münsterberg, or John Dewey been in charge, different standards would have prevailed and different results obtained.[116]

The debate, then, turned on the validity of the standards employed by Hanus and his associates. Was it legitimate to establish "purely theoretical ideals," not tested by wide and successful experiment, as standards by which to judge New York? Were many of those ideals, such as Hanus's plan to allow children to select their program of study after the sixth year, appropriate in a great city whose school population was largely foreign born? [117] In addition, Hanus was chastised for the imprecise questionnaire method he utilized and for his uncritical use of the Courtis Arithmetic Test, which though presumably measuring mathematical accomplishment, emphasized speed rather than accuracy.[118]

Hanus's final report admitted that "there are very few established standards whereby the efficiency of educational activities may be measured, and that accepted methods of studying such activities are, for the most part, yet to be found. The science of education is, as yet, in its beginnings. We have, however, used such standards as are available . . ."[119] But these standards, largely Hanus's observations of "progressive" schools, were not accepted by powerful sections of the New York educational world. Even in his grandest enterprise Hanus could not authoritatively apply the empirical and experimental methodology to the analysis of schools themselves. Indeed, considering his background of "practical" experience and observation, it is questionable whether Hanus ever felt at home with more clinical procedures. Almost plaintively he wrote Holmes in 1912: "I should be sorry if most of Dearborn's work in educational psychology should turn out to be laboratory psychology . . ."[120]

The establishment of education as a field of study at Harvard was not an inevitable outgrowth of the national emergence of pedagogy at the university level. It was an unexpected, somewhat accidental development; an unplanned response to local pressures; a tentative and unenthusiastic commitment to a limited form of teacher-training in which formal pedagogy played a minor and ancillary role. Eliot later recalled that its permanence was in doubt throughout the nineties and was assured only when Hanus received tenure in 1901.[121]

By 1912 the character of the education curriculum had become clear. The Faculty of Arts and Sciences had abdicated, because of apathy and the pressures of more congenial responsibilities, its early, central role in teacher education. Eliot had given neither unqualified support nor consistent enmity to education; thus it emerged without the guiding hand of the president. Hanus became the central influence in the formative years. Aided by the elective system, a fertile environment for curricular entrepreneurs, Hanus gradually broadened and deepened the content of the new field. From an initial concern with the educational implications of traditional subjects such as philosophy and history, Hanus's curriculum came to encompass both the committed temper of social reform and the more detached style of research.

Education had survived and had prospered. But it had not become a "discipline," and it became more difficult to speak of common educational "principles" when the curriculum became increasingly specialized. Education had become many pursuits, not a single one. But the Harvard program did not command the respect enjoyed by programs at several other universities. And the earlier suspicions of the Faculty of Arts and Sciences had not abated. President Lowell, moreover, proved less hospitable to the division than Eliot.

Hanus was not chairman of the division during the years of rapid expansion from 1912 to 1920. He had trained few scholars, had left no creative scholarship to influence those who followed, had taught none of the new courses on "research" and "reform," and had not been very successful in attracting philanthropy to the division. Had his earlier, incomplete forays into these subject areas accelerated the development of the expanded curriculum? Or were the new concerns imported largely from without by men such as Dearborn and Inglis?

Yet to judge Hanus as a scholar or scientist would be to miss much of the point of his career and his generation. He, like Ellwood Cubberley, Paul Monroe, and William Heard

Kilpatrick, had sought to build a discipline of education.[122]
But his background, like that of most of the others, was woe-
fully inadequate to the task. Enthusiasm and confidence
could not make up for what he lacked in technical training. He had the temperament of the promoter, the entrepre-
neur, the "doer." A colleague once called him the leading
representative of "thorough examination and careful interpretation of tendencies in actual school work."[123] He
came, increasingly, to look on "actual school work" from the
perspective of the administrator. Administration was well
suited to Hanus's personality. It served as a context for the
discussion of "aims and values" in an operative setting; it
made good use of the extensive knowledge of schools and
schoolmen which he had accumulated through observation
over the years; it enabled him to think inductively but not
experimentally. He could, as a result, gather facts from
school reports and induce from them rules of good practice.
To that extent he was empirical. But such an elementary no
tion of induction and educational "science" never touched
the challenging and complicated psychological experiments
that men like Dearborn defined as "science."

Thus Hanus neither developed nor systematically sought a
method of discovering educational principles subject to experimental verification. As an "influential" he could argue,
promote, plead. Often he was listened to, as when Massachusetts established the Commission on Industrial Education. But if his conclusions were challenged as "mere opin
ion," as they were in New York, there was little further he
could say. Experimental science, not ethical judgments or
commonsense imperatives, was in the academic saddle in the
early twentieth century. Hanus was unable to bridge completely the gap between speculative, introspective, deductive
educational science, on the one hand, and empirical, inductive, experimental educational science on the other. Yet his

attempt did destroy much of the confidence in the deductive tradition; and most of the problems he failed to solve are still as troubling today.

Perhaps a larger department early in the century might have enabled Harvard to overtake Columbia, Chicago, or Stanford. Hanus, aware of both his limitations and the rapidly expanding domain of education, incessantly argued for more specialized faculty members. Yet neither Eliot nor Lowell saw fit to assist the struggling division. Eliot called Teachers College an "exaggerated and undesirable standard," [124] while Lowell was never convinced that courses in education were necessary at all. Both seemed to make support contingent on the prior development of the field to the level of academic respectability. A perfected subject was the prerequisite for their support, but education could not be developed without the resources such support might provide. The subject matter did not impress Lowell or Eliot, support did not come, and other institutions with less critical standards stepped in to meet the growing demand. Harvard, like other liberal arts institutions, rapidly lost influence in American public education during the early twentieth century. For Harvard to influence the schools, her presidents would have had to risk commitment to education despite, or perhaps because of, its contemporary limitations as a field of study. Hanus never benefited from such leadership, which would only come at a later time and from other men.

NOTES AND REFERENCES

ANNOTATION PROCEDURES

The endnotes of this volume provide full citation for all material that can be consulted outside the Harvard University Archives.

For archival material, used extensively in this volume, the following annotation policies were adopted in the interest of reducing the number of endnotes:

(1) In general, material from the Harvard Archives that is unavailable in other depositories is identified in the text and is *not* referred to in the endnotes.

(2) Endnote references to archival material occur only: (a) when the nature and approximate date of the source are not clear from the text; (b) when the material cited emanates from a governing board of Harvard University; (c) when personal correspondence is cited.

(3) Fully annotated copies of this volume have been deposited in the Harvard Archives.

Contributors to a volume such as this of necessity consult the same primary sources. It seems appropriate, therefore, as a prelude to the endnotes, to present a brief checklist of archival sources.

A SELECTIVE CHECKLIST OF
HARVARD ARCHIVAL MATERIAL

OFFICIAL

(Note: Harvard University is subject to the jurisdiction of two governing boards: The Board of Overseers (1637) currently composed of 30 members, elected in groups of five, annually, for a term of six years, by the alumni of the University; and The Corporation (1650), a self-perpetuating body composed of the President, Treasurer, and five Fellows.)

1) Corporation Record: Minutes of the meetings of the President and Fellows. These are for the most part a record of actions taken and are useful in establishing the exact form and time of the action, but they are not a record of debate. The Corporation Record is complete.

2) Overseers' Record: Actions of the President and Fellows are subject to approval by the Board of Overseers; the Record, also complete, is, like the record of the meetings of the Corporation, minutes of meetings of the Board of Overseers, and useful chiefly for the same purpose although its record of debate is sometimes fuller.

3) Overseers' Reports: The Overseers are empowered to visit the various departments, graduate and professional schools, and other operations of the University. These numerous visiting committees, each chaired by a member of the Board of Overseers, report to the Board at regular intervals. These reports, sometimes in manuscript, sometimes (particularly if the subject were controversial and of wide interest) printed, constitute a very significant source of information on curricular change.

4) Harvard College Papers: Papers collected, mounted, and bound, pursuant to a Corporation vote of 6 February 1850, chronologically arranged, form the basis of this collection. After 1869, the file is continued in the Eliot Papers, the designation which will be used, when appropriate, below. The Eliot Papers, 1869–1909, are largely in transfer boxes, the first numbered 66. Correspondence is filed chronologically through 1893, numerically from

1893 to 1903, and alphabetically from 1903 to 1909. The latter two periods are indexed by correspondent.

5) Publications of the University: These fall into the following categories:

(a) Annual Report of the President and Treasurer. The file is complete from 1825.

(b) Annual Catalogue. The file is complete from 1819.

(c) Departmental announcements.

Beginning in 1901 these were grouped under the title of University Publications, New Series, and in 1904 under the title of The Official Register.

6) Faculty sources:

(a) The Record (minutes of meetings) begins in 1725.

(b) Reports and Papers.

(c) Papers of the Dean of the Faculty of Arts and Sciences (which supersedes the office of the Dean of the Faculty) constitute an invaluable source for later Harvard history but are of limited use in the Eliot period because of their perfunctory nature.

UNOFFICIAL

Harvard University Archives maintains an unequalled collection of unofficial source material. This embraces a virtually complete file of examinations and student publications; a somewhat more spotty file of student notes, student themes, course syllabi, and reading lists; faculty papers which include correspondence, lecture notes, and manuscripts. The historian will also find useful a complete file of printed class reports, comprising autobiographical data submitted by members of the class and class statistics, which are issued at regular intervals by the respective class secretaries.

NOTES

THE ECONOMISTS STUDY SOCIETY:
SOCIOLOGY AT HARVARD, 1891–1902

This study of the development of sociology at Harvard has been done from the inside out, in that it started with documents in the Harvard College Archives relating to academic decisions and course content and moved from them to the intellectual and biographical background of the protagonists, the teachers, and only then and only briefly did it venture into the realm of general intellectual history, the history of education, and the histories of sociology and economics. Two factors dictated this method: first, Harvard's Social Ethics Department and its Economics Department offered separately administered courses in sociology whereas most American universities fused the ethical and economic interests into a single sociology curriculum; and second, the paucity of general works of value on the development of sociology in American thought or in the American university made it impossible to construct from the secondary works a conceptual framework in which to fit the developments at Harvard.

The study, then, started with an examination of the course descriptions in the Harvard Catalogues, in the annual bulletins of the Division of History, Government, and Economics, and in course syllabi preserved in the Archives. These various descriptions served to identify much of the thematic content of the courses and some of their specific subject matter. Unfortunately, since the seemingly precise terminology of sociological jargon identifies rather vague and generalized concepts, many of the course descriptions seem to fit courses of the present day as well as they fit those of the nineties. Thus, my method has been to read the description and then, from other documents when possible (such as student notebooks, or teachers' lecture notes) but more often from published works of the lecturer, to identify the specific nature of the subject matter that the jargon was naming. Examination questions also served to identify the subject matter of courses, although the researcher must, if he is not to be misled, take care not to construe the questions as calling for answers that depend upon more modern academic interpretation. Examinations also indicate which aspects of the course the instructor wanted to stress, and they, like the course descriptions, can lead to specific points or themes found in the instructor's published work and thus prove that those points or themes were included in the courses.

Most valuable for understanding the intellectual background of this period and of the development of sociology at Harvard were works by and about the faculty at Harvard in this period. For more general background, the most fruitful source has been the debates and discussions lodged in articles, notes, and reviews published in the scholarly journals of the period. The *Quarterly Journal of Economics* (1886–1905), *Journal of Political Economy* (1892–1905), *Publications of the American Economic Association* (1886–1905), and *Economic Journal* (1890–1905) provided ample insight into the terms and heat of the debate between the deductive and the inductive schools. I found Joseph Dorfman, *The Economic Mind in American Civilization, 1865–1918*, III (New York, 1949); Sidney Fine, *Laissez Faire and the General Welfare State: A Study of Conflict in American Thought, 1865–1901* (Ann Arbor, Mich., 1956); and Joseph A. Schumpeter, *History of Economic Analysis*, ed. Elizabeth Boody Schumpeter (New York, 1954) most useful as references to the background of economic thought. However, none of them clarifies the relations of sociology to economic thought.

This study concerns itself with the impact of European thought upon American academic sociology, and the journals seem to be the only place where that impact may be examined. For much of the background on European social thought in this period, I am indebted to H. Stuart Hughes, *Consciousness and Society: The Reorientation of European Social Thought, 1890–1930* (New York, 1958). Both books consulted on the history of American sociology (Howard W. Odum, *American Sociology: The Story of Sociology in the United States through 1950*, New York, 1951; and L. L. and Jessie Bernard, *Origins of American Sociology: The Social Science Movement in the United States*, New York, 1943), by arbitrarily limiting their investigations to those phenomena which bore the title sociology or social science, disregard the sociological impulses within academic economics. Neither book examines any European influences aside from those of Spencer and Freud. And as the documents in the Harvard Archives show, it was the variety of ideas gathered from England, France, Germany, and Austria and not the ideas of a single European thinker nor those of American thinkers working *in vacuo* which formed the pattern of social science instruction at Harvard.

1. See, for example, the "Discussion" of Albion W. Small's paper, "The Relation of Sociology to Economics," read at the Seventh Annual Meeting of the American Economic Association, December 28, 1894. Discussion by Simon N. Patten, Franklin H. Giddings, Lester F. Ward, and William James Ashley. Abstracts in *Publications of the American Economic Association* 10:106–117 (March 1895).

2. College Record, XI, p. 268 (January 6, 1871), p. 271 (February

10, 1871), Harvard University Archives (hereafter HUA); Overseers' Reports, Miscellaneous Series, III, March 8, 1871, HUA.

3. College Record, XI, pp. 71–72 (May 7, 1868), HUA; Frank William Taussig, "Economics, 1871–1929," in *The Development of Harvard University Since the Inauguration of President Eliot, 1869–1929*, ed. Samuel Eliot Morison (Cambridge, Mass.: Harvard University Press, 1930), pp. 187–188.

4. Ephraim W. Gurney to Charles W. Eliot, August 30, 1869, Eliot Papers, HUA; Taussig, "Economics, 1871–1929," p. 188; Joseph Dorfman, *The Economic Mind in American Civilization, 1865–1918*, III (New York: The Viking Press, 1949), 63–65; Henry James, *Charles W. Eliot: President of Harvard University, 1869–1909* (Boston: Houghton Mifflin Co., 1930), I, 254; II, 121–122. For biographical information on Dunbar, see Frank William Taussig, "Introduction," in *Economic Essays by Charles Franklin Dunbar*, ed. O. M. W. Sprague (New York: The Macmillan Co., 1904); Davis R. Dewey in *DAB*, vol. V, s.v. "Dunbar, Charles Franklin."

5. Charles Franklin Dunbar, "Economic Science in America," *North American Review* 122: 153–154 (January 1876).

6. Charles Franklin Dunbar, "The Academic Study of Political Economy," *Quarterly Journal of Economics* 5:398–399 (July 1891).

7. *Ibid.*, p. 409.

8. *Ibid.*, p. 411. On the problem of the inapplicability of scientific economics to legislation, see [Charles Franklin Dunbar], Review of *Some Leading Principles of Political Economy newly expounded. By J. E. Cairnes*, New York, 1874, *North American Review* 120:214–216 (January 1875).

9. Charles Franklin Dunbar, "The Reaction in Political Economy," *Quarterly Journal of Economics* 1:12–13 (October 1886).

10. Dunbar, "The Academic Study of Political Economy," p. 402.

11. J. Laurence Laughlin, *The Study of Political Economy: Hints to Students and Teachers* (New York, 1885), pp. 53–54.

12. Alfred Bornemann, *J. Laurence Laughlin: Chapters in the Career of an Economist* (Washington, D.C.: American Council of Public Affairs, 1940), p. 3.

13. *Ibid.*, p. 11; Dorfman, *The Economic Mind*, III, 272.

14. Bornemann, *Laughlin*, p. 12; J. Laurence Laughlin, ed. *Principles of Political Economy, by John Stuart Mill* (New York, 1884), pp. iii–iv.

15. Bornemann, *Laughlin*, pp. 3, 15.

16. Alfred Bornemann in *DAB*, vol. XXI, Supplement One, s.v. "Laughlin, J. Laurence"; Dorfman, *The Economic Mind*, III, 271–274.

17. See, for example, Dunbar, "The Academic Study of Political

Economy," p. 398; Laughlin, *The Study of Political Economy*, ch. iii.
18. Dunbar, "The Reaction in Political Economy," p. 7.
19. *Ibid.*, pp. 25–26.
20. Taussig, "Introduction," in *Economic Essays*, pp. xi, xvi.
21. Dunbar, "The Academic Study of Political Economy," *passim*.
22. *Ibid.*, p. 401.
23. Harvard College Reports, 1882–83, pp. 24–25; Treasurer's Report in Harvard College Reports, 1882–83, p. 11; Charles W. Eliot to Henry Lee, March 5, 1883, E. L. Hooper to Charles W. Eliot, May 19, 1883, Charles Franklin Dunbar to Charles W. Eliot, March 12, April 25, and May 3, 1883, Charles W. Eliot to J. Laurence Laughlin, November 15, 1887, letterpress copy, all in Eliot Papers, HUA; Dorfman, *The Economic Mind*, III, 271. Compare explanation of Laughlin's leaving Harvard in Bornemann, *Laughlin*, p. 15.
24. Barbara Miller Solomon in *DAB*, vol. XXII, Supplement Two, s.v. "Brooks, John Graham."
25. John Graham Brooks, *The Social Unrest: Studies in Labor and Socialist Movements* (New York: The Macmillan Co., 1903), p. 122.
26. Solomon, "Brooks."
27. Brooks, *The Social Unrest*, p. 4.
28. *Ibid.*, *passim*.
29. Richard T. Ely, "Report of the Organization of the American Economic Association," *Publications of the American Economic Association* 1:6–7 (March 1886).
30. Frank L. Tolman, "The Study of Sociology in Institutions of Learning in the United States: A Report of an Investigation Undertaken by the Graduate Sociological League of the University of Chicago," in four parts, *American Journal of Sociology* 7:797–838 (May 1902), 8:85–121, 251–272, 531–558 (July, September, January 1902–03); L. L. Bernard, "The Teaching of Sociology in the United States," *ibid.*, 15:164–213 (September 1909).
31. *Endowment Funds of Harvard University, June 30,1947* (Cambridge, Mass.: Harvard University Press, 1948), p. 139; Frederick T. Persons in *DAB*, vol. XIV, s.v. "Paine, Robert Treat."
32. For biographical data on Edward Cummings, see Jeffrey R. Brackett in *DAB*, vol. IV, s.v. "Cummings, Edward"; e[dward] e[stlin] cummings, *i: six non-lectures* (Cambridge, Mass.: Harvard University Press, 1953), non-lectures one and two.
33. In all quotations from student lecture notes, I have changed the manuscripts' lower case letters to capitals at the beginning of sentences, inserted in the main text words originally written above or alongside the text, and written out all obvious abbreviations.
34. Richard T. Ely, *Ground Under Our Feet: An Autobiography* (New York: The Macmillan Co., 1938), pp. 154–155.

35. For a discussion of European social thought in this period see H. Stuart Hughes, *Consciousness and Society: The Reorientation of European Social Thought, 1890–1930* (New York: Alfred A. Knopf, Inc., 1958), esp. chs. i, ii, iv, and viii.

36. Edward Cummings, "A Collectivist Philosophy of Trade Unionism," *Quarterly Journal of Economics* 13:166 (January 1899).

37. Harry Elmer Barnes in *Encyclopedia of the Social Sciences*, vol. IX, s.v. "LeBon, Gustave."

38. See Lucius Moody Bristol, *Social Adaptation: A Study in the Development of the Doctrine of Adaptation as a Theory of Social Progress* (Cambridge, Mass.: Harvard University Press, 1915), pp. 185–192; Harry Elmer Barnes, "The Philosophy of the State in the Writings of Gabriel Tarde," *Philosophical Review* 28:248–279 (May 1919); Michael M. Davis, Jr., *Psychological Interpretations of Society*, Columbia University Studies in History, Economics and Public Law, XXXIII, no. 2 (New York: Columbia University Press, 1909), ch. vi.

39. Edward Cummings, "Charity and Progress" [address delivered at The National Conference of Unitarian and Other Christian Churches, Saratoga, N.Y., September 1897], *Quarterly Journal of Economics* 12:39–41 (October 1897).

40. Edward Cummings, "A Collectivist Philosophy of Trade Unionism," p. 153.

41. Edward Cummings, "University Settlements," *Quarterly Journal of Economics* 6:279 (April 1892).

42. *Ibid.*, p. 277.

43. Edward Cummings, "Social Economy at the Paris Exposition," *Quarterly Journal of Economics* 4:216 (January 1890).

44. The books were: American, Elgin Ralston Lowell Gould, *The Social Conditions of Labor* (1893) and Frederic J. Stimson, *Labor in Its Relation to Law* (1895); German, A. E. F. Schäffle, *The Theory and Policy of Labour Protection* (tr. 1893); United Kingdom, Charles Booth, *Life and Labour of the People in London* (1889–1902), L. T. Hobhouse, *The Labour Movement* (2nd ed., 1897), William H. Mallock, *Classes and Masses: or, Wealth, Wages, and Welfare in the United Kingdom* (1896), David F. Schloss, *Methods of Industrial Remuneration* (1892), John Alfred Spender, *The State and Pensions in Old Age* (1892), Thomas George Spyers, *The Labour Question: An Epitome of the Evidence and the Report of the Royal Commission on Labour* (1894), and Beatrice Potter [Webb], *The Cooperative Movement in Great Britain* (1891).

45. See, for example, Francis Greenwood Peabody, *The Religious Education of an American Citizen* (New York: The Macmillan Co., 1917), pp. 64–65, 72–73.

46. See, for example, Thomas Nixon Carver, "Sociology," in A

Guide to Reading in Social Ethics and Allied Subjects: Lists of Books and Articles Selected and Described for the Use of General Readers, Publications of the Department of Social Ethics in Harvard University, no. 3 (Cambridge, Mass.: Harvard University, 1910), pp. 29–31; Thomas Nixon Carver, The Essential Factors of Social Evolution (Cambridge, Mass.: Harvard University Press, 1935), esp. pp. 102–108.

47. Charles W. Eliot to Edward Cummings, March 22, 1898 and April 10, 1900, Henry Lee Higginson to Charles W. Eliot, January 6, 1900, Eliot Papers, HUA.

48. John Cummings, "Ethnic Factors and the Movement of Population," Quarterly Journal of Economics 14:171–211 (February 1900); cf. reply by William Z. Ripley, ibid., 14:426–428 (May 1900).

49. John Cummings, "Ethnic Factors," pp. 200–201.

50. Ibid., pp. 209–210.

51. Ibid., p. 211.

52. Ely, Ground Under Our Feet, p. 151.

53. William James Ashley, What Is Political Science? An Inaugural Lecture [at the University of Toronto, November 9, 1888], pamphlet (Toronto, 1888), pp. 10–11.

54. Ibid., pp. 17, 14.

55. Ibid., pp. 17–18.

56. Ibid., p. 19.

57. Ibid., p. 21.

58. William James Ashley, "On the Study of Economic History" [inaugural address at Harvard University, January 4, 1893], Quarterly Journal of Economics 7:117–118 (January 1893).

59. William James Ashley to Margaret Hill, 1886, quoted in Anne Ashley, William James Ashley: A Life (London: P. S. King and Son, Ltd., 1932), p. 35.

60. Frank William Taussig, "A Suggested Rearrangement of Economic Study," Quarterly Journal of Economics 2:230 (January 1888).

61. Ashley, What Is Political Science? p. 19.

62. Ashley, "Study of Economic History," p. 132.

63. William James Ashley, "The Present Position of Political Economy," Economic Journal 17:482 (December 1907); see also William James Ashley, Review of Arnold Toynbee, by F. C. Montague, Baltimore, 1889, Political Science Quarterly 4:532–533 (September 1889).

64. William James Ashley to Margaret Hill, 1886, quoted in Anne Ashley, Ashley, p. 36.

65. Anne Ashley, Ashley, p. 36.

66. William James Ashley, "Review of Stubb's Village Politics," Labour Standard, I (1881), quoted in Anne Ashley, Ashley, p. 55.

67. Anne Ashley, *Ashley*, pp. 70–80, 135–136.

68. W. J. Ashley, "The Present Position of Political Economy," p. 487.

69. A. W. Coats, "The First Two Decades of the American Economic Association," *American Economic Review* 50:555–559 (September 1960); Ely, *Ground Under Our Feet*, p. 163; Constitution, By-Laws and Resolutions of the American Economic Association, in Ely, "Report of the Organization," pp. 34–35.

70. Coats, "The First Two Decades," pp. 563–564, notes 15–16; Francis A. Walker to Edwin A. Seligman, September 24, [1887?], John Bates Clark to Edwin A. Seligman, April 25, 1887, Henry Carter Adams to Edwin A. Seligman, April 27, 1887, all in "The Seligman Correspondence, I & II," ed. Joseph Dorfman, *Political Science Quarterly* 56:108–111, 271 (March and June 1941).

71. Frank William Taussig to Edwin A. Seligman, October 14, 1890, in "Seligman Correspondence, I," p. 122. The officers in 1890 were Francis A. Walker, president, and Ely, secretary.

72. See, for example, Charles Franklin Dunbar, "The Career of Francis Amasa Walker," *Quarterly Journal of Economics* 11:445 (July 1897); note also the reaction to Dunbar's election in J. Laurence Laughlin, "The Study of Political Economy in the United States," *Journal of Political Economy* 1:11 (December 1892).

73. Coats, "The First Two Decades," pp. 560–563.

74. See, for example, John Bates Clark to Edwin A. Seligman, April 25, 1887, and Richard T. Ely to Edwin A. Seligman, June 23, 1885, in "Seligman Correspondence, I & II," pp. 110–111, 281.

75. Charles Franklin Dunbar to Charles W. Eliot, September 17, 1889, March 25, April 16, and July 19, 1890, Edwin A. Seligman to Charles W. Eliot, January 7, 1890, Edmund J. James to Charles W. Eliot, May 6, 1890, all in Eliot Papers, HUA.

76. William James Ashley to Edwin A. Seligman, April 8, 1903, in "The Seligman Correspondence, IV," ed. Joseph Dorfman, *Political Science Quarterly* 56:587 (December 1941); for some account of some of the ideas appearing in the nineties that contributed to the forming of the Business School, see Wallace B. Donham and Esty Foster, "The Graduate School of Business Administration, 1908–1929," in *The Development of Harvard University*, pp. 533–534.

77. The report of the Committee is fully quoted, along with the minority report, in "Political Economy as Taught at Harvard," *American Economist* 5:91 (February 7, 1890).

78. Charles Franklin Dunbar to Charles W. Eliot, March 25, 1890, Eliot Papers, HUA.

79. Charles Francis Adams to Charles W. Eliot, November 16, 1889, Eliot Papers, HUA.

80. On Ashley's views on protection and their peculiar relation to

his views on reform, see the chapter on Ashley in Bernard Semmel, *Imperialism and Social Reform: English Social-Imperial Thought, 1895–1914, Studies in Society*, ed. Ruth and David Glass (Cambridge, Mass.: Harvard University Press, 1960), esp. pp. 207–212.

81. W. J. Ashley, "Study of Economic History," pp. 135–136, 121, 131.

82. William C. Cunningham, *Christianity and Economic Science* (London: John Murray, 1914), esp. ch. v.

83. William C. Cunningham, "The Perversion of Economic History," *Economic Journal* 2:491–493 (September 1892).

84. W. J. Ashley, "Discussion" of Albion W. Small's paper, "The Relations of Sociology to Economics," p. 116.

85. W. J. Ashley, *What Is Political Science?* pp. 5–6.

86. Thomas Nixon Carver, "The Place of Abstinence in the Theory of Interest," *Quarterly Journal of Economics* 8:40–61 (October 1893); *idem*, "The Theory of Wages Adjusted to Recent Theories of Value," *ibid.*, 8:377–402 (July 1894).

87. Thomas Nixon Carver, *Essays in Social Justice* (Cambridge, Mass.: Harvard University Press, 1915), p. 27.

88. Thomas Nixon Carver, *Recollections of an Unplanned Life* (Los Angeles: The Ward Ritchie Press, 1949), pp. 53, 85, 88, 90, 100. I have relied on Carver's autobiography for all personal and biographical details of Carver's life.

89. Herbert Heaton, *A Scholar in Action: Edwin F. Gay* (Cambridge, Mass.: Harvard University Press, 1952).

90. Frank William Taussig, "The Present Position of the Doctrine of Free Trade" [Presidential Address before the American Economic Association, 1904], *Publications of the American Economic Association*, 3rd series, 6:63–64 (February 1905).

91. *Ibid.*, pp. 64–65.

92. For Taussig's biography and background, see Joseph A. Schumpeter, Arthur H. Cole, and Edward S. Mason, "Frank William Taussig," *Quarterly Journal of Economics* 55:337–363 (May 1941); Redvers Opie, "Frank William Taussig: 1859–1940," *Economic Journal* 51:347–368 (June–September 1941); Edward S. Mason in *DAB*, vol. XXII, Supplement Two, s.v. "Taussig, Frank William"; Irving Dilliard in *DAB*, vol. XVIII, s.v. "Taussig, William [father]"; *Encyclopedia of the History of St. Louis: A Compendium of History and Biography for Ready Reference*, ed. William Hyde and Howard L. Conard (St. Louis, 1899), vol. IV, s.v. all "Taussigs" and "Wuerpels" [F. W. Taussig's mother's family into which F. W. Taussig's sister married]. For Taussig's thought, see Dorfman, *The Economic Mind*, III, 258, 265–271; Schumpeter, Cole, and Mason, "Taussig," cited above; and the three studies in the volume of essays contributed to

Taussig in 1936—Jacob Viner, "Introduction: Professor Taussig's Contribution to the Theory of International Trade," pp. 3–12; Joseph A. Schumpeter, "Introduction: Professor Taussig on Wages and Capital," pp. 213–222; and Talcott Parsons, "Introduction: On Certain Sociological Elements in Professor Taussig's Thought," pp. 359–379, all in *Explorations in Economics: Notes and Essays Contributed in Honor of F. W. Taussig* (New York: McGraw-Hill Book Co., 1936).

93. Hermann Heinrich Gossen, quoted in John W. McConnell, *Economists Past and Present: Basic Teachings of the Great Economists* (New York: Barnes and Noble, Inc., 1959 [first edition, entitled *Basic Teachings of the Great Economists*, Garden City, New York: Doubleday and Co., Inc., 1943]), p. 160.

94. W. J. Ashley, "The Present Position of Political Economy," pp. 476–477.

95. Frank William Taussig, "The Love of Wealth and the Public Service" [Presidential Address before the American Economic Association, 1905], *Publications of the American Economic Association*, 3rd series, 7:1–3 (February 1906).

96. See Parsons, "On Certain Sociological Elements in Professor Taussig's Thought," in *Explorations in Economics*.

97. Carver, *Essays in Social Justice*, p. 35.

SOCIAL ETHICS AT HARVARD, 1881–1931: A STUDY IN ACADEMIC ACTIVISM

Peabody's course was reconstructed primarily from the published outlines of his lectures and the class notes of six students spanning the academic years 1889–90 to 1904–05. One of these notebooks is in the Harvard Divinity School Rare Book Room; the rest are in the Harvard University Archives. A professional tutor's outline and Peabody's published works provided additional evidence for determining what went on in his classroom. For the most part, however, I have worked from the lecture notes and tried to avoid reliance on the assumption that what Peabody said in his publications was the same as what he said in the classroom. The quotations found in the section of my essay which reviews Peabody's course in detail are from lecture notes. Before such a quotation or other piece of information was taken from a particular notebook it was cross-checked for general reliability against information in the other five notebooks. A good collection of student term papers written for Peabody's course is also located in the Archives. Similar although much less complete evidence allowed me to characterize the content of social ethics courses taught from 1913 to 1920.

I have been unable to locate any substantial collection of Francis Greenwood Peabody papers. A limited number can be found in the Archives. The papers of James Ford in the Archives are concerned mostly with his career as director of Better Homes in America and yielded little with regard to his teaching of social ethics. The scope of this essay as defined in footnote one restrained me from extensive use of the abundant course material in the large collection of Richard Cabot papers in the Archives. A great deal more can be done on the curious history of social ethics at Harvard during the 1920's. Cabot, a colorful and significant figure in the history of medicine, public health, social work, and intellectual history in general deserves a full-scale study.

1. The entire fifty-year span will not be covered in equal depth. Emphasis will be placed on the first thirty-two years, which may be termed the Peabody era, and the subsequent years will be sketched in to give a general idea of the shifting emphases and ultimate demise of Social Ethics at Harvard.

2. Franklin B. Sanborn, "The Social Sciences: Their Growth and Future," *Journal of Social Science* 21:6 (September 1886); Lester F. Ward, "Contemporary Sociology," *American Journal of Sociology* 7:477 (January 1902).

3. See Donald Fleming, *John William Draper and the Religion of Science* (Philadelphia: University of Pennsylvania Press, 1950), especially chapter xi, for an analysis of this assumption and its origins.

4. Jurgen Herbst, "From Moral Philosophy to Sociology: Albion Woodbury Small," *Harvard Educational Review* 29:233–234 (Summer 1959); and *The German Historical School in American Scholarship: A Study in the Transfer of Culture* (Ithaca: Cornell University Press, 1965), pp. 134, 155, 182–184. Herbst finds that another important stimulus to American professorial social action was the example set by groups of university professors in Germany such as the *Verein für Sozialpolitik*, see pp. 112, 142–148, 174.

5. "Sociology and Theology at Yale College," editorial, *Popular Science Monthly* 17:265–269 (June 1880).

6. Harald Höffding, "On the Relation Between Sociology and Ethics," *American Journal of Sociology* 10:676 (March 1905).

7. Ira W. Howerth, "Present Condition of Sociology in the United States," *Annals of the American Academy of Political and Social Science* 5:121 (September 1894).

8. Jurgen Herbst, "Francis Greenwood Peabody: Harvard's Theologian of the Social Gospel," *Harvard Theological Review* 54:46–52 (January 1961); for a guide to Peabody's extensive published works see his "Francis Greenwood Peabody: A Bibliography," *Proceedings*

15. Sanborn, "The Social Sciences," pp. 7–11; L. L. and Jessie Bernard, *Origins of American Sociology: The Social Science Movement in the United States* (New York: Thomas Y. Crowell Co., 1943), pp. 620–621, 638, 667; "Social Science Instruction in Colleges, 1886," *Journal of Social Science* 21:xxxiv–xxxvi (September 1886); see also L. L. and J. S. Bernard, "A Century of Progress in the Social Sciences," *Social Forces* 11:500 (May 1933) and Jeffrey R. Brackett, "Francis Greenwood Peabody," *Survey* 30:141 (April 26, 1913).

16. His predecessor in this position was Andrew Preston Peabody, a distant relative.

17. Herbst, "Harvard's Theologian," p. 55; Rand, "Philosophical Instruction," pp. 296–297.

18. Francis G. Peabody, "The Philosophy of the Social Questions," *Andover Review* 8:565–566 (December 1887); and "Social Reforms as Subjects of University Study," *Independent* 38:37 (January 14, 1886).

19. Peabody, "Social Reforms," p. 5.

20. Francis G. Peabody, "The Universities and the Social Conscience," in Henry C. King et al., *Education and the National Character* (Chicago: The Religious Education Association, 1908), pp. 23–24; Peabody, "Social Reforms," p. 5.

21. Peabody, "The Philosophy," pp. 561–562; Sydney Kaplan, "Taussig, James and Peabody: A Harvard School in 1900?" *American Quarterly* 7:320 (Winter 1955); Francis G. Peabody, "The Religion of a College Student," *Forum* 31:449 (June 1901).

22. Gladys Bryson, "The Emergence of the Social Sciences from Moral Philosophy," *International Journal of Ethics* 42:306 (April 1932). Subsequent and earlier periods are examined from the same point of view by Bryson in "Sociology Considered as Moral Philosophy," *Sociological Review* 24:26–36 (January 1932), and "The Comparable Interests of the Old Moral Philosophy and the Modern Social Sciences," *Social Forces* 11:19–27 (October 1932).

23. Booth, English shipowner, statistician, and social reformer, based his writings on organized, on-the-spot investigations. The first volume of his *Life and Labour of the People in London* was published in 1889, and the work was completed in 1903 with the publication of the seventeenth volume.

24. Francis G. Peabody to Charles Booth, October 8, 1903, September 29, 1904, May 12, 1905, Letters from F. G. Peabody Concerning a Social Science Exhibit, 1903–1906, HUA.

25. Letters to F. G. Peabody Concerning a Social Science Exhibit, 1903–1906, *passim*, HUA.

26. Francis G. Peabody, *The Social Museum as an Instrument of*

of the Unitarian Historical Society 13:86–97 (Part 2, 1961)
detailed analysis of Peabody's thoughts on social reform see Ba
Bernstein, "Francis Greenwood Peabody: Conservative Soci
former," *New England Quarterly* 36:320–337 (September 19

9. Herbst, "Harvard's Theologian," pp. 52–55; James Ford, '
Ethics, 1905–1929," in *The Development of Harvard Uni
Since the Inauguration of President Eliot, 1869–1929*, ed. ?
Eliot Morison (Cambridge, Mass.: Harvard University Press,
p. 223.

10. Levering Reynolds, Jr., "The Later Years (1880–1953
*The Harvard Divinity School: Its Place in Harvard University
American Culture*, ed. George Huntston Williams (Boston
Beacon Press, 1954), p. 180; cf. James Dombrowski, *The Earl
of Christian Socialism in America* (New York: Columbia Uni
Press, 1936), p. 69; Earl Morse Wilbur, "Reminiscences of a D
School Graduate of the Class of 1890," *Harvard Divinity
Bulletin* 20:92 (1954–55); Barrett Wendell, "Recollections o
vard, 1872–1917," MS. (1918), p. 43, Harvard University A
(hereafter HUA); for an example of this type of student activ
David B. Potts, "The Prospect Union: A Conservative Qu
Social Justice," *New England Quarterly* 25:347–366 (Sept
1962); "The Harvard Charitable and Religious Organization,'
pect Union Review 1:7 (October 24, 1894); Hugh Barbour,
Origins of Phillips Brooks House at Harvard," MS. (1943),
Phillips Brooks House Library, Harvard University.

11. Wilbur, "Reminiscences," p. 92; "Social Ethics," H
Crimson, October 13, 1892, p. 1.

12. Francis G. Peabody to Franklin B. Sanborn, quoted in Sa
"The Social Sciences," pp. 7–8.

13. See the data offered by Frank L. Tolman, "The Study
ciology in Institutions of Learning in the United States: A I
of an Investigation Undertaken by the Graduate Sociological I
of the University of Chicago," in four parts, *American Jour
Sociology* 7:797–838 (May 1902), 8:85–121, 251–272, 53
(July, September, January 1902–03), and L. L. Bernard, "The '
ing of Sociology in the United States," *ibid.*, 15:164–213 (Sept
1909). Even Albion W. Small, who resembled Peabody in ma
spects as a latter-day moral philosopher, noted with approval in
the increased methodological emphasis within sociology sinc
eighteen nineties. See Small's "Fifty Years of Sociology in the U
States," *ibid.*, 21:788–789, 815–820, 852–854 (May 1916).

14. Benjamin Rand, "Philosophical Instruction in Harvard
versity from 1636 to 1900," *Harvard Graduates' Magazine* 3
(March 1929); on sociology, see above, pp. 32–56.

University Teaching, Publications of the Department of Social Ethics in Harvard University, No. 1 (Cambridge, Mass.: Harvard University, 1908), pp. 1–3.

27. *Ibid.*, pp. 6–7.

28. David C. Rogers to Francis G. Peabody, January 11, 1906; Hugo Münsterberg to Peabody, April 13, 1903, and Peabody to Rogers, January 24, 1906, Letters to F. G. Peabody.

29. "A Significant Gift," *Harvard Bulletin*, June 21, 1905, p. 5; Francis G. Peabody, *The Approach to the Social Question* (New York: The Macmillan Co., 1909), p. 5.

30. Francis G. Peabody to Charles W. Eliot, November 10, 1896, Eliot Papers, HUA; Frank W. Taussig, "Economics, 1871–1929," in *The Development of Harvard University*, p. 193.

31. Jerome D. Greene, Henry J. Cadbury, and James Ford, "Minute on the Life and Services of Francis Greenwood Peabody," MS. (1937), p. 4, HUA; Stanley J. Lubin to Francis G. Peabody, August 3, 1905, Letters to F. G. Peabody.

32. Francis G. Peabody, "Alfred Tredway White," *Harvard Graduates' Magazine* 29:577–583 (June 1921); Ford, "Social Ethics," pp. 224–225.

33. Francis G. Peabody to Alfred T. White, February 3, 13, 1905, and Peabody to Robert W. DeForest, December 2, 1903, Letters from F. G. Peabody.

34. Peabody, *The Approach*, pp. 4–5, 34, 96–97, 135, 139, 183. Peabody acknowledged the permanent influence on his thought of the voluntary idealism of Fichte, see Herbst, "Harvard's Theologian," p. 60.

35. Peabody, *The Approach*, pp. 183–184.

36. There are several other dimensions to Peabody's encounter with Pragmatism. Professor James Luther Adams, who generously read and commented on my manuscript, contends that a key issue between Peabody and his colleague, William James, may lie in a quite different context. Professor Adams contrasts the "pietistic" individualism of James's pragmatism with the institutional emphasis of Peabody's ethical idealism. The few published letters from James to Peabody suggest both this intellectual tension and a warm personal friendship. See Ralph Barton Perry, *The Thought and Character of William James* (Boston: Little, Brown and Co., 1935), II, 269, 302, 331–332.

37. *Ibid.*, p. 131; Greene, "Minute," p. 2; Herbst, "Harvard's Theologian," p. 45.

38. Charles A. Ellwood, "How Should Sociology be Taught as a College or University Subject?" *American Journal of Sociology* 12:603 (March 1907); Ford, "Social Ethics," pp. 225–226.

39. For a collection of most of the ethical readings used during this period, see *Social Problems and Social Policy*, ed. James Ford (New York: Ginn and Co., 1923), pp. 1–149.

40. The American Social Science Association, founded in 1865, provides a case study in the expansion and fragmentation of the social sciences. Splitting off from this organization either directly or indirectly were the National Prison Association (1870), National Conference of Charities and Corrections (1874), American Statistical Association (reorganized, 1883), American Historical Association (1884), American Economic Association (1885), American Anthropological Association (1902), American Political Science Association (1903), and American Sociological Society (1905). When this process was completed, the parent organization had little left to do, see Bernard, "A Century of Progress," pp. 500–502.

41. Alfred T. White to A. Lawrence Lowell, 1917, quoted in Peabody, "Alfred Tredway White," p. 579.

42. A. Lawrence Lowell to James Ford, August 16, 1918, Ford Papers, HUA.

43. Richard C. Cabot, *Adventures on the Borderlands of Ethics* (New York: Harper and Brothers, 1926), pp. 91–99. Cabot divided his time between the Medical School and Harvard College until his retirement in 1933.

44. Interview with Gordon W. Allport, November 1961; Cabot, *Adventures*, pp. 102–107.

45. For Cabot's personal philosophy of life see his *The Meaning of Right and Wrong* (New York: The Macmillan Co., 1933).

46. Two others who left social ethics in the late twenties were William T. Ham, who joined the Economics Department in 1926, and Sheldon Glueck, who became a member of the Law School faculty in 1929, G. W. Allport interview; Ford, "Social Ethics," pp. 226–229.

47. Anonymous memorandum, ca. 1926, Ford Papers.

48. Ford, "Social Ethics," pp. 227–228.

49. "Field of Concentration in Sociology and Social Ethics, 1930–31," *Official Register of Harvard University* 28:2 (January 28, 1931), HUA; *Concentration in Sociology and Social Ethics 1929–30*, pamphlet (Cambridge, Mass.: Harvard University, 1929), p. 1, HUA; interview with Arthur M. Schlesinger, Sr., August 27, 1963.

50. "Concentration in Sociology and Social Ethics," MS. (March 5, 1928), p. 1, HUA; *Concentration*, p. 2.

51. For Sorokin's views on sociology at this time see his article, "Sociology as a Science," *Social Forces* 10:21–27 (October 1931).

52. Richard C. Cabot to James Ford, October 17, 1930 and ca. late October, Ford Papers; Ralph Barton Perry to Clifford H. Moore,

ca. 1930, Correspondence of the Committee on Concentration in Sociology and Social Ethics, 1928–31, HUA; Cabot to Ford, January 21, 1931, Ford Papers.

53. Richard C. Cabot to James Ford, October 17, 1930, Ford Papers; *Endowment Funds of Harvard University, June 30, 1947* (Cambridge, Mass.: Harvard University Press, 1948), pp. 68, 82; Gordon W. Allport to Ford, with copy of memorandum attached, December 17, 1930, Ford Papers.

54. Pitirim A. Sorokin to Richard C. Cabot, January 22, 1931, and Cabot to James Ford, ca. January 1931, Ford Papers; Cabot to Ralph Barton Perry, June 3, 1930, Correspondence of the Committee; *Report of the Committee on Sociology and Social Ethics on the Organization of a Division of Sociology and Social Ethics*, pamphlet (Cambridge, Mass.: Harvard University, 1931), p. 1, HUA.

ALBERT BUSHNELL HART:
THE RISE OF THE PROFESSIONAL HISTORIAN

The most important materials for a study of Hart's ideas about American history are to be found in his published articles and books. Because he wrote so profusely, he expressed these ideas many times on both scholarly and popular levels; a complete collection of his articles, bound by year (a gift of Hart to Harvard), is in Widener Library. A complete list of all his books, both original and edited, again prepared by Hart, is in the Harvard University Archives. In addition to published material are his course outlines and guides for study, and scattered student notes, also in the Archives. The course outlines, again a complete collection, furnish information about course content and specific explanations of his techniques of teaching. These guides give detailed outlines of lectures and are equal in importance to the course notes in forming a clear idea of the progression of both his ideas and his methods.

The collection of Hart's letters is unfortunately limited by the fact that almost all the letters date from the later and less productive period of his life. According to Clifford K. Shipton, there was a verbal agreement made by Hart with Harvard that all of Hart's papers were to come to the University. But unfortunately these papers were sold by his sons, through book dealers in Newburyport, at the time of Hart's death, and more than half of the material was never recovered. It is this material which would have dealt, for instance, with the American Historical Association, the *American Historical Review*, and the American Nation series. The personal letters do furnish some insights into Hart's private life, but show very little of his professional interests. There are two folders in the Eliot papers which reveal some of Hart's attitudes toward his work, his professional aspirations, and the nature of his loyalty to Harvard. Secondary sources, while useful for background, do not deal directly with Hart.

1. Samuel Eliot Morison, *Three Centuries of Harvard* (Cambridge, Mass.: Harvard University Press, 1936), p. 347.

2. The biographical information in this and the following paragraph is taken from the folder entitled "Biographical Directions" and from "Reminiscences of Albert Bushnell Hart, dictated to Gertrude Warner, April 29, 1937, Hart Papers, Harvard University Archives (hereafter HUA).

3. Harvard University Catalogue, 1877–78, p. 72; Harvard University Catalogue, 1879–80, p. 103.

4. Albert Bushnell Hart (hereafter ABH) to A. Lawrence Lowell, January 18, 1923, Hart Papers, HUA.

5. ABH, "American Progress," 1870 [?] (the uncertainty about the date is Hart's), Hart Papers, HUA.

6. Morison, *Three Centuries of Harvard*, p. 349.

7. Harvard College Class of 1880, *Fiftieth Anniversary Report* (Norwood, Mass.: Privately Printed, 1930), p. 38.

8. Oswald Garrison Villard, *The Fighting Years* (New York: Harcourt, Brace and Co., 1939), p. 82.

9. Harvard College Class of 1880, *Secretary's Report*, II (Buffalo, N.Y., 1883), 48–49.

10. Samuel Eliot Morison, "Edward Channing: A Memoir," *Massachusetts Historical Society, Proceedings* 64:266 (May 1931).

11. Harvard College Class of 1880, *Fiftieth Report*, p. 39.

12. See the letters exchanged by ABH and his wife; the folder entitled Condolences to Mrs. Hart, ca. 1897; also the letters of the sons and their wives to Hart; and the letters of one son, Albert, to his mother, Hart Papers, HUA. Some information from an interview with Clifford K. Shipton, Custodian of the University Archives, December 5, 1962.

13. C. K. S. [Clifford K. Shipton], "Albert Bushnell Hart," *American Antiquarian Society, Proceedings* 53:123 (October 20, 1943).

14. Walter P. Rogers, *Andrew White and the Modern University* (Ithaca, N.Y.: Cornell University Press, 1942), p. 124.

15. Ephraim Emerton and Samuel Eliot Morison, "History, 1838–1929," in *The Development of Harvard University Since the Inauguration of President Eliot, 1869–1929*, ed. Samuel Eliot Morison (Cambridge, Mass.: Harvard University Press, 1930), p. 150.

16. Charles K. Adams, *A Manual of Historical Literature* (New York, 1882), p. 1.

17. George E. Howard to Herbert Baxter Adams, May 30, 1883,

in *Historical Scholarship in the United States, 1876–1901: As Revealed in the Correspondence of Herbert Baxter Adams, The Johns Hopkins University Studies in Historical and Political Science*, LVI, no. 4, ed. W. Stull Holt (Baltimore, Md.: Johns Hopkins Press, 1938), p. 65.

18. J. Franklin Jameson, "Introduction," in *Historical Scholarship in America: Needs and Opportunities*, ed. Committee of the American Historical Association on the Planning of Research (New York: Ray Long and Richard R. Smith, Inc., 1932), p. 4.

19. Charles W. Eliot, "What Is a Liberal Education?" *Century*, n.s., 6:208 (June 1884).

20. Ephraim Emerton, "The Practical Method of Higher Historical Instruction," in *Methods of Teaching History*, ed. G. Stanley Hall, 2nd ed. (Boston, 1884), p. 50.

21. Charles W. Eliot to Edward Channing, June 23, 1880, quoted in Morison, "Edward Channing," p. 263.

22. *Historical Scholarship in the United States*, p. 8.

23. David D. Van Tassel, *Recording America's Past: An Interpretation of the Development of Historical Studies in America, 1607–1884* (Chicago: Chicago University Press, 1960), p. 176.

24. Henry Adams to Francis Parkman, December 21, 1884, in *Henry Adams and His Friends: A Collection of His Unpublished Letters*, ed. Harold Dean Cater (Boston: Houghton Mifflin Co., 1947), p. 134.

25. ABH, "The Teacher as Professional Expert," *School Review* 1:4–14 (January 1893).

26. J. Franklin Jameson, "The Influence of Universities upon Historical Writing," *Chicago University Record* 6:298 (1901–02).

27. ABH, Richmond *News*, February 11, 1941, Clipping in HUA.

28. Edward Channing, *A History of the United States*, I (New York: The Macmillan Co., 1905), v–vi.

29. Edward N. Saveth, "Scientific History in America: Eclipse of an Idea," in *Essays in American Historiography: Papers Presented in Honor of Allan Nevins*, ed. Donald Sheehan and Harold C. Syrett (New York: Columbia University Press, 1960), p. 1; W. Stull Holt, "The Idea of Scientific History in America," *Journal of the History of Ideas* 1:352–362 (June 1940).

30. Henry Adams, *The Education of Henry Adams* (Boston: Houghton Mifflin Co., 1918), p. 303.

31. Saveth, "Scientific History in America," p. 4.

32. Holt, "The Idea of Scientific History," pp. 352–354.

33. ABH, "Imagination in History," *American Historical Review* 15:232–233 (January 1910).

34. Jameson, "The Influence of Universities," p. 294.

35. Emerton, "The Practical Method of Higher Historical Instruction," pp. 59–60.

36. Holt, "The Idea of Scientific History," p. 356.

37. Ibid., p. 359.

38. ABH, "Imagination in History," p. 245.

39. ABH, National Ideals Historically Traced, 1607–1907, The American Nation: A History, XXVI (New York: Harper and Brothers, 1907), p. xiii.

40. ABH, "Imagination in History," pp. 234, 235.

41. Ibid., p. 233.

42. Report of the Committee on Secondary School Studies, Appointed by the National Education Association (Washington, D.C., 1893), p. 169.

43. Saveth, "Scientific History in America," p. 2.

44. See obituaries on ABH, esp. Harvard Gazette 39:103–104 (December 18, 1943).

45. "Historical News, Personal: Hart Obituary," American Historical Review 49:193 (October 1943).

46. ABH, "The Historical Opportunity in America," American Historical Review 4:1 (October 1898).

47. Harvard College Class of 1880, Secretary's Report, VII (Boston: Privately Printed, 1905), 33.

48. ABH to Theodore Roosevelt, January 11, 1896, Hart Papers, HUA.

49. ABH, National Ideals, pp. 23, 27, 30.

50. ABH, rev. of Franklin H. Giddings, Democracy and Empire (New York, 1900), Outlook 64:506 (June 30, 1900).

51. ABH, rev. of Franklin H. Giddings, Democracy and Empire (New York, 1900), Independent 52:608 (March 8, 1900).

52. ABH, "The Hope of Democracy," Tufts College Graduate 5:61 (July 1907).

53. ABH, "The Future of the Mississippi Valley," Harper's New Monthly 100:422 (February 1900).

54. ABH, "Why the South Was Defeated in the Civil War," New England Magazine, n.s., 5:375–376 (November 1891).

55. ABH, "The Outcome of the Southern Race Question," North American Review 188:51 (July 1908).

56. ABH, The Southern South (New York: D. Appleton and Co., 1910), pp. 371–375.

57. Theodore Roosevelt to ABH, December 18, 1907, Hart Papers, HUA.

58. Herbert Baxter Adams, Methods of Historical Study, The Johns Hopkins University Studies in Historical and Political Science, II, nos. 1–2 (Baltimore, Md., 1884), p. 59.

59. Herbert Baxter Adams, *The Study of History in American Colleges and Universities*, U.S. Bureau of Education Circulars of Information, no. 2 (Washington, D.C., 1887), p. 17.

60. Stewart Mitchell, "Henry Adams and Some of His Students," *Massachusetts Historical Society, Proceedings* 66:294–312 (1936–1941).

61. Henry Adams, *Education of Henry Adams*, pp. 304, 307.

62. Mitchell, "Henry Adams," p. 309.

63. Villard, *The Fighting Years*, p. 104.

64. Samuel Eliot Morison, "Albert Bushnell Hart, 1889–1939," *Massachusetts Historical Society, Proceedings* 66:435–436 (1936–1941).

65. ABH, "Methods of Teaching American History," in *Methods of Teaching History*, p. 3.

66. ABH, *National Ideals*, pp. xiii–xiv.

67. ABH, *25th Annual Record of the Ancient and Honorable Artillery Company* (Boston, 1897), p. 77.

68. ABH, *National Ideals*, pp. 68–70.

69. ABH, *Introduction to the Study of the Federal Government* (Boston, 1891), p. 23.

70. ABH, *Handbook of the History, Diplomacy, and Government of the United States, for Class Use* (Cambridge, Mass.: Harvard University, 1901), p. 10.

71. ABH, ed. *American History Told by Contemporaries*, III (New York: The Macmillan Co., 1900), viii.

72. ABH to Charles W. Eliot, December 13, 1907, Eliot Papers, HUA.

73. Merle Curti, "The Democratic Theme in American Historical Literature," *Mississippi Valley Historical Review* 39:15 (June 1952).

74. William S. Davies to ABH, November 7, 1923, Hart Papers, HUA.

75. John W. Burgess, "On Methods of Historical Study and Research in Columbia University," in *Methods of Teaching History*, pp. 216–217.

76. ABH, "Methods of Teaching American History," p. 4.

77. ABH to A. Lawrence Lowell, November 23, 1932, Hart Papers, HUA.

78. ABH, *Report of the Committee on Secondary School Studies*, p. 168.

79. ABH to Samuel Eliot Morison, March 30, 1936, Hart Papers, HUA.

80. ABH, "Methods of Teaching American History," p. 1.

81. Emerton and Morison, "History, 1838–1929," p. 168.

82. ABH, "Methods of Teaching American History," p. 28.

83. Edward Channing and ABH, *Guide to American History* (Boston, 1896), p. 24.

84. ABH, "Methods of Teaching American History," p. 16.

85. ABH to Charles W. Eliot, July 12, 1895, Eliot Papers, HUA.

86. James A. James, rev. of ABH, *Manual of American History, Government, and Diplomacy* (Cambridge, Mass., 1908), *American Historical Review* 13:920 (July 1908).

87. Villard, *The Fighting Years*, p. 104.

88. ABH to Charles W. Eliot, December 10, 1895, Eliot Papers, HUA.

89. ABH to Charles W. Eliot, March 26, 1908, Eliot Papers, HUA.

90. ABH to A. Lawrence Lowell, February 17, 1922, Hart Papers, HUA.

91. H. B. Adams, *The Study of History*, p. 246.

92. ABH, "The Historical Service of John Fiske," *International Monthly* 4:560 (October 1901).

93. Harvard College Class of 1880, *Secretary's Report*, VI (Boston: Privately Printed, 1900), 42.

94. ABH, "The Historical Opportunity in America," p. 18.

95. ABH, "The Teaching of Today, II: The Proposed Enrichment of the Grammar School Course—What Form It Would Properly Take," Boston *Evening Transcript*, November 5, 1894.

96. ABH to Charles W. Eliot, January 26, 1907, Eliot Papers, HUA.

97. Emerton, "The Practical Method of Higher Historical Instruction," p. 38.

98. Emerton and Morison, "History, 1838–1929," p. 157.

99. ABH, "The Historical Opportunity in America," p. 11.

100. See *Doctors of Philosophy and Doctors of Science Who Have Received Their Degrees in Course from Harvard University, 1873–1926* (Cambridge, Mass.: Harvard University, 1926), pp. 79–86.

101. ABH to Charles W. Eliot, February 4, 1907, and August 26, 1908, Eliot Papers, HUA.

102. Herbert Baxter Adams, *The College of William and Mary*, U.S. Bureau of Education, Circulars of Information, No. 1 (Washington, D.C., 1887), pp. 73–74, quoted in *Historical Scholarship in the United States*, p. 94n.

103. ABH to Charles W. Eliot, May 10, 1905, Eliot Papers, HUA.

104. ABH to Charles W. Eliot, August 26, 1908, and November 19, 1898, Eliot Papers, HUA.

105. Harvey Wish, *The American Historian: A Social-Intellectual History of the Writing of the American Past* (New York: Oxford University Press, 1960), p. 274.

106. ABH to A. Lawrence Lowell, October 12, 1917, Hart Papers, HUA. Lowell replied that he doubted that there was room for expansion in the department at that time.

107. ABH to Charles A. Beard, October 12, 1917, Hart Papers, HUA.

108. J. Franklin Jameson, "The American Historical Association, 1884–1909," *American Historical Review* 15:8, 18 (October 1909).

109. John T. Short to Herbert Baxter Adams, October 1, 1881, in *Historical Scholarship in the United States*, pp. 47–48.

110. Herbert Baxter Adams to Andrew D. White, February 4, 1890, in *ibid.*, p. 127.

111. J. Franklin Jameson, "The American Historical Review, 1895–1920," *American Historical Review* 26:3 (October 1920).

112. ABH, "The American School of Historians," *International Monthly* 2:316 (September 1900).

113. See Howard A. Clark to Herbert Baxter Adams, May 22, 1900, and James Schouler to Herbert Baxter Adams, December 1, 1900, in *Historical Scholarship in the United States*, pp. 279–280, 289–290.

114. Lester J. Cappon, "Channing and Hart: Partners in Bibliography," *New England Quarterly* 29:321, 327–328 (September 1956).

115. Channing and Hart, *Guide to American History*.

116. Cappon, "Channing and Hart," pp. 319–320.

117. *American History Leaflets: Colonial and Constitutional*, Nos. 1–36, ed. ABH and Edward Channing (New York: A. Lovell and Co. succeeded by Parker P. Simmons, 1892–1913).

118. ABH, ed., *American History Told by Contemporaries*, III, vii.

119. *American History Leaflet*, No. 11 (September 1893), back cover.

120. ABH, "The Historical Opportunity in America," p. 13.

121. ABH, "Editor's Introduction to the Series," in Edward Potts Cheyney, *European Background of American History, The American Nation: A History*, I (New York: Harper and Brothers, 1904), xv.

122. *Ibid.*, p. xvii.

123. Max Farrand, "The American Nation: A History," *American Historical Review* 13:592 (April 1908).

124. ABH, *Slavery and Abolition, 1831–1841, The American Nation: A History*, XVI (New York: Harper and Brothers, 1906).

125. Morison, "Albert Bushnell Hart," p. 348.

126. Harvard College Class of 1880, *Fiftieth Report*, pp. 38–39.

WILLIAM JAMES AND THE NEW PSYCHOLOGY

The major portion of the material from which this essay was compiled is located in the Archives. University material such as Overseers'

Reports, Presidents' Reports, Treasurers' Reports, course catalogues, and so on, helped to provide the fundamental data necessary for chronological accuracy. The analysis of James's and Royce's courses is drawn primarily from midyear and final examinations and student notes. James's own lecture notes and notebooks in the William James Collection, Houghton Library, Harvard University, are unfortunately closed to graduate students as a result of the legal terms of the bequest. Nevertheless, the assumption that examinations generally reflect course content is substantiated by the survival of a group of highly detailed and well-thought-out student notes.

Invaluable for an understanding of the intellectual context in which James moved are his numerous essays in psychology and philosophy, his superb letters, and the two-volume edition of Ralph Barton Perry's *The Thought and Character of William James*. In addition, recollections by colleagues and students such as Josiah Royce, George Santayana, and G. Stanley Hall proved invaluable in creating a human image of James's truly pluralistic personality.

Finally, histories of psychology and philosophy by Edwin Boring, A. A. Roback, Richard Müller-Freienfels, Sterling Lamprecht, and others contributed to an evaluation of the wider context of intellectual history in the second half of the nineteenth century.

1. Ralph Barton Perry, *The Thought and Character of William James, Briefer Version* (Cambridge, Mass.: Harvard University Press, 1948), p. 85.

2. *The Letters of William James*, ed. Henry James (Boston: The Atlantic Monthly Press, 1920), I, 118–119.

3. Perry, *Briefer Version*, p. 107.

4. René Descartes, "Discourse on Method," in *Discourse on Method and Meditations*, trans. Laurence J. Lafleur (New York: Liberal Arts Press, 1960), p. 25. Originally published in 1637.

5. See A. A. Roback, *A History of American Psychology* (New York: Library Publishers, Inc., 1952), p. 137.

6. Francis Bowen (Harvard University, A.B. 1833, A.M., LL.D. 1879) was trained in moral and natural philosophy. His disdain for scientific considerations was not unusual for someone of his background. Bowen held the Alford Professorship of Natural Religion, Moral Philosophy, and Civil Polity from 1853 to 1889.

7. After receiving literary and theological training at Bowdoin, Everett took his D.D. at Harvard in 1859. Everett served as Bussey Professor of Theology, 1869–1900, and as Dean of the Divinity School, 1878–1900.

8. Overseers' Reports, Academical Series I, October 11, 1871, pp. 29–30, Harvard University Archives (hereafter HUA).

9. Overseers' Reports, Academical Series I, November 1, 1873, p. 5, HUA. Cabot had been lecturer in philosophy, 1869–1871, and instructor in logic, 1874–75.

10. This synopsis is based primarily upon Ralph Barton Perry, *The Thought and Character of William James* (Boston: Little, Brown and Co., 1935), *passim*, and upon Sterling P. Lamprecht, *Our Philosophical Traditions* (New York: Appleton-Century-Crofts, Inc., 1955), pp. 453–462. Unless otherwise specified, quotations are from Lamprecht.

11. William James, "Some Omissions of Introspective Psychology," *Mind* 9:22–23 (January 1884).

12. Perry, *Thought and Character*, II, 737.

13. Overseers' Reports, Academical Series II, October 11, 1876, p. 4, HUA. The similarity in style and thought between James's writings and such reports indicates that he may have assisted in their preparation. Definite proof is not available.

14. For details of Hall's claim to priority over James, see Roback, *American Psychology*, p. 129.

15. Harvard College Reports, 1875–76, Treasurer's Report, p. 39.

16. As early as 1876 James complained to his friend Charles Renouvier about the time consumed by laboratory work, *Letters of William James*, I, 188; Perry, *Briefer Version*, pp. 183–184.

17. Perry, *Thought and Character*, II, 11.

18. *Ibid.*, I, 475.

19. *Ibid.*, I, 476.

20. Robert S. Harper, "That Early Laboratory of William James," MS. (1948), HUA.

21. Overseers' Reports, Academical Series II, October 10, 1877, p. 9, HUA.

22. G. Stanley Hall, "Philosophy in the United States," *Mind* 4:97 (January 1879); Perry, *Thought and Character*, I, 435.

23. Overseers' Reports, Academical Series II, October 9, 1878, pp. 5–6, HUA.

24. Perry, *Thought and Character*, I, 435.

25. George Herbert Palmer, "Philosophy, 1870–1929," in *The Development of Harvard University Since the Inauguration of President Eliot, 1869–1929*, ed. Samuel Eliot Morison (Cambridge, Mass.. Harvard University Press, 1930), p. 30.

26. Overseers' Reports, Academical Series II, 1878–79, p. 5, HUA.

27. Hall, "Philosophy," pp. 90, 93, 98. Hall also praised James Elliot Cabot of the Board of Overseers for his part in advancing psychology at Harvard.

28. James, in addition, gave "voluntary instruction" in "Physiology and Hygiene," which was open to all students.

29. William James, "What Pragmatism Means," in *Pragmatism—A New Way for Some Old Ways of Thinking* (New York: Longmans, Green and Co., 1909), p. 67.

30. Royce was trying to uphold, for different reasons, the partial validity of Bowen's distinction between the areas of science and philosophy.

31. James, "Some Omissions," pp. 1–26.

32. Harper, "Early Laboratory," pp. 16–17.

33. See William James, "What Psychical Research Has Accomplished," in *The Will to Believe and Other Essays* (New York: Longmans, Green and Co., 1927), pp. 299–327.

34. Overseers' Reports, Academical Series II, October 20, 1886, HUA.

35. It is not uncommon to find James beginning a letter to Royce with the words "Beloved Josiah." Royce was assistant professor of philosophy, 1885–1892, and professor of philosophy, 1892–1916.

36. Along with James and Hall, Ladd was one of the most significant pioneers in American psychology. His *Physiological Psychology* went through six printings by 1897, and in 1892 he founded the Yale Psychological Laboratory. For more information see Roback, *American Psychology*.

37. Perry, *Briefer Version*, p. 174.

38. William James to Charles W. Eliot, October 20, 1889, Eliot Papers, HUA.

39. This outline represents a condensation of some of the major topics treated in Philosophy 2, 1889–90. It is by no means complete. In addition, student notes contain numerous diagrams and charts of experiments, as well as anatomical drawings.

40. Perry, *Thought and Character*, II, 10–11.

41. James had indeed been the only psychology instructor in the United States.

42. Box N of the James papers in Houghton Library, Harvard University, contains scores of letters by friends, colleagues, and students concerning James's effect and conduct as a teacher. Allowed to scan these materials before it was realized that graduate students, as a result of the terms of the bequest, were not allowed access to the James Papers, I gained an impression of almost unanimous praise for James as a teacher of unusual ability and success.

43. Memorandum of Dickinson S. Miller in *Letters of William James*, II, 11–16. Miller was obviously more impressed with James; it is unfortunate that he did not describe Royce in greater detail.

44. For a list of both University and private contributions, see Harper, "Early Laboratory."

45. Santayana received his A.B. from Harvard in 1886 with highest

honors in philosophy. His Ph.D., completed in 1889, had included advanced study in psychology with Professor James. Santayana remained in the Harvard Philosophy Department until 1912.

46. It is worth noting that James had begun his *magnum opus* with great enthusiasm in 1878; by 1890, mental exhaustion and his growing dislike of experimental psychology caused him to rejoice at its completion. He never again devoted the burden of his writing to psychology.

47. The 1890–91 Catalogue specifically mentioned experimentation for the first time in the description of Philosophy 2.

48. The opening of all the new facilities was actually delayed until the fall of 1891.

49. Memorandum of Dickinson S. Miller, pp. 12–13.

50. William James, "Psychology at Harvard University," *American Journal of Psychology* 3:278 (April 1890).

51. Edmund B. Delabarré, a student in the seminar of 1888–89, published two such articles: "On the Seat of Optical After-Images" and "Colored Shadows," *American Journal of Psychology* 2:326–328, 636–643 (February, August 1889).

52. Perry, *Thought and Character*, II, 114–115.

53. *Ibid.*, II, 139.

54. Münsterberg took his D.Phil. at the University of Leipsic in 1885 and his M.D. at the University of Heidelberg in 1887. He gained renown for his criticism of Wundt.

55. Perry, *Thought and Character*, II, 140.

56. Although he took his Ph.D. in psychology at Clark University in 1891 under G. Stanley Hall, Nichols had attended James's seminar in 1889.

57. *Letters of William James*, I, 301.

58. William James to Henry Holt, July 24, 1891, in *ibid.*, I, 314.

59. Memorandum of Dickinson S. Miller, p. 15.

60. Perry, *Thought and Character*, II, 152–154.

61. *Ibid.*, II, 147.

62. Münsterberg in 1893 wrote a detailed description of the Dane Hall Laboratory: ". . . We have fine laboratory rooms, we have the most ample and complete collection of psychological apparatus in the world, we have three instructors . . . for Psychology, and have, in addition to the average of fifty students who are engaged in the course of laboratory practice, a dozen young men of advanced standing, most of whom spend the largest part of their working hours upon investigations in the laboratory.

". . . A stroll through the workrooms, even outside of working hours, permits one to see clearly this high development from a glance at the apparatus stored in the glass cases. Four great groups of contrivances can thereby be easily distinguished. First, the apparatus intended to illustrate the relations between mind and body through representations of the brain, nerves, sense-organs, etc. Costly models of brain, eye, and ear, all with detachable parts, valuable models of nerve paths, fine preparations in wax, dissected parts in alcohol, etc., —all are here. Here belong also the anatomical diagrams and the histological nerve-preparations with excellent microscopes. All this has a significance for demonstration only, and accordingly has nothing to do with experimental problems proper. The three remaining sections are for that.

". . . the section for the psychology of the senses is by all means the most imposing. Eye and ear have equal recognition. A copious collection composed of tuning-forks, an organ, a harmonical, pipes, resonators, etc., etc., serve for psychological acoustics. Color-mixers of various sorts, costly prisms, apparatus for after-images and color-blindness, a dark room, perimeters, etc., serve for psychological optics. And yet the lower senses are not forgotten. Complicated touch and temperature apparatus, and instruments for the study of sensations of movement and pressure belong to the list.

"Of greatest value is the rich collection of instruments of the third section. They serve for the time measure of psychical acts, from the simplest impulses to the most complicated processes of judgement . . . They allow us to estimate minute distinctions which are inaccessible to self-observation . . . Our clocks have about the same function as the microscopes of the anatomist. With his microscope he can distinguish the thousandth part of a millimeter; with our chronoscope we can measure the thousandth part of a second. But every question craves new contrivances, and so, together with our valuable clocks, we find the best kymographs, instruments for reaction, and registering tuning-forks of every sort. In this section almost nothing is left to be desired.

"In the fourth section is included all that apparatus which serves . . . for the investigation of higher mental processes, such as the perception of space and time, memory and attention, association and formations of judgements, discrimination and fusion. These stand in the foreground, but feelings and emotions, impulses and the acts of will, are also accessible regions . . . here the newest instruments show their power. Apparatus for the study of aesthetic feelings or the expression of the emotions, and much that is similar, has just now crossed the ocean. It is . . . in this department that the tiny mechanical workshop of our laboratory has proved most useful. Copious supplies of wood and glass, of brass and cotton wadding, of all varieties of paper and iron tools, of wires and tubes, and of physical and chemical paraphernalia, enable us to . . . adapt the instruments to our questions. Such is our laboratory after the expenditure of over four thousand dollars, equipped in the best possible manner . . ." Hugo Münsterberg, "The New Psychology, and Harvard's Equipment for Teaching It," *Harvard Graduates' Magazine* 1:202, 205–206 (January 1893).

63. This course had actually been offered since 1890, but the earliest surviving indications of content are from the year 1892–93.

64. Münsterberg even kept a record of the visitors to the Dane Hall Laboratory. The list grew from seven in 1892 to 36 in 1894 and included such notables as Professor J. M. Baldwin, founder of the Princeton Laboratory of Psychology; Professor J. M. Cattell of the University of Pennsylvania Department of Psychology; Professor Helmholtz of the University of Berlin; and Professor John Dewey.

65. Harvard College Reports, 1891–92, p. 66.

66. Hugo Münsterberg, "The New Psychology," pp. 208–209. See also Herbert Nichols, "The Psychology Laboratory at Harvard," *McClure's* 1:399–409 (October 1893).

THE EDUCATION OF EDUCATORS AT HARVARD, 1891–1912

The strategies employed to pursue this study grew largely from the sources available. The Harvard University Archives contain no lecture notes of the first education professors and very few student notes. An attempt to solicit notes from surviving education students before 1910 yielded but one set. Two distinct consequences followed. First, the content of the early education courses had to be inferred from Hanus's published writing. Those innovations in his thinking crucial to this study occurred within that writing. Thus the essay became, strictly speaking, an intellectual biography rather than an analysis of the education curriculum. My assumption is that the two are very similar. Second, the paucity of curriculum sources forced the essay into areas where primary sources did exist: the origins of the education curriculum; the reasons for its survival; the opposition to it; finances and the relevance of Boston reform movements. Of necessity, the essay eventually became concerned not only with education as a subject of academic study but with education as an emerging profession.

Thus many interesting doors of inquiry were opened, almost accidentally, by the absence of primary sources on the curriculum. But the extraordinary lack of secondary literature on both the education profession and the curriculum hindered efforts to place Harvard developments within a more comprehensive national framework. There has been almost no historical awareness of the remarkable generation of men who, in the nineties and thereafter, built up the university study of education in America. An important first effort at understanding is Jesse Sears and Adin Henderson, *Cubberley of Stanford* (Stanford, 1957). Readers should also see Bernard Bailyn's review in the *Harvard Educational Review* 28:283 (Summer 1958). One historical study of the content of education is Merle Borrowman's *The Liberal and Technical in Teacher Education* (New York, 1956). Unfortunately this suffers, as do so many books in the field, from a method which imposes contemporary categories of educational analysis on a past where they did not exist. Charles Brauner's *American Educational Theory* (Englewood Cliffs, N.J., 1964) is a lively and suggestive recent interpretation.

1. *The Substance of Two Reports of the Faculty of Amherst College to the Board of Trustees* (Amherst, Mass., 1827), p. 8.

2. *Fifty-Fourth Annual Report of the Board of Education Together with the Fifty-Fourth Annual Report of the Secretary of the Board, 1889–90* (Boston, 1891), p. 10.

3. The New England Association of Colleges and Preparatory Schools, *Addresses and Proceedings at the Fourth Annual Meeting* (Syracuse, N.Y., 1889), pp. 22–32.

4. John Tetlow to Charles W. Eliot, March 19, 1890, Eliot Papers, Harvard University Archives (hereafter HUA).

5. John W. Dickinson to Charles W. Eliot, March 19, 1890, Eliot Papers, HUA.

6. John Tetlow to Charles W. Eliot, March 19, 1890, Eliot Papers, HUA.

7. "The Harvard Normal," editorial in *Journal of Education* (Boston), 33:328 (May 21, 1891).

8. Records of the Faculty of Arts and Sciences, I, p. 46 (October 7, 1890), HUA.

9. *Official Report of the Fifth Annual Meeting of the New England Association of Colleges and Preparatory Schools* (Boston, 1890), p. 34.

10. See Edwin P. Seaver, "The Professional Training of Teachers," in *Sixty-First Annual Meeting of the American Institute of Instruction* (Boston, 1890), pp. 66–76, 107.

11. Gabriel Compayré, *Lectures on Pedagogy*, trans. W. H. Payne (Boston, 1887), p. 4.

12. See John Ogden, "What Constitutes a Consistent Course of Study for Normal Schools?" *Addresses and Proceedings of the National Education Association* (Worcester, Mass., 1874), p. 217.

13. Herbert Spencer, *Education: Intellectual, Moral, and Physical* (New York, 1861), p. 110.

14. Quoted in Merle Borrowman, *The Liberal and Technical in*

Teacher Education: A Historical Survey of American Thought, Teachers College Studies in Education, XIII (New York: Bureau of Publications, Teachers College, Columbia University, 1956), p. 65.

15. See, for example, Alexander Bain, *Education as a Science* (London, 1859).

16. William H. Payne, *Contributions to the Science of Education* (New York, 1886), pp. 4, 14, 50, 68.

17. Nicholas Murray Butler to Charles W. Eliot, July 27, 1890, Eliot Papers, HUA.

18. Josiah Royce, "Is There a Science of Education?" Part I, *Educational Review,* I (January 1891); Part II, *Educational Review,* I (February 1891).

19. Paul H. Hanus to Robert E. McConnell, October 9, 1927, Hanus Papers, HUA.

20. Harvard College Reports, 1889–90, p. 12.

21. Records of the Faculty of Arts and Sciences, I, pp. 59–62 (November 11, 1890), HUA.

22. *Ibid.,* pp. 68, 72 (December 2, 16, 1890).

23. Paul H. Hanus, *Adventuring in Education* (Cambridge, Mass.: Harvard University Press, 1937), p. 121.

24. The biographical information about Hanus is all taken from his *Adventuring in Education.*

25. Paul H. Hanus to Charles W. Eliot, April 10, 1891, Eliot Papers, HUA.

26. See *First Annual Catalogue of the State Normal School of Colorado,* 1890–91 (Denver, 1891), p. 19.

27. Hanus, *Adventuring,* p. 101; Hanus to Charles W. Eliot, April 10, 1891, Eliot Papers, HUA.

28. Charles W. Eliot to Paul H. Hanus, March 25, 1891, quoted in Hanus, *Adventuring,* p. 107.

29. Report of the Committee on Education, June 1, 1904, in *Reports of the Visiting Committees of the Board of Overseers of Harvard College from January 8, 1902 to July 30, 1909 Inclusive* (Cambridge, Mass.: Harvard University, 1909), p. 783, HUA.

30. Charles F. Dunbar to Charles W. Eliot, March 16, 1892, Eliot Papers, HUA.

31. Barrett Wendell to Charles W. Eliot, February 1, 1899, Eliot Papers, HUA.

32. Byron S. Hurlbut to Charles W. Eliot, August 28, 1901, Eliot Papers, HUA.

33. Barrett Wendell to Charles W. Eliot, February 1, 1899, Eliot Papers, HUA.

34. Paul H. Hanus, "The Study of Education at Harvard," *Educational Review* 7:250 (March 1894).

35. Hanus, *Adventuring*, p. 120; Hanus to Robert E. McConnell, October 9, 1927, Hanus Papers, HUA.

36. Josiah Royce to Charles W. Eliot, July 18, 1893, Eliot Papers, HUA.

37. Albert Bushnell Hart to Charles W. Eliot, November 22, 1898, Eliot Papers, HUA.

38. "Paul H. Hanus," editorial in *Journal of Education* (Boston), 51:168 (March 15, 1900).

39. Paul H. Hanus to Robert E. McConnell, October 9, 1927, Hanus Papers, HUA.

40. Hanus, *Adventuring*, p. 126.

41. Byron S. Hurlbut to Charles W. Eliot, August 28, 1901, Eliot Papers, HUA.

42. Byron S. Hurlbut to Charles W. Eliot, September 11, 1901, Eliot Papers, HUA.

43. Byron S. Hurlbut to Charles W. Eliot, August 28, 1901, Eliot Papers, HUA.

44. Harvard University Catalogue, 1894–95, p. 91.

45. Josiah Royce to Charles W. Eliot, April 7, 1891, Eliot Papers, HUA.

46. Joseph Torrey, Jr., to Charles W. Eliot, May 29, 1901, Eliot Papers, HUA.

47. LeBaron R. Briggs to Charles W. Eliot, December 17, 1890, Eliot Papers, HUA.

48. Paul H. Hanus, "The Training of Teachers and the Study of Education," *Journal of Education* (Boston), 34:356 (December 3, 1891).

49. Paul H. Hanus, "Education as a University Study and the Professional Training of College-Bred Teachers," in *A Modern School* (New York: The Macmillan Co., 1904), pp. 261, 264 [first pub. as "The Study of Education and the Professional Training of College-Bred Teachers," *Harvard Monthly* 37:1–12 (October 1903)].

50. Hanus, "Study of Education," p. 247.

51. Byron S. Hurlbut to Charles W. Eliot, August 28, 1901, Eliot Papers, HUA.

52. Charles W. Eliot to Paul H. Hanus, January 3, 1898, Hanus Papers, HUA.

53. Paul H. Hanus, "The New Division of Education," *Harvard Graduates' Magazine* 14:611 (June 1906).

54. Paul H. Hanus, "The Professional Training of the Teacher," Part III, *Journal of Education* (Boston), 67:6 (January 2, 1908).

55. Arthur O. Norton, "The Scope and Aims of the History of Education," *Educational Review* 27:443 (May 1904).

56. *Ibid.*, p. 454.

57. See Bernard Bailyn, *Education in the Forming of American Society* (Chapel Hill, N.C.: University of North Carolina Press, 1960), pp. 5–8.

58. *Ibid.*, p. 10.

59. Paul H. Hanus, "A Recent Tendency in Secondary Education Examined," in *Educational Aims and Educational Values* (New York, 1899), p. 31 [first pub. in *School Review* 3:193–205 (April 1895)].

60. Paul H. Hanus, "Educational Aims and Educational Values," in *Educational Aims*, p. 17 [first pub. in *Educational Review* 9:323–334 (April 1895)].

61. Hanus, "A Recent Tendency in Secondary Education," p. 32.

62. Hanus, "Educational Aims," p. 19.

63. *Ibid.*, pp. 8, 11.

64. *Ibid.*, pp. 14–15, 16.

65. See George H. Locke, rev. of Paul H. Hanus, *Educational Aims and Educational Values*, *School Review* 7:493 (October 1899).

66. Adelaide H. Thierry, *When Radcliffe Was Teen Age* (Boston: Humphrics, 1959), p. 87.

67. Paul H. Hanus, "Graduate Testimony on the Elective System," *Harvard Graduates' Magazine* 10:354 (March 1902).

68. Paul H. Hanus, "University Inspection of Secondary Schools and the Schools Examination Board of Harvard University," *School Review* 2:263, 265 (May 1894).

69. J. L. Meriam, rev. of *A Modern School*, in *School Review* 13:198 (February 1905), James E. Russell to Paul H. Hanus, October 27, 1903, Hanus Papers, HUA.

70. See Donald Fleming, *William H. Welch and the Rise of Modern Medicine* (Boston: Little, Brown and Co., 1954), p. 131.

71. Joseph Mayer Rice, "Obstacles to Rational Educational Reform," *Forum* 22:387, 392 (December 1896).

72. Joseph Mayer Rice, "Educational Research," *Forum* 34:117 (July–September 1902).

73. Charles W. Eliot to Paul H. Hanus, August 3, 1897, Hanus Papers, HUA; Paul H. Hanus, rev. of Karl August Baumeister, *Handbuch der Erziehungs und Unterrichts-lehre für höhere Schulen* (Munich, 1895–1898), *Educational Review* 17:48 (January 1899).

74. Paul H. Hanus, "Report on Educational Progress," *Journal of Education* 44:395 (December 10, 1896).

75. Charles W. Eliot to Paul H. Hanus, January 3, 1898, Hanus Papers, HUA.

76. Paul H. Hanus, "Obstacles to Educational Progress," in *A Modern School*, p. 220 [first pub. as "Our Chaotic Education," *Forum* 33:222–234 (April 1902)].

77. *Ibid.*, p. 224.

78. *Ibid.*, p. 233.
79. *Ibid.*, pp. 234–237.
80. *Ibid.*, p. 238.
81. Hanus, "The Study of Education at Harvard," p. 253.
82. Paul H. Hanus, "What Should the Modern Secondary School Aim to Accomplish?" in *Educational Aims*, p. 79 [first pub. in *School Review* 5:387–400, 433–444 (June, September 1897)].
83. *Ibid.*, pp. 99, 104.
84. *Ibid.*, pp. 91, 95, 97.
85. Paul H. Hanus, "Secondary Education as a Unifying Force in American Life," in *Educational Aims*, p. 127 [first pub. as "Secondary Education," *Educational Review* 17:346–363 (April 1899)].
86. Paul H. Hanus, "Attempted Improvements in the Course of Study," in *Educational Aims*, p. 47 [first pub. in *Educational Review* 12:435–452 (December 1896)].
87. Paul H. Hanus, "Industrial Education, under State Auspices, in Massachusetts" [address delivered January 9, 1908], in *Beginnings in Industrial Education* (Boston: Houghton Mifflin, 1908), pp. 38–39.
88. *Ibid.*, p. 40.
89. Paul H. Hanus, "The Professional Training of the Teacher," Part I, *Journal of Education* (Boston), 66:660 (December 19, 1907).
90. Hanus, "A Recent Tendency in Secondary Education," p. 28.
91. See also Henry W. Holmes, "Does the Present Trend Toward Vocational Training Threaten Liberal Culture?" *School Review* 19:477 (September 1911).
92. Hanus, *Adventuring*, pp. 166–167.
93. Paul H. Hanus, "Industrial Education" [1908], in *Beginnings in Industrial Education*, pp. 11–14.
94. Hanus, "Industrial Education Under State Auspices," p. 35.
95. Harvard University Catalogue, 1892–93, p. 86.
96. *Circular of Information 1891–92, New York College for the Training of Teachers* (New York, 1889), p. 21; *Circular of Information 1892–93, New York College for the Training of Teachers* (New York, 1891), p. 19.
97. *Catalogue, 1899–1900, Columbia College* (New York, 1899), p. 153.
98. *Calendar of the University of Michigan for 1901–02* (Ann Arbor, Mich., 1901), p. 85; *Calendar of the University of Michigan for 1906–07* (Ann Arbor, Mich., 1906), p. 105.
99. *Calendar of the University of Michigan for 1898–99* (Ann Arbor, Mich., 1898), p. 81.
100. Allen S. Whitney, *History of the Professional Training of Teachers at The University of Michigan for The First-Half-Century*

1879 to 1929 (Ann Arbor, Mich.: George Wahr, 1931), pp. 65–75.

101. Christian A. Ruckmich, "The History and Status of Psychology in the United States," *American Journal of Psychology* 23; Table IV facing p. 528 (October 1912).

102. Charles W. Eliot to Paul H. Hanus, August 3, 1903 and Hanus to Robert E. McConnell, October 9, 1927, Hanus Papers, HUA.

103. "Report of the Committee on Education," pp. 905, 907.

104. Lawrence A. Cremin, David A. Shannon, and Mary Evelyn Townsend, *A History of Teachers College, Columbia University* (New York: Columbia University Press, 1954).

105. Arthur Mann discovered no interest in formal education among the Boston reformers he studied. Arthur Mann, *Yankee Reformers in the Urban Age* (Cambridge, Mass.: Harvard University Press, 1954), p. 102.

106. Paul H. Hanus, "Education," *Harvard Graduates' Magazine* 10:262 (December 1901).

107. Harvard College Reports, 1896–97, p. 46.

108. Hanus, *Adventuring*, p. 148.

109. Neva R. Deardorff in *DAB*, XXII, Supplement Two, s.v. "Lee, Joseph."

110. Harvard College Reports, 1907–08, p. 9.

111. Paul H. Hanus to Charles W. Eliot, July 19, 1907, Hanus Papers, HUA.

112. Harvard College Reports, 1906–07, p. 139.

113. Paul H. Hanus to A. Lawrence Lowell, February 6, 1912, Hanus Papers, HUA.

114. Boston *Evening Transcript* quoted in "Quotations: New Courses at Harvard," *School and Society* 4:519 (September 30, 1916).

115. Hanus, *Adventuring*, p. 204; Harvard College Reports, 1917–18, p. 28.

116. "The New York Inquiry," editorial in *Journal of Education* (Boston), 76:546–547 (November 21, 1912); "The Hanus Report," editorial in *Journal of Education* (Boston), 77:154 (February 6, 1913).

117. [William H. Maxwell?], "Good and Bad in New York Schools," *Educational Review* 47:68 (January 1914); Jacques W. Redway, "Knocking the New York City Schools," *Journal of Education* (Boston), 77:371 (April 3, 1913).

118. "What is the Trouble with the New York Inquiry?" editorial in *Journal of Education* (Boston), 77:662 (June 12, 1913).

119. Paul H. Hanus, *School Efficiency: A Constructive Study Applied to New York City* (Yonkers-on-Hudson, N.Y.: World Book Co., 1913), p. xxvii.

120. Paul H. Hanus to Henry W. Holmes, May 18, 1912, Hanus Papers, HUA.
121. Charles W. Eliot to Paul H. Hanus, July 10, 1901, Hanus Papers, HUA.
122. Bernard Bailyn, "Education as a Discipline: Some Historical Notes," in *The Discipline of Education*, ed. John Walton and James L. Kuethe (Madison, Wis.: University of Wisconsin Press, 1963), pp. 125–131.
123. Meriam, rev. of *A Modern School*, p. 198.
124. Charles W. Eliot to Paul H. Hanus, February 18, 1906, Hanus Papers, HUA.

INDEX